My Place In Time

By Opal Phillips Johnson

Psalms 103:16 states
When the wind has passed over it, it is no more, and its place remembers it no more.

No sadder words have ever been written. We realize this is true when we visit a cemetery. There we see the many gravestones of people not remembered. My dream has always been to write about *A Place in Time* that holds not only memories but life experiences that have molded and made us into the adults we are today. Although our parents have gone on to be with the Lord, their love, determination and hard work made this place worth remembering.

My Dedication

This book was written to give my grandchildren and great-grandchildren a glimpse into their grandmother's life in the late 1940's and early 1950's. We had very few conveniences that people have today, yet we were happy and content. You don't miss what you don't have.

1. I dedicate this book to the one who gave me eternal life, my Lord and Savior, Jesus Christ.

2. To my parents, who gave me physical life, my mother, Lemmie Effie Phillips, and my father, Coy E. Phillips. Their life was much harder than mine, but somehow they sacrificed and struggled, managing to raise eight children. They taught us values, integrity, how being poor in no way made you less important than if you had been blessed with wealth. My mother taught us to be independent and determined to fulfill our dreams. A friend paid her the best compliment at her funeral. He said, "Your mother was the kindest woman I ever knew."

3. My lifetime mate for fifty-six years, Warren Johnson. He took his vows seriously in that country church many years ago. He's always supported me in all my many endeavors, and most importantly he's loved me unconditionally. So I LOVE YOU, BABE – this book is your life, too.

4. I dedicate my efforts to another group I love dearly, my immediate family- First, to our three children and their spouses. Adrienne and Jimmy Otto, Eric and Emily Clarke Johnson, then Tammy, (to whom I'm so very grateful for your help with this book) and her husband, John Hurst.

The next generation, David Frank Childs, Matthew Childs, (who's now with the Lord), Adrienne Kim "Kim" Childs, and Andrew Childs (their father is John Childs). Next, Lindsey Katherine Johnson and Blake Warren Johnson (their mother is Lisa Tabor), Adam Clarke, and Andrew Clarke. Lastly is Candice Eley and

My Place In Time

Amy Edmiston (their father is Eddie Hill) and Max Edmiston, Heather and Chris Wright, and Maria Blair and Brian Moore.

We've been doubly blessed to have four great-grandchildren. Candice is the mother of two, Anna Marie Eley and Brian Jacob Eley (father, Christopher Eley). Amy has Adeline Grace, (Addie Bug) and another daughter, Britton Faith, born May 25th 2011. They are truly a joy to have in our lives.

5. This group I dedicate to is my siblings and their families. We've lost three siblings and one brother-in-law. My oldest sister Louise Walker and her husband Frank Walker are now deceased. Pat Wentworth, (Patricia Ann), left us almost ten years ago. Also our youngest brother Dan is no longer with us. I believe they are all in a wonderful place with our Lord.

Next, our extended family, which still meets together at least twice a year. If I miss anyone, please forgive me. My brother Morris Phillips and his wife Janice have two children, Pam married Steve King and they have given three grandchildren to Morris and Janice. They are Stephanie, Mitch, and Sam. Their son Tony Phillips and his wife Kim, have two children, a daughter, Bayli, and a son, Austin.

My oldest living sister, Joan, is married to Tommy Wyatt and they have two children, a daughter, Melinda, and her husband Kenny Thompson who have three children, Ali, Spencer, and Ridge. Steve Wyatt is married to Karen and they have one daughter, Ivy Lane.

My youngest living brother Sam, is married to Deborah and they have two daughters, Samatha, whose husband is Shae Hensley and they have one son together, Samuel Philip. Mary Beth married Darrell Scott and they have two daughters, Lauren and Kayce Belle.

I previously mentioned my sister, Pat Wentworth, had passed away but her husband Carver Wentworth is still very much a part of the family.

Lastly, my youngest sister Cheryl married Doug Harvey over twenty-five years ago and they have two children, Jonathan and Laura.

These are my identity, a glimpse of who I am and where I came from. We meet regularly and have such great times.

6. Warren's family was, and is, very dear to me. His mother, Katherine Maine Johnson and Walter L, his dad are both departed, along with his only brother Bruce Johnson.

Marlene Randall and her family are still with us and are a great blessing. Marlene is more like a sister than a sister-in-law. Marlene has seven boys: Phil Randall, Lance Randall, Brad Randall, Tim Randall, Jessie Randall, Clayton Randall, and Ethan Randall.

Bruce Johnson and his wife Jeanette had three children: David Johnson, Dawn Johnson and Dean Johnson (or as we know him "Deaner.")

7. Lastly, I dedicate this to my best friend Bennie Farmer. We've been friends for over forty years. She's a prayer partner and a very special person. We've been going to lunch together once a week for over twenty years. She's truly blessed my life, and I'm a better person for having her as a friend. May God bless her and keep her in his love.

8. This book is a memorial to my dear departed friend, Mildred Tucker Clary. She was a friend, "In season and out of season." "Millie you were the best."

May God be glorified in my efforts to tell my story. Remember it's my memories and not every one remembers the same. I also pray *I will not be one of those, whose place remembers it no more*, at least for a little while. Nevertheless, my life will then be with the Lord, rejoicing and praising Him forever and ever. Amen.

Table of Contents

Acknowledgements	12
Little Cabin in the Woods	13
The Beginning	13
The Early Years	13
Believing	15
Moving Day	17
School Days	18
Brothers and Sisters	21
Bicycles and Fish Fins	22
The Garden and Flour Sacks	25
Wash Days	25
Hog-Killing Weather	27
Temper, Temper	28
Let There be Light	29
Turkey Tom	33
More School Days	34
Dating	37
A Close Call	38
Sweet 16 and Square Dancing	39
Cotton Pickin' Days	44
Senior Year	51
Nashville - The Beginning	62
Doubts	75
Boys, Boys, Boys!	77
Our 1st Apartment	81
The One!	88
New Friends	94
The Wreck	94
Going Steady	96
Warren Meets the Phillips Clan	97
Morris	108
The Rehearsal	113
The Wedding Day	114
The Wedding Night	118

The Day After	119
The Journey to Minnesota	121
Homeward Bound	123
Our First Fight	125
Life with the Newlyweds	126
Grandpa Phillips	126
The Colons	132
Our First Thanksgiving	134
First Christmas Party	136
Christmas at the Phillips	141
Minnesota – January 1956	142
Slippin' an' a Slidin'	143
Home Again	145
Moving Again & New Furniture	146
Mildred	150
Billy Graham Crusade	153
Mildred & Johnny	154
Mama's Little Surprise	155
Mildred & Johnny - Again	157
New Car – 1955 Pontiac	158
Chattanooga	160
Phase II – November 1956 to August 1968	172
Newlyweds	173
Thanksgiving	175
Christmas - 1956	176
The Stork	178
First Apartment	179
Home Again	182
Back to Minnesota	185
A New Home	185
Labor Day	189
Adrienne	189
Part Time Job	193
Springtime	197
Timmy	197
Tennessee Bound	200
Home Again	203
Back to Work	204

Stay at Home Mom	206
Adrienne's First Birthday	207
Christmas 1958	207
Remodeling	210
Summer of 1959	212
Thanksgiving 1959	213
Tammy	215
Remodeling Begins	219
Trap Door	220
Finished Remodeling	221
Plymouth Fire Department	222
Hot Coffee	224
Pat's Visit	225
Routines	227
Train Ride	227
Bruce's Accident	231
More Remodeling	233
Dad	234
Morris and Janice	236
Smoky Mountains	237
Ruth and Little Debbie	243
Christmas Train Ride and a Surprise	245
Adrienne's First Day of School	250
Accident-Prone	251
Adrienne's Birthday Party	255
Christmas 1963	256
Church	257
Joan and Tommy	259
Stuck in the Mud	260
July 1964	261
Christmas 1964	263
Early 1965	264
July 1965	267
Fall of 1965	268
Christmas 1965	270
Eric	272
1966	277
July 1966	278

Early 1967	278
Summer 1967	280
Christmas 1967 and Pat and Carver	280
Spring 1968	283
The Move to Tennessee	285
Warren's New Job	287
Settling In	288
Christmas 1968	289
Mrs. Poppa John and Bible Study	290
More Accidents	292
Moving to Jackson (Almost)	292
Our Home on McCool	295
I'm Saved!	295
New Beginning	296
Christian Friends	297
Lay Witness Missions	299
Our Children	299
50th Anniversary	300
My Family	301
True Joy!	301
ABOUT THE AUTHOR	307

Acknowledgements

    I want to thank Warren, my husband, for his encouragement and his enduring love for me.

    I want to thank my daughter, Tammy, for all the time and effort she's put into getting my book ready for publication. She's edited, typed and helped reshape everything. A simple thank you is not enough.

Little Cabin in the Woods

My earliest memories are of a two room cabin in the woods. There were no roads, only wagon trails and paths. The cabin was a large living area with a huge rock fireplace. The furniture consisted of a rocking chair, two double beds, a chest of drawers, a small wardrobe and a trunk. The kitchen was smaller with a wood cook stove, a small homemade table and chairs, a pie safe and cabinet. There were oil lamps we used which sat on the mantel, giving a soft candle like glow. We had no refrigeration or even an ice box. Mama kept milk in a cold, cold spring down a path from the cabin.

The Beginning

Our Mama, Lemmie Effie Phillips, married very, very young; in fact, she was only sixteen years old. Louise, the eldest of the children, who was five years my senior, was born the following year. When Louise was only two years old, my mother gave birth to a son, Malcolm, who had serious complications and lived only for six weeks. The following year another son was born, but disaster struck again and he was stillborn. He was never named. I can only imagine how this must have been devastating to a mother so young.

The following year in 1935 I was born. This is where my story really begins.

The Early Years

"Mama, Mama," Louise cried, "can I name the baby? Please, please, let me call her Opal Mae after my doll. Look, right here on the back, it says Opal Mae." Mama looked and, sure enough, it said *Opal Mae* on a tag at the back of the doll she had gotten for Christmas.

"I'll ask your Daddy," she said. Later on Daddy agreed and my name became Opal Mae Phillips.

Eva, Mama's sister, came running up the path while I stood watching from the window. "Mama, she's here," I cried. "Is Coy back yet?"

"No, but he should be shortly," my mother answered. "He's been gone for hours. Mrs. Yarbro should be here soon. He was going by her house on the way to get Mr. Clyde to go for the doctor." Mrs. Yarbro was a midwife or granny woman as they were called in those days.

Eva told me to get my things ready and that I would be staying with them for a few days. Mamie was coming over very soon to help out. A knock at the door brought Mrs. Yarbro and my grandmother, Janie Horner, at the same time. Mama called me over to the bed and explained a little of what was going on. "You'll have to stay with Mamie for a few days," she said. "Connie and Louise will be there, so you'll have a good time." She went on to explain that the doctor would probably bring another baby. I was only three years old, so I understood very little of what she was saying. "Connie will be waiting for you and Louise, so be a good girl and don't cry," she said. Connie, who was my mother's youngest sister, was only a year older than Louise. "Your daddy will come to get you in a few days."

We met my daddy on the way to my grandmother's house. "Did Mrs. Yarbro get there yet?" he asked.

"She got there just before we left," Eva answered. "She'll be able to handle things even if the doctor doesn't make it in time," she continued.

Louise was eight and Connie, Mama's youngest sister, was nine. They were old enough to look after me and play together at the same time. Mamie and Pappy lived about two miles from our house. There was a gravel road leading to their house, but that's where it ended. A large spring supplied water for many families that lived in the area. It was called Temp Spring. This spring served almost like a social gathering place for people in the community. Families gathered there to make molasses in the fall. I used to watch in awe, as the horses pulled the paddles that stirred the vats full of sugar cane.

Bob, Mama's brother, had a Model T Ford. Fred, her other brother, was probably part-owner in it. I remember some years later going to town in it. This was a really big deal for Connie, Louise and me. We arrived at Mamie's house to find Connie all excited and ready to play. Their house was much bigger than ours. It not only had a large living area and kitchen; there was a breezeway and another bedroom. This was like an open hallway and could be very cold in the winter. Mama's two brothers, Fred and Bob, slept in this room. I remember being so fascinated with their room. They actually had a Victrola that you could wind up and listen to the most beautiful music.

I was so excited the next day when Daddy came and told us Mama had a new baby boy. I could hardly wait to get home and see him. He told us we would have to stay a few more days, until Mama got to feeling better. In those days women stayed in bed a complete week after childbirth. He came back the next day and told us they had decided to name the baby Morris Glen. I knew this would end my having the privilege of being the baby in the family.

Believing

My memories are vague for the next few years. I was five years old when I was disillusioned and heartbroken. This memory has stayed with me and is vivid until this very day.

It was about two weeks before Christmas, and in those days Christmas was much more exciting than it is today. We so looked forward to what Santa Claus would bring, including the apples and oranges we got in our stockings. This year, in particular, I just knew Santa would bring the things I had asked for. We always searched the Sears catalog and dreamed of things Santa would bring us. This year I wanted a beautiful doll and a green doll cradle.

"Opal," Mama called from the kitchen, "put on your coat and go with Louise and get in the stove wood for tonight." Daddy usually brought in the heavy wood for the fireplace, but we were expected to not only carry all the water from the spring but to also keep the box full of stove wood. We grabbed our coats and started down the path to get the wood.

"Louise, aren't you excited?" I asked.

"Why?" she wanted to know.

"It's almost Christmas, and Santa will bring our presents and candy!" I exclaimed. She didn't seem nearly as excited as I was, but she didn't let on that she knew there was no Santa Claus. However, the next day, I was to find out differently.

The next morning Mama announced she was going to Mamie's to help quilt and that Eva would be coming over along with Connie and Dorothy, Mama's middle sister, to stay with Louise and me. She said she would take Morris with her. They arrived shortly and Mama left on her outing. Louise and Connie started playing paper dolls, ignoring me as usual. "Eva, it's almost Christmas," I began. "Santa Claus will be coming in a very short while," I said.

"Aren't you a little old to still be believing in Santa Claus?"

"What do you mean?" I wanted to know.

"Your daddy is Santa Claus," she continued. "If you don't believe it, I'll prove it to you. Let's climb up in the loft, and I'll show you what I mean." I followed her up the make-shift stairs to the loft above the living area. There, in plain view, was a beautiful doll and green doll cradle. I was stunned because it was exactly like the one in the catalog I had told Mama I wanted Santa to bring me for Christmas. "Now do you believe it?" she asked. I knew she was right…that it was all make believe. I don't remember ever telling Mama and Daddy about what she had told me. Christmas was never the same after that. I know now the real meaning of Christmas, but at the time that's all we knew.

Our parents were not Christians when we were growing up so we never really knew the true meaning of Christmas until much later. Mama and Daddy both became Christians after I was grown up. This was my first real disappointment in life.

Opal Phillips Johnson

Moving Day

"Get up, you sleepy head!" Louise yelled at me, pulling me out of bed. "Don't you know what day this is?"

"Yes, I do. It's moving day." We had looked forward to this day for weeks.

Several weeks ago Daddy announced that he and his brother Omer had just bought 60 acres of land from Mr. Clyde Smith, and there were two houses on the property. Omer and his family would get one and we would take the other. They planned on dividing the property at a later date. Somehow, we ended up with the smaller house, but that was all right because it would be so much better than the cabin we were living in now. Daddy planned on adding a room as soon as possible.

The exciting thing about this place was the location. It was on the main road, and it was also fairly close to the school house, where Louise and I would be going to school. I was now six years old and would be starting school in the fall. On this particular morning there was so much excitement in the air.

By this time we had had another addition to the family about six months before. A beautiful little girl named Joan Marie. She was named after the singing sensations at the time: Jean, Jane and Joan.

"The wagons will be coming soon!" Mama yelled to the kids, who seemed to be more rowdy than usual. "Get your things together so we can load everything up." I remember the ride over to the house so well. It was only about two miles but seemed much further to a six-year-old. Mama let me hold Joan for part of the way while she walked along beside the wagon. We arrived shortly before noon. All four kids were yelling and having a gay old time.

"Mama, where will I sleep?" Louise asked, for the tenth time.

"We'll all be in the same room until Daddy gets the new room finished," she explained.

This house was built with logs and the ceilings were quite low in the main room. Even the two rooms were quite a bit larger than our other place. With help from neighbors and friends, the new room was finished quickly. Louise and I now had a room all by ourselves. What an exciting time.

School Days

I started school in a few months in a one-room schoolhouse about a mile from our home. We had one teacher that taught seven grades. When you got to eighth grade, you went to "town school." The teacher at the one-room schoolhouse just so happened to be my aunt, Aunt Kathleen. She was Daddy's brother, Kitty's wife. She was a teacher that did not spare the rod. I never remember getting whipped but vividly remember others receiving their fair share. The boys, especially, received paddlings on a daily basis. Needless to say, these seven years of my life hold memories best forgotten. We did walk home for lunch every day, where Mama usually had a hot lunch waiting for us.

Opal Phillips Johnson

Above: Tootsie, Dean, Opal

"Opal, be sure you come straight home this afternoon," Mama announced at lunch. "I don't want you sliding down that hill in the snow and getting yourself hurt."

"I will," I promised. After we were dismissed at three o'clock, everyone gathered outside to discuss sledding down the schoolhouse hill. Bobby brought his sled, or rather a bench, to use going up and down the hill.

"Opal, you're going to sled aren't you?" my cousin Exie asked.

"Mama told me to come home, but maybe just once," I said. What fun we had! Sledding one time turned into thirty minutes or longer.

All of a sudden, I saw Mama coming down the hill. She was moving rather fast and had a large switch in her hand. I knew what was coming, so I tried to cry and beg her out of whipping me, but to no avail. "I didn't mean to stay," I cried. "They

talked me into it and I was only going to sled down one time," I said.

"That's no excuse not to mind," she said as she switched my legs all the way home. I would run ahead, but she kept saying, "You might as well wait up or I'll get you when we get home." I learned a valuable lesson that stayed with me the rest of my life from that snowy day at Mt. Carmel schoolhouse hill. Our actions have consequences, and Mama meant what she said.

We had many, many experiences in the seven years I was enrolled at this little country school. Meanwhile, another sister was born and this little one was named Patricia Ann. I was nine years old and felt very grown up. Pat was almost my charge because I babysat her so much. We did sharecropping in cotton for Mr. Clyde. Mama would work in the fields, along with Daddy and Louise, while I would look after Morris, Joan and now the baby, Pat. I would take care of them either at the end of the fields, or sometimes at Mamie's house.

My Aunt Connie Horner and my sister, Louise in front of the one room school

Pat was a beautiful baby, but her hair just wouldn't seem to grow. She was completely bald until she was over a year old. Mama was beginning to worry, so she ordered something from a catalog that was supposed to make hair grow. Her hair finally began to grow, but it probably had nothing to do with the product Mama ordered. Pat ended up with a beautiful head full of blond hair. Pat probably had more colds and viruses than the rest of us. It's a miracle that we all survived with the little bit of medical care we received. It had to be a major illness to go to the doctor.

One of Pat's colds turned into severe croup and she almost died. I was about ten years old, but I vividly remember Mama and Daddy being up all night with her for a couple of days. Several neighbors came in and sat up with her. You could hear her breathing and gasping for breath all the way outside the house. By God's grace she survived with an over-the-counter medication called "Save the Baby." Mama used this medicine quite a bit.

Brothers and Sisters

I was quite a tomboy when I was ten or eleven. I played an awful lot with our neighbor, Mayme's boys, and with Morris, who was only three years younger than me. Usually, I could get Morris to do what I wanted, which was the complete opposite of Louise. She was five years older than me and wanted to boss me around continually. Therefore, a lot of the time I played with Morris and his little buddies. We climbed trees, looked for rocks on Pretty Rock Hill and swam in streams and creeks.

One time in particular, we were out roaming in the woods when we found a large stream of water which had been damned up. It was not too far from Mayme's house. We ran back to see if they would let us go swimming. "Oh, Mama, please," we both cried. "It's not very deep and

we'll be careful," we promised. "It's not over our heads, so there's no danger of drowning."

"Opal, you don't even have a bathing suit," she said. Morris could wear his cut-off jeans, but I had to have something different.

"I know," I cried. "I'll get Mayme to make me one." Mayme was a wonderful seamstress and could cut and make something from a picture.

"If Mayme will make it, I've got some feed sacks she can use," Mama said. Flour, feed and other grains came in printed cotton bags. I took the bags to Mayme and, needless to say, she whipped me up a bathing suit in about an hour.

We were then off to the stream to have an afternoon of swimming. I can still remember the vines that were hanging over the area where we were swimming. We would grab the vines and swing and drop into the water. Again, God's angels protected us.

Bicycles and Fish Fins

Daddy worked at several different jobs when we were growing up, and he could make a living at anything he set his mind to. His primary job later became brick laying. My grandpa, Sam Phillips, had done bricklaying and taught him the trade. Daddy also worked on pipelines and stayed away from home some. At this time though, he was doing quite well working on the river. At this particular time, he was digging mussel shells.

Morris was now nine years old and I was twelve. We had dreamed of a bicycle for years, but there never seemed to be a way to get one. We came up with an idea to cook out mussel shells and pay for it ourselves. Now, all we had to do was convince Daddy it was a good idea.

"Oh, Daddy, please let us get a bicycle." Morris and I both began to beg Daddy as soon as he walked in the door from work. "They have one at Western Auto and we could pay for it on time. We could pay $10.00 a month and have it paid for in five months," I begged.

"We can both use it and take one week for each of us," Morris chimed in. We finally convinced Daddy it would work and agreed to go to town on Saturday and get it. We could hardly wait for the weekend to come.

On Saturday, Daddy took his pickup truck and brought home a shiny red bicycle for Morris and me. The problems started right away, because neither of us wanted to be second to get our turn. So we decided we would both ride it. For our first outing I put Morris on the back and I was going to peddle. We decided to go to Grandma Phillips and pick apricots from their tree. Grandma and Grandpa Phillips lived down a gravel road about a mile from the Methodist church house, which had a cemetery. We had both heard our neighbor, Clay, tell ghost stories about this church and cemetery.

We had no problems on our trip there. We picked apricots, put them in a tow sack for Morris to hold, and started back. Just as we started past the church house, I heard a noise that sounded just like a baby crying. "Did you hear that?" I asked Morris.

"What?" he asked.

"That sounds like crying," I said.

"Yeah, I hear it."

About that time I heard a loud crash, like something fell inside the church. It could have been my imagination, but to this day I can still remember the sounds. "Hurry!" Morris cried. I was so scared, but I didn't want him to know how scared I really was. I started peddling as fast I could. Remember – this was a gravel road. We started down the hill toward Mrs. Myrtle's house, and the bike got in loose gravel, flipping both of us to the ground. Morris was crying at the top of his lungs.

"Let me see how bad you're hurt?" I remarked. After looking him over, I decided I was hurt much worse than he was. "Let's go to Mrs. Myrtle's and get her to stop my leg from bleeding," I continued.

The bike seemed okay. We pushed it over to the Crawley house, where Mrs. Myrtle met us at the door. "Come on in and let me fix that knee," she said. She cleaned and bandaged my knee and sent us on our way with a warning to be more careful on our new bike. I was able to ride again, so we continued our journey home. Mama wasn't too impressed with our story of the baby crying and said we had been listening to too many ghost stories. This was just the beginning of a series of skinned knees and arguments over our new bike.

We started our job at the river the following week. We were out of school for the summer, so we had a couple of months to earn the money we needed to pay for it. "Look, Opal, the shell boat is here," Morris cried as we arrived at the river to start cooking out shells.

"It sure is," I replied. "Maybe we can go on it after we finish." The horrible smell was the first thing that your noticed as you approached the shell camps – the stench almost took your breath away.

The men built the fires under the vats, cooked the shells and shoveled them onto the long tables to be finished by us. We had two jobs for that day. The first was to take the meat out and throw that in one pile. The second job was to throw the shells in other piles, which were sorted by shapes and sizes. We had finished our two jobs and had made $4.00. We were getting ready to leave when Grandpa Phillips asked if we wanted some fish he had just caught. "Of course!" I said. "Daddy loves fish." I took the long string of fish and we started to leave.

All of a sudden one of the fish stuck its fin right into my right arm and I started screaming at the top of my lungs. Several people came running over to where we were, including two men from the shell boat. "Little lady, you come with me and we'll get that thing out of your arm," he said. They took me on the boat, got out their first aid kit and began trying to get the fish fin out of my arm, succeeding after several minutes. They bandaged my arm and told me I would be fine now and to run along home.

"What on earth happened to you?" Mama asked as we came through the door. She could see I had been crying and my arm was all bandaged up. "I got a fish fin in my arm," I cried. When Daddy came home later, he was pretty upset to say the least.

"I'll pay for the darned bike myself," he said. "I don't want one of you getting yourself killed." He paid for the bike and we stayed away from the river for the rest of that summer.

Opal Phillips Johnson

The Garden and Flour Sacks

We were so poor growing up; there was very little money for extras. We always had plenty to eat, thanks to Mama and Daddy's ingenuity and foresight. We had about 25 or 30 acres of land so there was plenty of room for a large garden. We raised acres of potatoes, onions, tomatoes, peas, corn and every other vegetable you could think of. Mama spent many weeks preserving and canning all this produce for winter. We also raised and slaughtered several hogs to be cured in hams, sausage, and bacon for the winter months ahead. My daddy was an avid hunter, so we usually had an ample supply of squirrels and other wild game. The only things we had to buy were flour, meal, lard and coffee.

As I mentioned before, flour, meal and feed for the livestock were bought in feed sacks that were made of prints. These sacks Mama sewed into most of our clothes. She made us dresses and the boys homemade shirts. When I was 12, I think the thing I hated most was not having store-bought underwear. "Opal, where did you get those black bloomers?" Bob, Mama's brother, asked as I swung from a tree one hot summer afternoon. He laughed and said, "I've never seen black bloomers before." I didn't say a word, just walked inside and cried.

Eva, Mama's sister, now had two girls, whom were doted upon by Mamie and Pappy. Dorothy and her husband, J. C., decided they didn't want any little snotty-nosed kids; therefore, we were almost treated as outcasts. By this time, we now had another baby brother named Samuel. He was named after both grandpas. There were now six children in the family.

Wash Days

Wash day was a major event in those days. "Opal, get busy hanging those clothes on the line," Louise snapped. She was now

17 and thought she was our second mother. She was always so bullheaded and strong-willed that Daddy nicknamed her Bull. I hung the clothes on the lines that were strung from 5 or 6 trees. There were large poles on the lines to keep them from sagging from the weight of overalls, etc. "I'm doing the best I can!" I yelled back at her. "Mama, make her leave me alone," I cried. Mama separated us and told Louise to go put the last load through the wringer on the washer.

Mama was helping me get the last of the clothes in the basket on the line when we heard a blood-curdling scream. "Help!" Louise was screaming. "I'm stuck," she cried. We ran over to the washer and her arm was caught in the wringer. Mama quickly unplugged the washing machine and released the wringer to get her arm out. It was bruised and sore for several days, but nothing kept Louise down in those days.

Louise was now working at Slant and Slant, a shirt factory in a nearby town. She had to quit school when she finished eighth grade because there was no bus to take her to high school in nearby Decaturville at that time. This added to her sense of independence and self-will. She now had her own money, and most of the time we had to grovel and beg to get any of it. I have to give her credit though: sometimes she could be very good to me if she was in a good mood when she got her check. She would take me to buy clothes or sometimes to a movie. I had worn hand-me-downs most of my life from her and Connie, so this was a great treat to have something store-bought. Mama also made a lot of our clothes. "I won't wear this!" Louise screamed as she ripped the blouse apart. "Connie's looks better than mine and you know it." Mama had worked all afternoon making blouses for both Louise and Connie, and now Louise decided hers didn't look the same as Connie's.

"That's the last time I'll sew for you," Mama said, as she walked away. Louise knew she could talk her into it again sometime later. Mama stood her ground, but there was always a struggle between the two.

Opal Phillips Johnson

Hog-Killing Weather

"I think this is good hog-killing weather," Daddy said as he built a roaring fire one cold November day. "Get everybody up so we can get an early start." I could smell the sausage and coffee as I hopped out of bed to see what was going on. Daddy had already eaten, so he was leaving as I approached the table. Some of the neighbors were coming to help so he hurried to meet them at the barn. As usual, we had a huge pan of homemade biscuits, chocolate syrup, sausage, eggs and red eye gravy. By then Morris, Joan and I were seated on a long bench that held at least 4 kids on one side of the homemade table. We all talked at once; this morning it was more than usual. It was Saturday, so there was no school, although sometimes we missed school for such important occasions. We finished and all rushed to the barn, just in time to see three huge hogs hanging by their necks from a large pole. After hanging for a while, they were taken down and laid on plastic bags to be scalded and scraped. Daddy always let us help scrape the hair off using dull knives. After the insides were taken out, everything was cut up into hams, shoulders, middling, etc. Some of the meat was taken out to be ground up for sausage. This was always Mama's job, along with cooking out the lard.

"Do you think this has cooked long enough?" Mama asked as she continued to stir the boiling lard, filled with now bubbling cracklings.

"It looks about right to me," Daddy answered.

We watched as she removed several buckets of hot cracklings. This was a wonderful treat – eating cracklings right out of the kettle. The next best thing was the wonderful dinner Mama would cook, using the fresh tenderloin and liver from the day's hog killing. When you're twelve years old, it seems you're the one that's kept the busiest. The others were too young to help, and Louise thought she was too old for this kind of thing.

Temper, Temper

I had a rather bad temper, which flared quite easily when I was young. One night in this general time frame, Mama yelled from the kitchen, "Opal, I told you to get in some stove wood."

"Why can't Joan help me," I cried. There seemed to be a double standard on our chores. Morris helped Daddy with the outside chores, but he was never required to do much of anything in the house. On this particular night, my temper flared, because I seemed to have to do everything myself.

"Joan is too little to help," Mama said.

"I was bringing it in when I was her age," I cried. "She's such a baby!" I screamed as I picked up a piece of the wood and threw it at her. Luckily it missed her, but I knew I was in bad trouble. "I'm sorry, Mama," I began to cry. "I didn't mean to do it. Please, don't whip me." It was too late. She took me outside, cut a switch, and let me have a switching I'll never forget. I wish I could say it cured my bad temper, but it didn't.

I never seemed to have any space of my own. As we were growing up, I shared a room with Louise, and the rest of the time there always seemed to be someone around. I was now between 12 and 13 years old and longed for a place of my own. One day after Daddy had finished doing some work on the kitchen, I noticed there was some lumber left over. He had piled it up beside the house, probably to use at a later date. "Daddy, can I use your leftover lumber?" I asked.

"What on earth for?" he wanted to know.

"I want to build a room or a playhouse in the corner by the porch."

After much begging and pleading, he agreed. One stipulation was I would take it all down and clean it up sometime later.

I found a bucket of nails and a hammer and went to work. I worked for weeks making a lean-to on the corner of the house. I dreamed of how I would be able to be by myself and write my mystery stories. At this time in my life, my life's ambition was to be a writer. I used old tin for the roof. All in all, it was quite an accomplishment. I had a table and chair, blankets, and pillows for my bed. I begged Mama to let me sleep in it, but she would never agree to that. She was afraid a wind would come up and blow it down on me. I was able to spend several days in it, writing and pretending before disaster struck.

Louise decided it was an eyesore and she was going to get rid of it. She started knocking it down, and my temper rose bit by bit. I was so angry and determined to keep her from destroying my hideaway that I remember picking up a butcher knife from the kitchen table and chasing her around the house with it. I'm sure I would not have used it, but she ran screaming to Mama, "Help, help, Mama, make her stop!" I got another switching, and finished tearing my playhouse down myself. However, my desire for privacy and my own space continued.

Let There be Light

Electricity – probably my most memorable experience in my life.

"I guess we need to be thinking about getting the house wired," Daddy announced one spring morning. "They say we'll have electricity in a few months," he continued.

"I hope it won't cost too much," Mama replied. "The ones John and Eva are using are supposed to be the most reasonable," she remarked.

"We'll have to decide how many outlets we'll need in each room and have everything marked for them," Daddy said. I listened intently because I knew this would mean there would be all sorts of changes.

Up to this time we had studied by kerosene lamps, listened to radios with batteries, ironed with gas irons, cooked with a wood stove, and heated with a wood heater. Probably the most exciting thing we all wanted was a refrigerator. Mama had promised to make us ice cream. "We'll go to town on Saturday and look for a new stove and refrigerator," Mama said. She also wanted a washing machine and yet, I guess, those two things will have to wait for a little while.

She talked to the electrician the following day, and a date was set the next week to get the house wired. True to their word, Mama and Daddy went ahead and purchased a new stove and refrigerator and had them in place for the big event. I woke up so very excited: this was the day the electricians were scheduled to wire the house.

I was now thirteen years old and felt very grown up. I would be going to town school in the fall. I had grown quite tall by this age, around five feet seven inches. I was very thin and very self-conscious. Everyone was always teasing me about being so tall. "Opal, how's the weather up there?" someone was always saying. I went around feeling angry inside most of the time.

However, this beautiful spring morning in 1948, nothing could put a damper on my good spirits. How exciting to think that in a very short while we would have electricity. We could actually have all the ice we wanted for iced tea. "Mama," I yelled to get ahead of the rest of the chatter, "what time will they get here?"

"In a little while," she answered. "Get busy, finish breakfast and get this house cleaned up," she continued. After everyone had left the table from breakfast, I cleared the table and put water on to heat to wash the dishes. I suddenly remembered about the new hot water heater sitting in the corner of the kitchen. Mama and Daddy had gotten it when they purchased the refrigerator and stove. Kitchen sinks and hot water were essentials they had decided. I thought to myself, *It won't be long until I can turn on a faucet and have hot water.* Electricity was about to be the greatest thing to ever happen in our lifetime, I decided.

I finished the dishes, put on my jeans, which were too short for me as usual, a blouse Mama recently had made me, and ran outside to wait for the electricians to arrive. Morris, 10, Joan, 7, and Pat, now 4, were also hanging around outside waiting for the excitement to begin. Mama was busy inside taking care of Sam, who was only a year old. About this time, a pickup truck turned in our driveway and started up the hill to our house. "Mama, Mama, they're here!" we all screamed at once. By this time Daddy had left for work, so Mama was left in charge. Louise had left for work also. She was now 18 and worked at the shirt factory in Parsons. A lady that had worked at the factory for many years and lived in the neighborhood had agreed to give her a ride to work on a permanent basis.

I was sitting on the steps, when three people got out of the pickup truck. Two were older men, probably in their forties, but the other was a young man about eighteen. I was thirteen at the time and just beginning to notice the opposite sex. I remember thinking, Oh, what a good-looking boy. He walked over to where I was sitting, looked me straight in the eye and asked, "Is this Coy Phillips' house?"

I answered, "Yes, it is, and you're probably the ones that are going to wire our house, right? I'll run and get Mama." I ran inside and yelled, "Mama, Mama, they're here! You need to come out and talk to them."

"Just a minute, I need to put Sam down; then I'll be right out," she answered. "You'll have to keep an eye on him." She proceeded to lay Sam on the bed and went out the back door to talk to the workers. I placed a chair beside the bed and followed her out. She gave them instructions on where the outlets were needed, and they started to work. Mama went back inside to tend to Sam and finish ironing, but I stayed out where I could see what was going on.

I found out the boy's name was Mike and one of the electricians was his father. He was only helping during the late spring and summer and would go back to school in the fall. I also found out he would be a senior at Parsons High School. The wiring for our house took about a week. Each day I became more fascinated and intrigued with Mike. He actually treated me like I was someone important. I had a huge crush on him after only a couple of days. In fact, this was my first taste of puppy love.

The highlight of the week came the day before they were to finish our house. "Opal, do you want to go with me and show me where the other houses are that are scheduled to be wired?" he asked. There were three other houses they had agreed to wire.

"I'll ask Mama," I said. I rushed inside, completely out of breath. "Mama, can I please ride with Mike and show him where they need to go next? He says they'll finish ours tomorrow and will be ready to begin their other jobs. He needs to talk to the others about when they can start and needs me to show him where they live. Oh, please Mama, let me go," I begged. She had gotten to know Mike over the past week so I guess she figured it would be all right and she could trust him. I ran back out to his pickup truck and told him I could go.

    I'll never forget how grown-up I felt, riding in a pickup truck with an eighteen year old boy. I directed him to each of the houses, which took about an hour and one half. During the whole time we talked. He asked me questions about school, my likes and dislikes and just life in general. He even told my aunt, when we were at their house, that I was his helper. It was a day that has stayed vivid in my memory all my life. When I look back, I know it was because he treated me the way we all long to be treated. We like to feel important and special. That's very rare when you live in a large family and no one seems to have time for you. The following day was the last day I saw Mike. He didn't help with the other jobs in the neighborhood. His father said he had taken on a part-time job in Parsons. I wonder if he ever knew what his kindness had meant in my life.

    Our house had been wired for almost a month when the big day arrived. All the appliances were in place and plugged in, just waiting for power. Sometime just before noon, Morris came running through the house. "Guess what?" he yelled. "The lights are on!"

    We all started flipping lights and running to the refrigerator to see if the ice was freezing. Mama had promised to make us ice cream the following day with some mix she bought, called Junket ice cream mix. Today though, we were just going to have lots of ice for iced tea. We also kept turning the burners on the new stove on just to be sure it worked.

    "Mama, won't it be great not having to bring in wood to cook with?" I asked.

    "It sure will," she answered.

    Our first night of having electricity was absolutely awesome. After it got dark, everyone in the neighborhood had their porch lights on. "Can we please leave it on all night?" I pleaded with Mama.

Opal Phillips Johnson

"Just for tonight" she conceded.

We sat on the front porch with our light on and could see the glitter of all the other porch lights in the neighborhood. It was truly a day and evening I'll always remember. Now, almost fifty years later, I look around me and see so many things we take for granted. It was a time I cherish, but not a time I would want to go back to. I only hope my grandchildren can get a glimpse of what it was like without all the conveniences we have today. It took several years before we had indoor plumbing to put in a bathroom. Television sets were unheard of around our house until the early fifties. I always loved to read and dream of the places I would see someday. We've come a long way in our progress and technology, but I sometimes wonder if we have lost something along the way.

Turkey Tom

Even after having electricity, our entertainment consisted mostly of listening to the radio, reading, and listening to others tell stories. Our neighbor, Clay, who was Mamie's husband, was a master at telling ghost stories. He came up to our house on average of 2 times a week in the evenings after supper. He and Daddy would talk about things in general for a little while, but, inevitably, he would venture into one of his famous ghost stories. He told these for fact, but even as children we knew most of his tales were his vivid imagination.

One story in particular was about Turkey Tom, who supposedly haunted a cave a few miles from where we lived. He wore a bandanna around his neck and walked with a cane. We would gather around in awe, hanging on to every word until Mama announced it was bedtime. Many nights I would lie in bed too scared to go outside to the outhouse. Sometimes I could beg Louise into going with me, but most of the time I would just lie there miserable, until I finally went to sleep.

On occasion we got to go to the movies in Parsons. Our school bus driver would take the bus, and for a small fee we were picked up at our house and brought home after the movie. He also did this when the fair was in town, and this was a really big deal to get to go to the fair.

More School Days

When I was 13, I knew that I would be going to school in Decaturville in August. We started early and let out six weeks in the fall for cotton picking. "Mama, Aunt Kathleen says she has a present for me," I proudly announced one morning. "She said it's a graduation present from eighth grade. She also said I was one of her smartest students."

"That's nice," Mama commented, "but I wouldn't expect too much though."

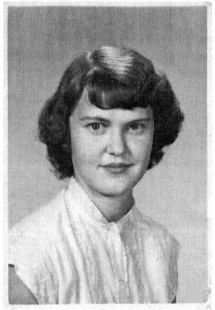

About a week later she stopped and left my present. It was a small locket that could also be used as a pendant. I was really proud of it until I found out later she had given her other niece something much nicer, along with an award certificate. There were 4 of us from Aunt Kathleen's school starting town school. There was a first cousin, Exie, another cousin, Alton, who was Mamie's son, and another distant relative, and, of course, me. I was literally scared out of my wits about starting to such a big school.

One of my classmates, in those days, reminded me of Nellie Olson from the "Little House on the Prairie" series. "Don't pay any attention to her," Mama would say over and over. "You're just as good as anybody, so hold your head up and remember that."

But she didn't have to listen to her brag and continually put people down. I made it fine for the first few days, but after that things went from bad to worse. The teasing and smart remarks from the "in crowd" seemed to get worse and worse. "Opal, don't you have enough money to buy Kleenex?' she would ask. I seemed to have a cold or allergies regularly. They would come up behind me and sniff, then snicker and walk off.

I found out right away that I had not been properly prepared for high school. We had memorized how to diagram sentences and created formulas for math, but I had no idea how they really worked.

"Opal, would you please come to the board and diagram this sentence?" asked Mrs. Flynn, my English teacher. I was petrified; I had no idea how or what to do. I walked to the board with tears in my eyes. I stood there a few seconds before she came over, laid her hand on my shoulder, and told me to sit down; someone else could do it.

After class was dismissed, I stood up to leave but before I got to the door, she said, "Opal, would you please stay for a few minutes?" She asked me when I had study hall. "I'd like to help you to understand the concept of sentence parts," she continued. From that time on she took me under her wing and taught me everything I know today about the parts of speech and other English concepts. She never put me on a spot but worked with me in her free time.

Mrs. Flynn also invited me and a couple of other girls to stay at her house when we had extracurricular activities at school. We had no way to get back to school plays, basketball practice, etc. She lived in a huge Greek Revival house, built sometime before the Civil War. She and her husband had a bedroom downstairs, so we would have the whole upstairs to ourselves. There were always two of us that stayed. I think I would have been terrified to stay by myself. Even with someone else in the room, I remember having trouble getting to sleep. There were so many creaks and unusual noises. She was so kind and made us feel so at home. I know now that she was one of those people that helped shape my life. In fact, her house was the first house where I was able to take a bath in a real bathtub.

She continued to work with me for the next couple of years with my homework during study hall and sometimes even during class. I learned English in a way I would never forget . I learned the parts of speech, how to diagram sentences, and all about term papers from Mrs. Flynn Pickens. I also learned to enjoy reading when I was in her classes, She made literature come alive for me.

I wish I could say I enjoyed my high school years, but as a whole, I didn't. I was a couple of inches taller than the boys, so I felt very self-conscious. I did go out for basketball because the coach asked me to because I was tall, but I was never very good. I always thought people were looking at my skinny, pied legs. I was always cold, so my legs looked red-checked. I did get a suit and I remember getting to play in a few games. I had only one boyfriend in high school. They all seemed so immature compared to the boys I met from Perry County.

Dating

By this time Louise was about 19 and dating guys from across the river. Mama would send me with her to keep an eye on her. I was only 14, but the next thing I knew, Louise's boyfriends were bringing someone for me. "Oh, Mama," she'd say, "she's only going to sit by them when we go to the movies. It's not really a date." There was usually a carload, which included my two cousins and different friends in the neighborhood. Most of the time we would go to a square dance some place. Dancing was my passion from the time I was 13. My cousin Exie and I would spend hours dancing to records and learning all the square dance steps. "Opal, I'll say I think we'll call you Clodie," Daddy announced one day. Clodie was the dance hall queen of Decatur County, so I was nicknamed Clodie for a time.

After Louise got her car, we didn't have to have dates for Saturday night and we would go to the V.F.W., where they had a band and dancing. A lot of single guys came, so we would just have a great time. This went on most of my high school years. I look back now and see how God protected us during that time. We had several automobile accidents but were never seriously injured. I cannot imagine how Mama survived having teenagers and babies at the same time. When I was 14, Sam was only 2, so it's hard to imagine how hard this must have been.

Mama had very strict rules and we had to be home by 11:30 p.m. on weekends. I remember one time in particular, Exie and I had dates and I wasn't really impressed with my blind date. He was shorter than I was. I had an ironclad rule - I would not date anyone shorter than me.

We went to a party in Perry County. It was a birthday party for a friend of the guy I was with. "We've got to be going," I announced about 10:45 pm. They kept eating and talking and ignored me. A few minutes later I said again, "We've got to go." This time they knew I meant it, so we left.

About 10 miles before we got home we had a flat tire. "We're already late," I cried. "If I don't get home by 12:00 a.m. Mama will ground me for months." I was so upset we drove the car the rest of the way home on the rim. He not only ruined the tire but also the rim. Mama was waiting up for us and needless to say she wasn't very happy but she did believe me. I never saw that boy again.

I dated very few boys my own age, mainly because they seemed so immature and the other reason being, I was so tall. I was 5 ft. 8 in. when I was 14 years old. Needless to say, there are very few boys that age that are that tall.

A Close Call

"Opal, Opal, please wake up! Don't die!", my sister Louise was screaming at the top of her lungs. I could hear her vaguely in the distance, but I couldn't seem to wake up enough to answer her. I struggled to come out of the coma-like state I was in. I could hear Louise, my cousin, Bobby and Lloyd talking, but I still could not comprehend what had happened or where I was. I raised my head up and realized I was lying in a ditch beside the car. Two other people were lying beside me with coats thrown over us because the weather was so cold in early December.

"What happened?" I asked, as I desperately tried to get up.

"Don't move," Louise said. "Stay there for a few minutes." My two cousins were now coming around and also asking questions.

"I should have gotten that muffler fixed," Lloyd commented. "I was planning on getting it done but decided to wait another week."

"I guess the fumes from the hole in the muffler were coming up into the backseat," Louise said. "We'll get them back in the car and take them on to Cordie's, and she can tell us what we should do," Louise said, half-crying.

"We'd better leave the windows down partway," Lloyd remarked. By this time my head was starting to hurt tremendously. We were all helped back into the car and taken to my aunt's house, which was about eight miles down the road. She seemed quite concerned and gave us aspirin and had us lie down for a while before we started back. I remember thinking, I've got to get to feeling better because I really want to go to Martha's Christmas party in a couple of days. I very seldom got invited to anything she had, so I really wanted to go.

I remember very little of the ride home. My head hurt so bad and I felt very sick to my stomach. My two cousins were in the same condition. "This hit you so suddenly," Louise said. "You were talking and suddenly you looked like you just froze. We couldn't get either of you to speak or move."

"You would probably have died if we hadn't noticed you when we did and got you to fresh air," said Lloyd.

When we got home, Mama was concerned, but I don't think she realized how close we came to death. We were never taken to the doctor, but I stayed in bed for the next three days, and I did miss Martha's Christmas party.

The rumor that circulated in the following weeks was that we didn't have carbon monoxide poisoning but had been drinking instead. "Well, just consider the source," Mama said, "but you won't be going back to Perry County for quite some time."

I was 15 when this incident happened. Louise was now 20 and thought she was madly in love with someone from Perry County. He would be going in service soon and she thought she should spend every spare minute with him.

Sweet 16 and Square Dancing

I had my 16th birthday party at the community center in Mt. Carmel, where young people could have parties or just hang out. I didn't have a steady boyfriend at the time so I remember having more girls than boys. However, sometime before it was over, the Perry County crowd showed up. One guy I was infatuated with brought me a necklace and earring set. This was my most treasured gift for many years.

Mama's rule about our going to Perry County didn't last too long. Just after my 16th birthday, we found out that one of the churches close to Daddy's brother's house was having a homecoming and dinner on the ground. "Oh, please let us go!" we begged. "We'll go over in a boat with our cousin and stay at Cordie's and come back early Sunday." She finally relented and said we could go if we promised to get back early Sunday afternoon, and we agreed to stay away from the wild bunch of boys that drank.

"Oh Louise," I began early the next day, "why don't we go shopping for new outfits? You get your check tomorrow and Palmers has some really cute things in." She seemed to be in a really good mood and said we would go look on Saturday. The big day was a little over a week away. Since Louise had been working at the factory, she could be quite generous if she was in the right mood.

Saturday morning rolled around and it was hectic as usual. This was the day Mama and Daddy went to town for feed and to buy the groceries. The children that got to go to town varied. Today was Joan and Pat's day and, of course, they had to take the two smaller boys. Sam was now 4, and a new brother, Danny Rickey, who was 1 year old.

Louise had gotten a car around her 20th birthday. She and I took off in her car before the others were ready to go in Daddy's pickup. There were always one or two kids in the back of the pickup. "Now, Opal," Louise began on the way to town, "you know I can't afford something real expensive, so remember that."

There were very few people in the store since we got there so early. Mrs. Palmer knew us quite well, since she had a daughter living in our community. "What can I do for you girls?" she asked.

"We're just looking," Louise answered.

"I got some new things in last week," Mrs. Palmer announced as she began to take several dresses off the racks. She held up a white organdy, with lace around the top, that was so beautiful. "This would look great on you, Opal."

I looked at Louise and asked, "Should I try it on?"

"Go ahead and see if it fits," she answered.

When I came out of the dressing room and looked in the mirror, I knew I had to have this dress. I looked at the price tag and realized it was probably more that she could pay. "Isn't it beautiful?" I asked. "And it looks like it was made for me." Mrs. Palmer agreed, of course.

"I'll give you a discount and you can charge it and make payments, if you like," she continued.

Louise had also tried on several dresses and found a two-piece outfit that looked great on her. "We'll probably need shoes too," Louise remarked as Mrs. Palmer was putting our dresses in bags. I found some white flats that looked great with my dress and Louise found some to go with her outfit.

All the next week I was so excited about our upcoming trip. We always had such a good time at Cordie's. They had a daughter about my age and usually we got along great. Her name was Sarah, but everyone called her Sari.

Saturday finally arrived, and we left bright and early. A friend took us across the river in his fishing boat. It only took about an hour if you went by boat, but by car it was probably a three hour drive. Sari and her brother were there to meet us when we got to the other side of the river. We had a wonderful time during the day and then that night they took us to a square dance in town. I absolutely never got tired of dancing.

The next morning, we put on our new outfits and left for the homecoming and dinner at the church. We were mingling and talking outside when I noticed this one boy looking at me. "Who is that?" I asked Sari.

"His Name is Glen Cross," she answered. "He lives up near Clifton."

"He sure is cute," I remarked.

All of a sudden, I noticed him walking over to where we were. I had been sort of dating for the past two years, but I had never been as impressed with anyone as I was with this young man. He was about my height and looked younger than his 18 years. His smile lit up his whole face. Today, I would say, he looked like Don Johnson, the movie star.

We talked for several hours, and he finally asked if he could drive me home. I talked it over with Louise, and she finally agreed it would be all right if we left fairly soon so we could get there by the time she did. We had a great time, talking and getting to know each other on our ride home. This began an off and on courtship that lasted until after I graduated from high school. We did not have telephones, so dating was rather difficult. Dates had to be made from one date to the next, and if something came up, there was no way to reach each other. Mama was not too pleased with me dating an older boy, but after a lot of discussion she came around. We dated regularly for the next several months. Several times he picked me up at school and drove me home.

"Oh, Exie," I told my cousin, one Saturday as we practiced some new dance steps, "I really think I'm in love with this guy. He's about the nicest guy I've ever dated."

"He's okay," she answered, "but I wouldn't tie myself down if I were you, with almost two more years of school. A lot can happen in that length of time."

He never asked me to go steady, so I dated different boys when he wasn't around. One boy I dated was somewhat older than I was; he was 21 and I was only 16. Needless to say, he was not on Mama's list of favorites. One of Louise's boyfriends had brought him along for me on one of their dates. His name was Ralph Anderson and he was quite a man about town. I only went out with him a few times and then double-dated with Louise and her boyfriend. Mama finally forbid me to sit by him or be any place around him. There was a local boy who had been trying to get me to date him and I didn't want to, so he tattled to Mama every time he saw me talking to a boy that was not on her list. He finally got me into serious trouble.

"Guess who's outside?" Louise asked just as Sunday night church was ending.

"I have no idea," I answered.

"Jim and Ralph," she replied. Louise had been dating Jim rather seriously for a while now.

"You know I can't get in the car with Ralph Anderson, or Mama will ground me forever."

"We'll just ride home with them and you can tell her tomorrow," she reasoned.

I really knew I shouldn't go but I thought I could talk myself out of trouble, and at this point, I wasn't even sure I would tell her. We went to Parsons to the Dairy Queen for a shake, but by the time we got home, Mama already knew who I was with.

Paul, the local friend and tattletale had gone straight from church to tell Mama I was in the car with Ralph. This was one I couldn't talk myself out of and I was grounded for the next month. I had no other contact with the forbidden fruit of boys until about six months later.

We were spending the weekend with Sari again and, of course, Saturday night was square dance time. There were about five of us girls that ran around together. The dance was held at a club in Clifton, Tennessee, and was a place that nice girls could go because there was no liquor sold or even allowed on the premises.

"It looks like it's going to be really crowded," Sari remarked as we parked the car.

"The more the merrier," I answered.

I was hoping Glen would be here, since I hadn't seen him for a month or more. I wasn't to be disappointed because just as we walked in the door, I heard someone call out my name. "Opal, over here!" I turned and saw Glen coming toward me. "Want to dance?" he asked as I finished hanging up my jacket.

"Sure," I answered, "I'd love to." We danced several sets and then decided to go get Cokes.

"Do you want to go outside and cool off?' he asked.

"That would be great," I agreed.

We started toward the door and who should come in but Ralph. I could tell immediately that he had been drinking. "What are you doing with my girl?" he asked as he grabbed my arm.

"Let go of her!" Glen answered, "And get this through your head, she's not your girl!"

"I suppose she's yours?" Ralph said as he swung at Glen. The next thing I knew Glen took a swing at Ralph and he was on the floor.

"Let's go," Glen said, as he took my arm and led me out the door.

"Let me tell Louise we're leaving," I said, while grabbing

my jacket from the rack. We told Louise we were going on to my aunt's house and would meet them there.

When I looked back, Ralph was getting to his feet and he seemed to have calmed down and I knew the trouble was over. I guess this would be considered a once in a lifetime experience. I've never forgotten how it felt to have two men actually fighting over me. It certainly wasn't something I bragged about but was most certainly a time I would never forget.

I dated Glen off and on through the rest of high school. I had loads of other boyfriends, but he had a special place in my heart, even after I graduated from high school and moved away to Nashville. I'll come back to that part of my life at a later time.

Cotton Pickin' Days

I guess I can understand a little of how it feels to be a transient worker. Daddy had an uncle that lived in one of the lower counties where they grew a lot of cotton. This was sometime before the machines to pick cotton came into being. The schools would let out around 6 weeks in the fall for cotton picking vacation. We packed up the whole family a couple of times and moved to Dyer County to pick cotton for those 6 weeks. Uncle Johnny had a cabin we lived in rent-free for the time we were there. The first time we went Joan was just a baby, which meant I was 6 years old. Mama would work and let me watch Joan at the end of the field in the shade.

"Coy," Mama announced one morning, "I'm going home. "This child is sick and I think it's probably the water." As I remember, Joan was about 9 months old at the time.

"We've only been here a little over 2 weeks and I hate to do Johnny that way. He needs us here since he has such few workers," Daddy answered.

We stayed around another week, but her condition seemed to worsen. "Pack up your things," Daddy announced one Saturday morning. "I've talked to Johnny and he's arranged for a driver to drive us home tomorrow." I'll never forget how excited we all were to be back at home.

Nine years later we had a similar experience. It seems our first episode was forgotten and Mama was ready to try again. Mamie and part of her family decided to go with us. We had a larger cabin this time, but it was nothing to brag about. I shared a room with all the girls and the boys slept in another room on the floor. Mamie and Mama did all the cooking. I can still remember how good the bacon smelled in the morning. We had a lot of fried chicken and biscuits for suppers and nothing ever tasted so good. Those were the good parts.

This time we stayed over a month and I guess we did all right money-wise because Daddy seemed to be pleased. We were able to buy school clothes to start back in the fall. There were at least 4 other times I left home to go away and pick cotton in the fall. The one I remember most vividly was when I was 14, and a cousin moved to one of lower counties to live.

"Mama," I begged one morning, "please let me go stay with Tootsie for a few weeks and make some money for my clothes for school. They're paying really good this year. Tootsie says I can make over $30.00 a week if the weather is good."

"How would you get there?" she asked.

"Gladys will meet me at the bus station if I can ride the bus. Joan could go with me," I said, doubting that she would go for that idea.

"Let me think about it," she answered, while putting supper on the table.

The next morning she announced that she had decided to let us go. "Daddy will drive you to Parsons on Saturday, and we'll write Gladys and Tootsie that you're coming so they can meet you." Tootsie was a cousin that lived in our neighborhood most of the time with her grandmother and two maiden aunts. I had spent several nights with Tootsie at her grandmother's, but this was a new experience.

Mama had decided I could take Joan along. I didn't feel

good about it but decided it was probably a good idea not to say anything about it. I proceeded to write Gladys a letter, telling her we were coming and would be expecting them to meet us at the bus station.

"I'm real excited about this," I remarked to Joan the next morning. "Aren't you?" I asked.

"I guess so," she answered "but I wish Mama would come too."

"It'll be great," I assured her, telling her all the good things I was looking forward to. I had this deep down feeling she would probably get homesick, but I hoped I was wrong and she would stay the month or so. I wanted to work and earn money for school clothes for fall.

On Saturday morning I jumped out of bed even before Mama had breakfast finished. "Mama," I began as I sat on the bench, watching her finish put the last of the biscuits in the pan, "have you finished packing Joan's things?"

"I think so," she answered, "but I suppose Gladys will wash for you regularly, and you probably won't need all you're taking with you."

The rest of the clan gathered around the table shortly for breakfast. There were now 6 children ranging in age from 19 to 2. Louise was 19, I was 14, Morris was 11, Joan was 8, Pat was 5 and Sam was 2. Dan and Cheryl were to come along later.

"Is Joan really going away for a month?" Morris asked. Mama seemed a little upset and told us all to be quiet and eat.

We left for the bus station around 10:00 a.m. in Daddy's pickup. We said our goodbyes at home and Daddy drove us to Parsons to meet the bus. I kept thinking Joan was going to start crying and back out, but she surprised me and was even a little excited about going.

We caught the bus at 11:30 a.m. and would be there around 1:00 p.m. I was a little nervous myself and afraid no one would be there to meet us. We had sandwiches in a bag and enough money to buy drinks from the machine when we got to the station. We ate our lunch on the bus and I tried to be in good spirits for Joan. "Isn't this fun?" I kept asking her. Riding on a Greyhound bus was quite an adventure for a 14 year old, let alone an 8 year old.

We arrived at the bus station right on schedule, and I could see Tootsie and her brother waiting for us even before we stopped. "Look, Joan, they're here!" I said excitedly. We took time to get us a drink and some candy from the machines before we left for the farm where they lived. We had no telephones at home so there was no way I could let Mama know we were there immediately, but I had promised to put a letter in the mail the next morning.

We drove about 15 miles from the station, through field after field of cotton. The fields were so white, they looked like they were snow-covered. Gladys was waiting for us on the porch and helped with our suitcases and showed us where we would sleep. Joan and I would sleep together in a room with Tootsie. She had gone to a lot of trouble to try to make us feel comfortable.

Our first hint of trouble came at suppertime. "I don't like cabbage and I don't like potatoes cooked this way," Joan whispered as we sat down to eat.

"Well, eat fried chicken and biscuits," I whispered back.

"I don't like white gravy."

"Then don't eat it," I snapped at her.

We started work the next morning, after eating a breakfast of foods Joan was not overly fond of. After a lot of coaxing, she ate a small amount.

I knew Joan was too young to work at the pace I did, so I told her she could go to the shade and rest anytime she wanted to. I worked so hard and I wonder now how I could have worked 8 to 10 hours a day - stooped over, pulling a loaded cotton sack. I averaged picking over two hundred pounds a day.

The first week went better than I had expected. It only rained one afternoon so we were able to work close to 5 days. I had made over $25.00 dollars, which was quite good in the year 1949. Gladys wouldn't take any money for room and board. This meant it was all profit. Joan had made a little less than $10.00. Each day we were there, Joan got a little more homesick. I just kept hoping she would stick it out and I could work a few more weeks. She cried every night for Mama and said she hated Gladys' cooking. I would talk to her and tell her if she would just try, it would be all right. I told her we would go shopping for clothes when it rained again or next Saturday afternoon. It did rain the following Wednesday and Lodie, Gladys' husband, and Tootsie's father took us all to Dyersburg to shop.

We had a great time shopping for school clothes. I remember buying a wool plaid skirt and several sweaters. We bought Joan a few things too, but she showed very little interest in anything except going home. We worked the rest of the week, despite her crying and begging to go home. I wrote Mama on Friday and told her we would be home the following Wednesday and to meet us in Parsons.

"This is the day we're going home!" Joan cried as she jumped out of bed all excited.
"It is," I agreed, wishing we could stay longer so I could make more money. I only had about $30.00 left, and I had to buy our bus tickets home. Joan had around $10.00.
We arrived in Parsons in the late afternoon tired, but excited to be home. Louise was there to meet us. "I'm really glad you're home," she remarked. "I'm tired of doing dishes."
"Aren't you glad to see us?" I asked her. I think she was but she just wouldn't admit it.

I had a couple of other interesting cotton picking vacations. These were with my aunt and uncle, J. C. and Dorothy Crossnoe. Dorothy was Mama's sister. They decided to go to Lake County and stay for a month or so in September of 1950. "Lemmie," Dorothy began one Saturday morning, "I thought we'd see if Opal wanted to go with us and make her school money for fall. Bobby and Alton are going too."
Alton was my age and Bobby a couple of years older. Mamie, their mother, had done a good job with them, and we got

along quite well. "I guess it would be all right," Mama answered. "She needs to make some money somewhere."

I was now 15 and felt very grown-up. Compared to today's teenager – I was. "Oh, Mama, this will be great," I cried. "I just know I'll do good." We left the next week, excited about our adventure. Bobby, Alton and I agreed to help with groceries and also to split the cooking and other housework. The man that owned the farm where we were going was named Cox. He was a really nice man and had a daughter exactly my age.

We arrived at our destination late in the afternoon. "This is great," I commented. "Look at how big the house is!" There were only two bedrooms, and the boys said they could sleep in the living-room on roll-a-way beds. I had a room all to myself, and I also made a friend the very first day named Lorraine Cox, and she and I got to be good friends in the next few weeks. By this time, we were both interested in boys, so this was our main topic of conversation.

The first week went off without any problems. Dorothy and I took turns cooking and the boys did dishes. "Opal," J. C. announced on Monday of the second week, "Dorothy doesn't feel good today so could you cook in her place? I can help you," he continued. I agreed but told him to get out of kitchen; I had rather do it myself.

I had never learned to work in the kitchen with anyone else. Mama would always say, "I'll go out and let you do it the way you want to." I had been cooking at home for almost a year before this episode. This pattern continued for most of the time we were there. I loved both of them, but I believe Dorothy was a little lazy, and J. C. pampered and petted her like a child. Later in life, J.C. died of cancer and several years later so did Dorothy. I loved them both very much. We stayed a full six weeks working in Lake County and did quite well financially.

"Opal," Dorothy announced one Saturday morning, "Mr.

My Place In Time

Cox is going to Tiptonville this morning. Do you want to go and spend some of your money on clothes?"

"Oh, could we?" I answered quickly. I had averaged over $30.00 a week, and even with expenses I had saved over $100.00.

Dorothy was a lovely person, but her taste was all in her mouth. I look back now at the clothes we bought for a 15 year old and cringe. They were way too old for me. I didn't know much different either so I wore most of them. Thank goodness, we didn't spend all my money, so Louise took me shopping at Palmers with the rest I had to spend on clothes.

On this trip in 1950, Dorothy wouldn't let me out of the house with anyone except Bobby and Alton. We went to the movies several times with Lorraine and a couple of her friends, but I wasn't allowed to have a boyfriend.

This trip went so well that we decided to go back the next year. We didn't have the same house the next year, but I liked where we lived in 1951 even better; it was closer to town. My cousin Exie and her family came down this particular year and they lived in town. They had a nice white house where you could walk to the movies and restaurants. I spent almost every weekend with them on this trip. We met several boys and really had a ball. I can't imagine how we had enough energy to do anything after picking cotton all day but somehow we did. I guess that's just being 16.

That year I bought great clothes and also saved enough to pay all the fees we had to pay at school. There were fees in every class, it seemed. It all totaled up to $30.00 or $40.00. This time in my life was difficult, to say the least, but when I look at how much I learned about life and the experiences I had, I wouldn't change anything.

One experience I forgot to mention happened on our second trip in 1951. I had tried to keep J.C. out of the kitchen when I cooked, but he persisted in trying to help me. One night he came in and was goofing around with a dishtowel, He kept snapping it at me and joking and laughing. I picked up one and yelled, "Two can play this game!" We snapped the dishtowels at each other a few times before disaster struck. I pulled my towel back and snapped it and the next thing I knew J. C. was on the floor. "J.C.!" I screamed to the top of my lungs. "Get up! Get up!" I cried. By that time Dorothy had gotten to the kitchen and was screaming too. Bobby ran in and grabbed a washcloth and placed it on J.C.'s temple. A couple of seconds later, he started coming around. I guess I had hit just the right spot on his temple.

"You could have killed him!" Dorothy said as she stroked his head.

"He started it!" I cried. "Are you going to be alright?" I kept asking.

"Should we get him to a doctor?" Bobby asked.

"I'm alright" J.C. kept insisting. He was fine, and there never seemed to be any adverse consequences. It really scared me, because sometime later I realized he really could have died.

Senior Year

In the fall of 1952, I started my senior year in high school. I did not go away for cotton picking vacation that year. I did work, but I stayed home and worked on a sharecrop of cotton Daddy had instigated for the Crawleys. We hoed it in the spring and picked it in the fall. After it was completed, we got a share of the profits. Daddy paid us for what we picked and he made a percentage too.

That year in the spring, I got a suntan you would die for today. I worked with a halter top and shorts and absolutely cooked my skin. I did this in late May and June. I had a suntan I'll never forget, but I now realize I had exposed myself to skin cancer for the rest of my life.

I was really excited about being a senior, but also a little apprehensive. I knew I really didn't want to work at the factory for the rest of my life, but there seemed to be so few alternatives. I would love to have gone to college or even to business school, but I also knew we could not afford it. *Opal, what are you doing after graduation?* was a question I avoided if at all possible. *I'll probably go to business school,* I pretended. I really loved typing and was quite good at it. I could type 120 words a minute. I had good grades in all my subjects except one. In home economics I always got a "B" no matter how hard I tried. Mrs. Pauline was the only teacher I had that I just couldn't relate to. She strictly had to have everything her way and there was no variation whatsoever.

One particular instance I remember vividly. "Opal, did you take your baby dress home?" Mrs. Pauline asked as she passed my desk early one Monday morning.

"I did," I answered, "but I didn't work on it. I only asked Mama how to fix the mess I have it in."

We were making baby dresses as a sewing project. I had already been sewing for 3 years. Mama taught me her sewing techniques when I was only 14. She didn't baste anything; she just pinned it in a couple of places and then sewed it. Well, needless to say, I preferred Mama's way. I finished my baby dress, turned it in and only got a B. In all my other classes, I always got straight A's. This infuriated me because I knew it was probably the best in the class, but she would absolutely give me nothing higher than a B.

"Opal," my cousin Exie said on the way home that afternoon, "I haven't finished my baby dress and she'll probably give me an F for the whole year because of this one project. What did you get on yours?" she asked. "Just a B," I said, "but that's par for her class."

I had my dress in a bag taking it home to probably throw it in the garbage. We had all made dresses exactly the same for this one project.

"There's no way I can turn mine in by next Friday," she commented. "She probably wouldn't know the difference if I used yours," she added.

"I don't know," I answered. "What if she found out? We would both get F's."

"She'll never know the difference," she begged.

I finally relented and handed her the dress. She turned it in the next day as her project. When Mrs. Pauline gave it back to her, she had an A. I was furious but there was absolutely nothing I could do about it.

Exie had a boyfriend from Perry County that picked her up

at school several times in her senior year. I rode with them on occasion rather than ride the bus. She approached me in study hall one Friday afternoon and announced that I could ride home with them that afternoon if I wanted to. "Sure," I answered, "if Howard will let me drive part of the way."

"I don't know about that," she said, "but you can ask him."

I had been driving Daddy's pickup on occasion. My last experience driving the pickup had not turned out too well. I hit the clutch instead of the brakes when I went to stop and lunged into the side of the porch. I knocked the lights out and burst the radiator. Daddy was not pleased, to say the least, and insisted I would have to pay the repairs eventually. He relented on this when he did the same thing a few months later. The pickup had only been repaired for a short time when the brakes didn't hold when Daddy started to stop beside the porch, and he did almost the identical damage I had previously done. He was furious but relented on my having to pay back the price of fixing it the first time.

So on this particular Friday when I insisted on driving Exie and Howard home, I was not known as the best driver around. "Can I drive?" I asked as we approached the car.

"After we get out of town," he agreed.

We did not have paved roads in 1952. They were gravel and dangerous if you drove too fast. A few miles from school, Howard stopped the car and I took the wheel. Another boy was with him whose name, I think, was Joe. Joe got in the front with me, and Howard and Exie got in the back seat.

"Opal, I don't think you should drive so fast," Joe said. "This gravel can be slippery." He had no more gotten this sentence out of his mouth when I turned a curve in the road too fast and the car started sliding. I had no idea how to get it back, and the next thing I knew we were in a ditch. Everyone was yelling at me so, naturally, I started to cry. "Stop crying!" Exie said. "It's not going to help."

"We'll have to get someone to pull the car out," Howard said as he assessed the damage. "I don't think the car is damaged, but we'll never get it out by ourselves."

"We'll walk over to the nearest house and see if someone has a tractor," Joe commented.

Exie and I got back in the car and sat down and waited.

My Place In Time

We eventually heard a tractor coming up the road and were able to get the car out in a short time with the help of a local farmer and his tractor. I thought I would be in bad trouble when I got home, but Mama was so glad I wasn't hurt that she was pretty lenient on this occasion.

My senior year does not hold too many fond memories. As I said before, I dated very few boys in my school, and my other boyfriends would not come to my functions at school. I remember asking Glen to come to my senior prom, but he said he couldn't come so I did not have a date. I wasn't the only one in this predicament; so many of my school friends did not have dates either. We all sat together with the boys we were just friends with.

"Opal," Mrs. Pike, our librarian, said as she approached me early one January morning. "Do you have any plans after you graduate?" she asked.

"No, I don't," I answered. "I'll probably just work at the factory with my sister."

"Would you be interested in working at an insurance company in Nashville?" she continued. "We have scouts coming next week to talk to the top girls in the class about coming to Nashville to test for training positions with National Life and Accident Insurance Company. Talk it over with your parents and get back to me as soon as possible," she continued.

The more I thought about this, the better it began to sound, so by the time I got home I was really excited. I tried to approach Mama at the right time when I had something serious to talk to her about. On this particular night I volunteered to cook supper and didn't get into an argument with Louise about dishes so when I approached her about the possibility of going to Nashville after graduation, she at least listened. I put up a really good argument. "It would be the opportunity of a life time. Only the smartest girls are asked to go and be tested," I continued. "There are 6 that will probably go, but that doesn't mean we will all get jobs," as I continued to make my case. "Mrs. Pike will drive us up there and they'll give us a free lunch. Oh, please Mama, say I can go!" I begged. "I might not even pass the tests, but I wish I could at least go and try," I said with tears in my eyes.

"I'll talk to your Daddy later," she said as she walked outside.

I really prayed she would give me this chance to do something different with my life. I would have loved to be able to go on to college, but I also knew that was an impossibility at this time, so this would probably be the next best thing. I spent a restless night, but just before I started to school, she said they had decided to at least let me go and test for the job. I guess down deep I knew they wouldn't have the heart to not let me go if I passed all the tests.

What an exciting time this was in my life! The scout came the following week and selected 6 that were eligible to go and told us the day we would be coming and exactly what to expect. One backed out the following day and decided not to try for it. Now there were five that planned to go the following Wednesday. I had known the other girls before, but now we all had something in common and started becoming fast friends right away.

"Mildred, wait up!" I called as I saw her getting off her bus the next day. "Are you excited?" I asked.

"Of, course," she said. "Aren't you?"

"I really am, but I'm so scared I won't pass."

"Oh, you will," she said as we departed for separate classes.

This was Mildred Tucker, who would probably be valedictorian, and I knew she would probably have no trouble passing. There was another Mildred going and her name was Mildred Hopper. There was also a girl named Sue and one named Betty. I had never been particularly close with any of them before, but I also knew that would probably change.

In the next few months before graduation, my life would change drastically. Wednesday finally arrived and we were all nervous wrecks by then. "Mama, are you sure this outfit is all right?" I asked for the tenth time as I finished getting dressed on this, the most important of days.

"It's fine," she kept telling me. Mrs. Pike planned to leave school around 8:00 a.m. hoping to get there by 11:00 a.m. Our first test and interviews were scheduled to begin at 11:15 a.m. and lunch was to be at 12:30 p.m.

As soon as we arrived at school, we all met in the library for last minute instructions. We were told again that we would not know the results for around two weeks and to just do the best we

My Place In Time

could and make the school proud. Girls were coming from schools all over the state of Tennessee. This was such a great opportunity for those of us who could not afford to go to business college.

There were 6 people in the car so it wasn't the most comfortable drive. However, it's hard for five 17 year olds to be quiet and subdued. "Mrs. Pike, can we stop for a Coke?" Sue asked, shortly after we had gotten started.

"I'll stop in about an hour for a Coke and bathroom break," she announced, hoping it would be the last time we asked for a while. After stopping for our break, we still drove into the parking lot around 11:00 a.m. We were assigned a conference room and told someone would be with us shortly. We filled out forms and interviewed with different department heads for the next hour. We were then given our assignments for the afternoon. We were to all meet back in the original conference room at 1:30 p.m.

I met Mildred outside the front door getting a breath of fresh air. "Where are you going this afternoon?" she asked.

"I'm taking typing tests and visiting the Key Punch Dept. on the 4th floor," I answered. "Where are you going?" I asked her, thinking maybe she would be with me.

"I'm going to tour the Accounting Dept. on 7th floor after I do some other tests with numbers," she answered. We started out for the cafeteria to meet the rest of our group. We were served a wonderful lunch and we were all glad to relax for a short time.

"Do you think you passed?" I asked one of the girls as we finished our tests and turned in the results to the lady in charge.

"I think so," she said, "but it's always hard to tell."

There were around 10 girls taking typing tests. After everyone had finished, the instructor said we would have a short break before we toured the Key Punch Dept. on 4th floor. I had never met a kinder lady than Mrs. Belew, the one in charge of training the girls for positions a few months down the road. "I hope to see everyone of you back after you graduate in May" she said as we left to meet our group in the lobby. We left National Life around 3:30 p.m. in the afternoon. Tired and drained, but also with a feeling of a sense of accomplishment. Now all we could do was hope for the best in the two weeks to follow.

We had made arrangements for someone to pick us up at

school around 7:30 p.m. Louise had promised to be there and I just hoped she didn't forget. We were all quieter on the way home, feeling tired and ready to just reflect for a while.

We stopped for supper around 6:00 p.m. and that gave us a new burst of energy. "It's going to be hard," Mrs. Pike announced after we got back in the car. "We'll just believe all of you passed and have jobs after you graduate." Louise was waiting for me when we got back to the school sometime after 7:00. "How did you do?" she asked right away.

"I think I did all right, but we'll just have to wait and see."

"I'll miss you, if you do go away to Nashville," she said out of the blue.

"Oh, yeah! Sure you will," I said. "You'll probably miss me because you won't have anybody to bribe to do dishes."

"That's probably true too," she answered.

The next two weeks dragged by, but we tried to make the most of the situation and not be too nervous. My boyfriend, Glen, came over on Saturday night and we went to a movie. I hadn't told him there was a possibility I would be moving to Nashville because I wanted to tell him in person. He was working on a boat during this time and was gone 30 days at a time, so I hadn't seen him for a couple of months before this.

His boat had docked in Perryville some 2 months before. Frank had taken Louise and I down on Sunday to see him and tour the place where he spent most of his time. When I told him about possibly moving to Nashville, he wasn't very happy, to say the least. "I'll never see you," he said.

"I'll probably come home almost every weekend," I answered. "We can ride the bus, if we can't get a ride with someone that is working there," I continued, "so it shouldn't affect anything very much." All the while knowing down deep that it probably would.

"You'll likely meet someone else and forget all about me," he said.

"That will never happen," I assured him.

"Would the group that went to Nashville a few weeks ago, please come to the library," the principal announced over the intercom early on Wednesday, exactly two weeks later. My knees went weak, as I left my French class and met the others in the library. Mrs. Pike came in just as the rest of us entered and took seats around a table. She sat down and looked at the letter she held in her hand. "We have 3 from the 5 that were accepted," she said sadly. "I wish it could be different, but it's not," she continued. As we all held our breath, she read the names of the ones that were accepted. "Mildred Tucker, Mildred Hopper," and then she paused before she said my name, "Opal Phillips."

Although we felt bad for Sue and Betty, we could not help but be elated that we were going. When I look back now, I know this was a day that changed my life forever. If I had not gotten this opportunity, my life would have taken a completely different turn.

I could hardly wait to tell Mama and Daddy about my good fortune. "I guess it'll be all right, but I can't help but worry about you," Mama said after I had delivered the good news. "There are so many things to think about," she said. "Where will you live is a main concern," she continued.

"Mildred and I thought we would stay at the Y. W. C. A. for a while," I answered. "It is supposed to be well-chaperoned and a safe place for girls or at least that's what Mrs. Pike says. It's right down the street from where we'll be working," I assured her. "We can eat our meals there or eat out part of the time." I rambled on. "We don't know exactly how much we'll make yet, but I know I'll be able to send some home to help Daddy out," I said excitingly. This all happened in January of 1953, and we would not graduate until May.

The next few months would be spent in planning our future in Nashville. Everything went on as usual. We had our Senior Prom, a play production to make money for a Senior trip and, of course, just the excitement of graduation itself. Mildred and I were good friends now and asked to be in rooms together when we went to Chattanooga for our class trip. We were planning to leave right after graduation and arrive there sometime early in the morning.

"Mama, are you going to graduation?" I asked a couple of weeks before.

"I'll try to go," she said, "that is, if Louise will let us go with her. Daddy will stay here with the boys, but I will try to go."

I reserved 8 seats on the floor for my family the next day,

but I knew there would only be 3 or 4 there. "Are you packed for your trip?" Louise asked as I was getting ready for school a couple of days before graduation.

"Which one?" I asked. "We're leaving for Nashville in less than a week after I get back from Chattanooga, so I'm also trying to get everything ready for that," I continued. The day before, Louise had taken me to Parsons to buy a suitcase. "Do we have to buy this awful-looking brown one?" I wanted to know, hoping she would change her mind and buy me the white Samsonite one.

"You can charge it and buy it yourself," she said, "but I'm not paying that much for luggage."

"Maybe I'll get it for Christmas," I said matter of factly.

"You'll never get out of debt anyway," she said as she paid for the brown suitcase.

I guess it'll have to do I thought as we walked out of store. At least it's good-sized and I can take a lot of stuff in it. I knew she was right about all the things I had already charged, getting ready for my new life.

Daddy had borrowed a hundred dollars from the local bank so I could get by until I got a check. I knew I would have to make payments on that, plus I had bought several new clothes at Palmers Department Store and charged them. "Mama, I simply love the things you've made for me," I commented as I packed my brown suitcase, especially my white dress. It fits so good," I went on.

Louise interrupted, "You'd better be getting your things ready for your class trip," she said, "And quit spending all your time getting ready for Nashville. You'll have time to finish up that after you get back."

"I guess you're right," I agreed as I packed a small bag for our class trip. I knew we would probably wear jeans most of the time. One of the chaperones had said we would probably eat at a nice place one night, so we should bring at least one dress. We had raised enough money as a class to pay for the motel and one banquet. Breakfast was also included in the package deal. I received some money for graduation gifts, but I was hoarding it to have to take to Nashville.

"This is the day," Mama said as I sat dawn to breakfast. "On the day of graduation, I hope everyone behaves themselves on this trip," she commented.

"I can't believe it's really here," I answered. "Time has dragged by since January," I remarked.

"You know how much I am going to worry about you in Nashville, practically on your own?" she said. "You also know I've trusted you for a long time, and I have to trust you now to make right decisions," she continued.

"We'll be fine," I assured her, both on this trip and in Nashville. "You just worry too much," I said as I left the table to get ready for the most exciting day in my life.

We were only going to school for a few hours, and I was catching a ride with one of my friends today so I wouldn't have to ride the bus and stay all day. "They'll be here around 10:00 a.m. and we should be home by 2:00 p.m.," I reminded her. "We'll have to get there early tonight, but I guess Louise knows that."

"I'll be ready to leave by 6:00 p.m.," Louise answered.

Graduation went off without any major problems. Mildred made a speech because she was valedictorian, and another speech was given by a girl, also named Mildred. I came in third with a 97.6 average for four years. This was even with my B's from Mrs. Pauline. The ceremony was eventually over and at last we were given our diplomas.

We met at a chartered bus in the school parking lot about an hour later. Still on cloud nine, Mildred and I took our seats, two seats back from the driver. We knew the rowdy ones were going to be in the back of the bus, and we wanted to keep out of trouble at all cost. Our big adventure was coming up in a couple of weeks and we wanted smooth sailing for that.

"I've never been to Chattanooga," I said to Mildred as we relaxed after getting started around 11:00 p.m.

"I haven't either," she commented.

There was great excitement on the bus for the first hour of our trip. We sang and talked until we were hoarse. Sometime around 2:00 a.m. Mildred and I both went sound asleep. In a couple of hours, I awoke to someone yelling, "We're coming into Chattanooga! Everybody had better wake up."

Sometime in the wee hours of the morning, we checked into our motel tucked into the side of Lookout Mountain. "You can sleep until around 8:00 a.m.," our chaperone announced. "We'll be having breakfast at 9:00 a.m. in the main dining room," she continued. "The bus will leave at 11:00 a.m. for our tour, so be sure and be on time or you'll be left," she said as we all dragged ourselves to our assigned rooms for the next three days. Everything went quite smoothly for the first-twenty four hours, mainly because everyone was totally wiped out. We had free time in the late afternoon before our banquet at 7:00 p.m.

The banquet was over around 9:00 p.m. and that's when everything seemed to break loose. Many of the wild and popular group sneaked boys into their rooms. Somehow they had gotten booze and the partying began. I am truthful in saying we were not involved in it, but we knew a party was going on across the hall. They disturbed the other guests in the hotel by all the noise they were making. The chaperones were called in and at one point there was talk of our group being asked to leave. The worst part of it was the fact that our bus driver was drinking with some of the boys. He was a chartered bus driver and was reported because of his behavior. However, he was allowed to finish the tour, which seemed strange to me.

The trip itself was quite fun, mainly because most of us had never taken a real vacation before. It was my first time to stay in a motel, and I'm sure it was for a lot of the others. We found out later there was talk of ending Senior trips because of the way our trip turned out.

We got home safely on Tuesday, quite tired and worn out. I knew now I had less than two weeks before I would be leaving home for good. It felt good in some respects but in other ways, I was terrified. I promised Mama we would come home every weekend if at all possible. Joan was now eleven, Pat was eight and Morris was fourteen. No one seemed very sad that I was moving away. "I'll probably have to do the dishes now," Joan said. Louise thought she was too old to do much of anything anymore. Besides, she was working at the factory. I had cooked supper almost every night for the past couple of years, so I knew Mama would miss that part of my being gone.

"Opal, what kind of concoction have you cooked up tonight?" Daddy would ask as we gathered around for supper.

My Place In Time

There were now 9 in the family so it wasn't an easy task to cook, because you had to cook so much. When we had fried chicken, we had to cook three chickens. Morris was our biggest eater at this time. I guess he was a typical teenager when it came to food. He could eat almost a whole chicken by himself. Louise, my oldest sister, was now 23, I was 17, Morris, 14; Joan, 11; Pat, 8; Sam, 5; and the youngest was Dan, who was only 2.

We had a small grocery store that Daddy built in the corner of the house. I'm not sure they ever made any money on it because the kids ate up the profit.

"Mama, do you want me to do the sales tax statement for you?" I asked as I finished packing my brown suitcase.

"It has to be mailed in next week," she answered.

"I'll do it before I go to bed," I replied.

This was one of the worst parts of having the store - trying to keep up with the paperwork. I had been helping Mama with that for the past two years. Mama was so tired and exhausted by mid-afternoon that she would do anything not to have to cook supper. I loved to cook and she would let me use anything we had in the store to get me to do it. We didn't carry produce or meat, only canned goods, dried beans, Cokes and candy.

We were the second small grocery store in the community over the years. Since we lived thirteen miles from town, there was a real need for one. The Crawleys ran one for many years, but they also sold gasoline. I think we probably lost money in the long run because Daddy was so generous to give credit to everyone, and more than a few did not pay their debts. The store lasted a few years and I'm sure Mama was glad it closed. Daddy's brother, Omer, opened one shortly after ours closed. Several years later the Crawleys opened another one.

Nashville – The Beginning

"I can't believe you're really leaving," Louise said as she drove me to catch the bus to Nashville early one Saturday morning around the last of May. Mildred and I had decided to go up on

Saturday so we could get everything settled and be ready to start our jobs on Monday. I don't know what we would have done if the Y. W. C. A. had been full and we couldn't have gotten rooms. I guess we would have caught a bus back home. We did not have phones, so there was no way to call and find out, so we just took our chances.

"I'll be home next Friday night, so be sure and be here to pick me up," I reminded her. "I wish I could have seen Glen before I left, but he won't be on leave from the boat for a couple more weeks; maybe I'll see him then. You know my birthday is in a couple of weeks," I remarked, hoping she would remember to buy the Samsonite luggage I wanted.

Mildred was already at the bus stop when we arrived. "I hope the bus isn't late," she said. "I've been here for an hour already."

"We've got time to get a Coke," Louise commented, "that is, if we hurry."

"The bus is coming!" someone yelled from the restaurant where we were getting our Cokes.

"It's early," I said. "I guess we'll have to get a Coke at the stop in Linden."

We took our small bags with us but let the driver store the big ones under the bus. We said goodbye to Louise, Mildred's sister, Nancy, and her mother and took our seats up close to the front of the bus. We had a couple of stops, one in Linden and the other in Centerville, before arriving in Nashville around 1:00 p.m.

We had scouted out the city on our second visit with Mrs. Pike, after we had been told we had the jobs with National Life so we halfway knew where we were going. "Are we going to lug our bags 4 blocks to the Y?" I asked Mildred as we collected our belongings.

"I guess so," she answered. The other choices are to get a cab or wait for a bus and that could be hours.

We carried our heavy bags the 4 long blocks to the Y.W.C.A. located at Church and Union. The lady at the front desk was nice and friendly, but if she hadn't been, I think I would have turned around and left. "We have a wonderful room on third floor and it's close to the showers and convenient to the elevators," she said. It was to be $10.00 a week, not including meals, and we had to pay two weeks in advance. We thought we might eat in our room part of the time so we decided not to buy the meal tickets. We both had brought quite a bit of goodies from home so we knew we wouldn't starve for the first few days.

National Life & Accident Insurance Co. HQ

One of the counselors or room mothers, escorted us to our new residence. "It's just down the hall," she said, as we carried our heavy luggage the last leg of our journey. She gave us each keys and told us to guard them very carefully. She also gave us a typewritten page of rules and regulations that must be strictly adhered to. If not, we would be asked to leave. This was supposed to be a safe and homey environment. We had to be in by 10:30 p.m. unless we had permission from a councilor who would make arrangements for us to get in the front door. All doors were locked and secured by 11:00 p.m. on week nights and 12:00 a.m. on weekends. There was a T. V. and family room on the second floor, where we could go any time until 11:00 p.m. We sat our luggage down and took a good long look at our new home.

She said to call the front desk from the phone in the hall if we were in trouble or saw anything suspicious going on. She left and closed the door. I'll never forget the sinking feeling I had in my stomach as I looked around that room. There were two twin beds, a couple of chests, a small closet, and a half bath with commode and sink. There was only one mirror and that was over the sink. "We can make it look better," Mildred said as we started to unpack. She always seemed to have a positive attitude, which helped to get us through the next few days. I had taken some of my graduation money and bought a radio. It was a red Sylvania and turned out to be a lifesaver over the next couple of years. We could listen to music, the news or just have it for company. Neither of us was used to having a TV so it would be a treat to go to the family room and watch TV after supper. So began our first week living away from home.

Our first weekend was quite exciting. We showered, got dressed and went downstairs to check out the cafeteria and discovered the prices weren't as high as we had expected so we decided to eat supper there. "Let's splurge and go to a movie," Mildred said as we finished our dessert. "I saw that 'From Here To Eternity' was playing at the theater on Church Street," she continued.

"What time does it start?"
"At 7:00 p.m., I think."
"We'll be back a little after 9:00 p.m. Then we can watch TV for a couple of hours." Our evening went pretty much as planned, and we were ready for bed before 11:00 p.m. I remember lying in bed and talking about an hour or more before finally going to sleep. This was one of many nights we would share our hopes and dreams with one another.

The next morning we were up and dressed by 8:00 a.m. "Let's go out and have breakfast," Mildred said as she finished doing her hair.

"Sounds good to me."

"We'll walk around for a while after we eat."

We walked to the corner and ate at Krystal. The waffles were wonderful there. Afterwards we walked up Church Street past the McKindrick Methodist Church. "Look," I commented, "we'd have time to get dressed and come back to church. Would you like to?"

"That might be fun, it's such a beautiful church; I'd like to see the inside." We crossed the street and walked back past Harvey's Department Store, past Castner Knott, before crossing the street at the corner ending up back at the Y.

We had both admired the clothes in both the big stores on our way back. "It'll sure be different shopping here than at Palmers," I commented. "I can't wait to have some money."

"Maybe someday we can buy a sewing machine," she said. "Then we could make our clothes and it would be a whole lot cheaper." This was a dream we would realize in a year or so.

We went to church, had a sandwich at Wilson Quick Drug Store on the corner beside the Y on our way home. There you could have a grilled cheese sandwich, chips and a Coke for around fifty cents. Later, Wilson Quick would become our mainstay when we were trying to conserve our money. We spent the rest of the afternoon talking, reading, listening to the radio, and eventually going down to watch TV before retiring around 10:30 p.m. We knew we had to be at work by 8:00 a.m., which meant getting up at 6:00 a.m.

It was hard to get to sleep on this particular night, mainly because we were so anxious about the next day. We absolutely did not have any idea what to expect. On this particular Monday morning, we both awoke with a start when the alarm went off at 6:00 a.m. Mildred looked outside our door and gasped, "There are 10 or more people in line to shower," she said as she closed the door, so we decided to do a sponge bath and from then on to get our showers at night.

We dressed and decided to eat in the cafeteria this

morning, mainly because we wanted to have plenty of time on our first day. "I wish we were working together," I commented as we walked the couple of blocks to National Life. "At least on the same floor would be nice." We already knew what departments we would be working in, this having been decided from our tests we had taken several months before. I was to report to 4th floor, the Key Punching Department, and Mildred was to be on 7th floor, working with numbers or accounting. We parted on the elevator after making plans to meet at lunch in the cafeteria. "If our lunch times aren't the same or if something comes up, I'll call you," she said, as I left the elevator.

I felt very much alone, as I proceeded to a reception desk to ask how to find a "Mrs. Belew." She would train us for the next few weeks before we would be placed on a team as a Jr. Clerk. The receptionist directed me on how to find my assigned position. There were several girls lined up at her desk, when I got there. "Gather around," she said "and I'll talk to you all together. You must be Opal," she said as she looked my way. "We have two others that haven't arrived yet so we'll wait about anything important until they get here. We usually train about 10 girls at one time," she commented. "However, this time we may have twelve. It takes about 3 weeks for the training, then we place the girls on teams, as openings come up."

I knew any fears I might have had were not warranted after I met Mrs. Belew. She was so kind and talked so soft and gentle. I knew immediately it would be a joy to work for her. I found out later that everyone called her Mother Hen and her girls her chicks. The other two girls arrived, and we were assigned our desks and had our first meeting about our new jobs.

Before we realized it, it was lunchtime. "I'll escort you to the cafeteria," she said. "You probably wouldn't get lost, but I'll do it for a couple of days. Mildred had called and we would be having our lunch hour at the same time, so we were excited about that. Mrs. Belew escorted her chicks to the lunchroom, where I found Mildred already there. "How's it going?" I asked as we went through the line.

"I think I'll like it," she answered. There's an awful lot to learn, we both agreed.

My Place In Time

At 4:30 p.m. we met back in the main lobby and started our walk back to our new home. We talked continually for the next few hours before deciding what we would do for supper. We both knew we had to conserve our money, so agreeing on an economical place was no problem.

Tuesday morning, our second day, was much the same as the previous one, except we were "learning the ropes" so to speak. In the cafeteria, one of the girls came over to our table, introducing herself as Mary. We introduced ourselves and continued to talk for a few minutes before she brought up the subject of the Tuesday Y Club. Someone else had mentioned it, but we needed more details. There was a monthly membership of $5.00, but that includes dinner, dances both on Tuesday and Saturday, and transportation to U. S. O. dances on both the Air Force and Army Bases, Seward and Fort Campbell. By this time, we had observed that Nashville was invaded by servicemen. "I hate to part with $5.00," I said to Mildred after Mary left the table, "but it sounds like a way to meet people, and you know how I love to dance." We talked about it on our way from work and decided to try it for a month.

"We'll get four meals out of it," she commented, "besides getting to go to the dances."

"There are also other benefits I had read in a brochure she had given us," I answered. My birthday was in a few weeks, and you get a special birthday cake and a small gift, or so it said in their literature. We left it at that, and decided to go that night and try it out. This gave us something to look forward to for the rest of the day.

Our second day went much the same as our first, except some of the fear and apprehension was gone. We had an hour for lunch so we met in the lobby and went to Krystal for lunch, then walked around window shopping for a few minutes before going back to work. Our group was learning how to read an insurance rate book and check the applications the agents had mailed in against the book. The day passed quickly and before we knew it, we were on our way back to the Y, excited about our upcoming evening.

"What are you going to wear?" I asked.

"Probably just a skirt and blouse," she answered. "They said it was casual," she continued.

"I have a sundress with a jacket, I think I'll wear that. Mama made it for me a couple of weeks ago and I haven't worn it yet, and, besides, it'll probably be quite warm at the dance," I reasoned. I was proud of my tan and thought I could take the jacket off, if it got too warm at the dance. The dinner was to start at 6:00 p.m. so we had almost two hours to get showered and dressed.

We entered the community room recognizing several girls we had met on our floor. Tables had been set up for around one hundred people. There was a head table with about fifteen seated there. This was strictly girls for the dinner and program, which would be concluded by 7:30 p.m. and the dance would start downstairs in the ballroom at 8:00 p.m. The food was quite good, nothing elaborate, but better than Krystal.

While we were eating dessert, there was a program about techniques in applying makeup. Mildred and I were introduced as new members. Our dues were collected, and we received tickets for the dance and found out there would be a fashion show from Castner Knott the following week. "This is really fun so far," I commented to Mildred. "I hope the dance will be too," she replied. We ran upstairs to our room to freshen up before catching the elevator to the ballroom on the first floor. Boys were only allowed on the first floor.

When we walked into the ballroom, I was not prepared for the number of servicemen scattered around the room. On Tuesday night, there was not a band, only jukebox type music. The bands were reserved for the Saturday night dances. There were 4 or 5 chaperones there and just before the dancing was to begin, one lady took the microphone and made a short speech about the rules. There would be no drinking, no foul language, no inappropriate behavior. Anyone not obeying the rules would be escorted out. In one area of the room, there was a small refreshment area: Cokes and food must be kept in this part of the ballroom. The music started promptly at eight o'clock. We stood around watching people do the waltz and slow dance to the first several numbers. This type dance was not new to me, except most of the ones I went to in high school were square dances. There were always a few slow dances, but that wasn't the main thrust of the dances at the V.F.W. Club, where I had gone almost every Saturday night for the past few years.

We didn't stand by ourselves too long before guys approached us to dance. The boys outnumbered the girls, so we didn't lack for someone to dance with. Some were better dancers than others, so you could decide if you wanted to dance with them more than once. We danced almost continually until suddenly they announced the last dance.

We were back in our room by 10:30, discussing the events of the evening. We didn't meet anyone we were particularly impressed with, but both agreed the evening was a lot of fun, and we were looking forward to next week. "I wish we could go on Saturday night," I said as we hopped into bed.

"I do too," she commented, but we both know we'll have to go home on weekends for a while.

"Maybe later we'll get to stay up here every other weekend," I said as we turned out the light. We both knew how early six o'clock came.

On Thursday night we packed our bags for the weekend, mostly with our laundry, to be done while we were home. When we finished work on Friday, all we had to do was pick up our bag on our way to the bus station. We were able to get a bus around 5:00 p.m. After two or three stops, we would be in Parsons by 8:00 p.m. I had written a couple of letters, so I hoped they would be there to meet me. The round trip ticket from Nashville to Parsons was around $5.00. Our money was getting quite scarce after just one week. "We have 3 more weeks before we get paid," Mildred commented as we sat on the Greyhound on our way home.

"I'll probably have to get a little more money," I said.

"If we don't, we probably won't eat," she replied. I just hoped Daddy could let me have a little more money until we got our first check.

Louise was there to meet me and Mildred's sister, Nancy, was there too.

"I'll see you on Sunday," I said as we loaded our luggage in the cars.

"The bus leaves at 3:00 p.m., so I'll probably be here around 2:30 p.m.," she said as we waved goodbye.

I was glad to be home and suddenly realized, I had missed everyone. I talked non-stop the 13 miles home telling Louise about everything that had happened, especially the dance.

The weekend went by quite fast, and before we knew it, we were back at the Y unpacking our suitcases. We had nice clean clothes, and each of us had gotten a little more money. Both of us had brought food so we could eat in our room part of the time, and this would help us save money. "Let's see if we can stay up here for a weekend next week," I commented.

"We'd better make it in two weeks; that will give us a weekend to convince them," she replied.

"You're probably right," I agreed. This would help us save money by not having to pay $5.00 for bus fare. We both agreed and decided we could also go to the Saturday Y Dance.

We went home the following weekend, planning to stay in Nashville the next weekend, if at all possible. Mama was pretty hard to convince, but by Sunday morning I had her on my side, and she talked Daddy into letting me stay up for at least one weekend.

We later began to stay in Nashville every other weekend, which worked out quite well. When we brought our luggage into the lobby on our second week as residents of the Y.W.C.A., I had a wonderful surprise. "Opal, you have a package," the lady at the front desk announced. She handed me a large package that had arrived in the mail on Saturday.

"Who is it from?" Mildred asked excitedly.

"It's from Glen," I answered as I looked at the top of the package.

We took the elevator to the 4th floor as I looked forward to opening my package. We dragged our luggage inside the door, and I laid my treasure on the bed until I could find the scissors to cut it open. "Oh, guess what it is!" I said, as I ripped the rest of the paper off.

"Just tell me," Mildred said, a little impatiently.

"It's a camera, with a flash and everything!" I yelled. "Isn't it great?" "He remembered my birthday; its Tuesday you know. I can't believe I'll be 18."

"Mine is in August, I'll be 18 then," Mildred said.

Glen had put a card in the package which said he cared for me and wished we could see each other more. This made me a bit homesick, but I was so excited about the camera, it didn't last very long. I used this camera for the next five years, even after I was married.

Work was basically the same. We had completed our training and were now waiting to be placed on a team. The rumors were always floating around about who the bad team leaders were, but we had no say about where we were placed. I just hoped and prayed that I got one of the better ones.

We were into our third week at the Y when the unexpected happened. "Opal," Mrs. Belew announced as I walked to my desk in mid to late June, "you're being placed on a team starting tomorrow." Of course, the big question was, *where* and *who's the team leader*. "You'll love her," she continued, "and the assistant team leader is a jewel. The leader is Mrs. Baskim and the Assistant is Louise Carlton." I would be the Junior Clerk, low person on a team of eight. I was so excited. At least this was permanent. We had been working on different teams, when other girls were out.

The next morning, I cleaned my things out and settled in as part of a team. The girls were all great and made me feel right at home, especially Louise Carlton. Louise and I hit it off right away and quickly became very good friends. She took me under her wing and told me who was nice and who to avoid on the 4th floor. I found out later that she was an avid dancer, who was in the advanced courses of the Arthur Murry dance classes. I had seen her at the Y dances and knew she was a great dancer. She was about 24 years old, about the same age as my older sister Louise. Everything went great for the next few weeks. I made friends with the girls and was doing quite well, except for an occasional bout of homesickness.

Mildred and I were both sick of living at the Y by this time. We still enjoyed the dances, but we knew we could continue being in the club even if we moved, We had spoken to several people and told them we were looking for a nice place, possibly a boarding house. This paid off because shortly after that, Mrs. Belew called me to her desk. "Opal, I think I know just the place for you and your friend," she announced. "Katherine Boyce, the dietitian in the cafeteria, lives in a big house in West End with her mother-in-law. She and her husband are living there temporarily trying to save money to buy a house. She rents rooms to about 10 girls and at the moment she has a room for rent. Ms. Boyce is a widow and the girls all seem to think she's great. I don't know all the details, but if you are interested, I'll call Katherine so you and Mildred could meet with her on your lunch hour."

"It sounds great to me, that is, if the price is right. I'll have to call Mildred and see if she's available at lunch." Mrs. Belew said I could use her phone so I called and made arrangements to meet on our upcoming lunch hour to talk to Katherine Boyce about a new place to live.

We had both seen Katherine in the cafeteria on several occasions but had never been formally introduced. After meeting her we discovered what a nice person she was. She explained all the details to us: "The rent is $12.50 per week, which includes 2 meals. There are 6 bedrooms upstairs, but one is rented to a couple. They are quite private. She's not well and is bedridden most of the time. Her husband works but knows his wife is taken care of. As far as the girls, most of them work right here at National Life. They're about your age and seem to get along quite well. If you're interested, you could ride out with me this afternoon and look at the room and talk to Mrs. Boyce."

The bus line was only a couple of blocks from the house. "We'd love to," we both answered and made arrangements to meet her after work.

Upon arrival at the Boyce house, we met her husband, Graham, a lawyer, who arrived a few minutes later to pick her up. Mrs. Boyce seemed to be quite nice and the rooms were great. There were only two bathrooms for twelve people so we knew that might not be an easy situation. We both agreed it was much better than the Y. Besides her son, Graham, Mrs. Boyce had a daughter in her mid-twenties, named Martha Ann. We took the room and decided to move in the following weekend.

We didn't have an awful lot to move, just mostly our clothes.

My Place In Time

We had given notice we were leaving as soon as we decided to take the room. We had paid up until the end of the week at the Y so it all worked out great. We were both excited when Saturday morning rolled around. We each had a couple of heavy suitcases that we lugged to the bus stop to move to our new residence on Richland Avenue, two blocks from the bus stop on West End Avenue. This was one of the most beautiful areas in the city of Nashville. It was a few miles from Centennial Park and a few blocks from the city of Bellemeade. When we arrived at the house, Graham was there and helped us settle into our new home.

The next few weeks took some adjusting. The first room we had had a porch attached and the back stairs led downstairs from our porch. Well, needless to say, everyone was using our room as a cut-through to the porch or to go downstairs. We had only been there a short time when we went to Mrs. Boyce and asked to be put on a list for another room. I think we had to stay in the porch room for a month or so before another room became available.

Everything was scheduled. We signed up for baths either in the morning or at night. Breakfast was promptly at 6:00 a.m. and dinner was at 6:30 p.m. - there were no variations. If you weren't there, you didn't get supper. She had a wonderful black lady that did the cooking. "Have you ever eaten such good rolls?"

Mildred asked one night at supper. They're wonderful, everyone agreed. We were all expected to use good manners, by saying "Please," "Thank you" and "May I be excused?" as the rule of thumb.

The next few weeks went great by getting to know the girls and getting adjusted to our new surroundings. My new friend and co-worker, Louise Carlton, only lived two blocks from us. "Opal," she announced one day at work "would you like to come over and help me practice some new dance steps?"

"That would be great," I said, excited about the prospect of learning to dance the Arthur Murray way. We set a time after work the next day, and I met her at her apartment as scheduled. We spent a couple of hours dancing and having a great time when she asked if I would like to go to a place she and her boyfriend went to a couple of times a week to just dance and meet friends.

"I'd love to!" I answered quickly. "Could Mildred come too?"

"Of course," she answered. "We'll pick you up around 8:00 p.m. tomorrow night."

Mildred was also excited about going, and this started a trend for the next year or so. If we didn't have anything to do, we would go to Coopers. It was a nice place with a juke box and always plenty of people to dance with.

Doubts

On one of the weekends we went home, my life almost had a drastic change. Glen came over on Saturday night and we went out and I had a great time. "If you were home more, we'd be able to see each other more," he said. I agreed but knew I couldn't afford to come every weekend. I still had not met anyone special, although I was enjoying the dances we went to very much.

Mildred and I had been going to the bases on U.S.O. tours. They would pick us up at the Y and take us to dances on the Army and Air Force Bases. It was all great fun, but I was suddenly very homesick. It only took one word to Mama and Louise about me being homesick before they were planning for me to come home and get a job at the factory where my sister Louise worked.

"Irene, the lady I ride with, could get you a job real easily," Louise said, the following weekend, as we were riding home from the bus station.

"I guess I really want to come home. I know I would save money by staying at home."

"I'll get you an interview for next Friday, if you can take a day off and come in Thursday night," she continued.

Everything was arranged, and I managed to get off work the following Friday to go to the shirt factory and interview. They were hiring so there was no problem getting hired for a position. The following Monday, I went back to National Life and gave a two week notice. "I can't believe you're doing this!" Mildred kept saying. "I just know you'll be sorry," she reasoned.

"I'll get to see Glen more, and I know I'll have more money to spend."

"Money isn't everything, and, besides, you might meet someone you'd like better than Glen," she argued.

"I doubt that," I concluded.

I took another day off the following weekend so I could tour the plant and get acquainted with where I would work. I went with Louise in the morning on Friday. I remember walking through the plant with all the noise from the machines, people yelling, bolts of material everywhere, and I suddenly felt sick. My head was pounding, and I started to cry. "Take me back to Louise," I said to the lady that was taking me on the tour.

"What's wrong, Opal?" she asked, as I approached her machine.

"I just can't do it!" I cried. "Please, I want to go home. I'm going back to National Life and try to get my job back," I said as I sobbed.

"Okay, if that's what you want to do, but you'll have to wait around till quitting time to go home."

"That's all right," I answered. "I'll walk uptown and come back later."

On the following Monday, I walked into my boss's office and asked if I could have my job back and not quit as planned. They seemed delighted that I had decided to stay. Mildred was overjoyed when I told her so, of course, we had to go out to eat and celebrate. It turned out she was right; we did meet a couple of really nice guys the following week.

Boys, Boys, Boys!

It was early September and one of those beautiful fall Sunday afternoons. "Let's walk to Centennial Park," Mildred announced after we'd finished lunch.

"That's a long walk," I commented.

"Oh, it's only about a mile or so," Robbie, one of the other girls, chimed in. "I'm game if everyone else is." It turned out Mildred and I were the only two that decided to go.

We walked around the park for a while and ended up feeding the ducks by the pond. "Look, those two soldiers over there are eyeing us. Pretend you don't notice them," she said. We got up and walked to a bench where they followed us. They came over and started a conversation about the park and how beautiful the weather was in Tennessee. It turned out they were both from Iowa, and one said it was probably getting cold there already. They asked where we lived and if they could come out later that evening. Their names were Jack Emgee and Bob Hurkle and were both paratroopers.

We told them we didn't pick up boys in the park, but they could come to our house and have iced tea on the porch. Mrs. Boyce was really nice about letting us have boys over. We could even invite them in to listen to music or play cards. She had a hard and fast rule that you had to be in by 10:00 p.m. on weeknights and 11:30 p.m. on weekends. If not, the door was locked and you had to ring the doorbell to get her to let you in. They came as promised about 7:00 p.m. and stayed around until 9:30 or 10:00 p.m. before leaving for the base.

We made dates with them for the following Saturday night to go to a movie. I dated Jack, and Mildred dated Bob for the next couple of months. I knew from the start that Jack had a girlfriend in Iowa, so it was strictly a lot of fun and they would be transferred the last of October. I forgot about Glen during this time and had fun.

We had picnics in the park, went to movies, dances at the Y, and sat on the porch playing cards. One night in particular, we got home about 9:30 p.m., Mildred and Bob were sitting on the swing, while Jack and I were standing beside the front door. I must have been leaning on the doorbell because the next thing I knew Mrs. Boyce came to the door. "Did you forget your key, Opal?"

"No, I have it."

"We'll be in before 10:00 p.m.," Mildred commented.

Five minutes later, Ms. Boyce came back to the door. "Do you need something?" she asked.

"No," I answered, this time getting a little annoyed. "It's still only 9:45 p.m."

"I know," she replied.

The next morning she asked me: "Opal, why were you ringing the doorbell last night?" I suddenly realized why she had kept coming to the door. Everyone thought it was really funny but me; I was really embarrassed.

We dated Jack and Bob for the next couple of months. Jack was the first boy I'd cared anything about since Glen. I went home almost every other weekend and didn't lack for dates while I was home, but usually during this time when we got back to the boarding house on Sunday night, Jack and Bob were waiting for us. It was a whirlwind of dances at the Y, movies, picnics, and just spending time talking.

I remember being so tired during the day at work that I would actually go to sleep behind my rate book. We knew they would be leaving to go to another base, but it seemed to come too quickly. We kept in touch with a few letters, but that didn't last very long.

I continued to have fun on my weekends at home, but somehow the weekends at home got fewer and far between. Nashville was such a different lifestyle and I was beginning to love it. Jack and Bob left on Oct. 27th and I met someone on the first of November that I thought at the time I was totally in love with.

"How about going to a movie?" Mildred asked on a particular Saturday afternoon. I had been feeling really low for the past couple of days. "This movie will cheer you up; I hear it's great."

I agreed and we took the bus downtown to the State Theater to the movies. "Do you want to wait until after the movie to get something to eat?" I asked.

"That would be great," she agreed.

We window shopped for the next thirty minutes until the theater opened. After we got popcorn and were seated, we noticed two soldiers standing in the entrance. The lights were still on so they walked over and asked if the seats next to us were taken. What a coincidence; they're open. We talked for the next 15 minutes before the movie started. We probably annoyed the people behind us during the movie because they kept talking and asking us questions. We found out their names and where they were from and other pertinent facts. The one sitting by me was named Bob Smitt and the other boy by Mildred was named Ray something. They were both from St. Paul, Minnesota. They kept talking about our southern drawl, and we had to ask them almost everything twice because it was so hard to understand them.

After the movie, they asked if we had eaten and would we like to get something to eat across the street at Wilson Quick Drug. We didn't think there would be any harm in that. We ate and stayed there talking until we knew our last bus would be leaving. "We'll walk you to your bus stop, or we could drive you home," Bob suggested.

"I think we'd better ride the bus," I volunteered.

At least give me your address and phone number, Bob piped up. I wrote my name , phone number and address on a scrap of paper, thinking it was probably a waste of time, because I'd probably never hear from him again.

"I'm not very interested in Ray," Mildred said as we settled in our seats on the bus heading back to West End Avenue.

"I could tell that," I commented.

"Bob is really interesting and I hope he calls or writes." I wasn't to be disappointed. I received a letter from him on Wednesday of the following week. He said he would call me later in the week and maybe I would consider going out with him.

By this time two new girls, named Helen and Jean, had moved in. Helen was a student at Vanderbilt and Jean was a nursing student at Baptist Hospital. These new friends were a new development in our lifestyle - Helen had a car. It seemed as if she had more money than we did, and we found out a little later that her family had money. She not only had a car but received a dividend check from her grandmother for stock she had given her. She had loads of good jewelry. On one particular occasion when I was going out, she put a necklace on me to complete my outfit. I found out later that necklace turned out to be worth over $2,000. I wouldn't have worn it if I had known!

We decided to go to the drive-in movie on Thursday night and I missed Bob's phone call. He called back the following night, but I had made plans already. My sister Louise and my cousin Georgia were coming up for the weekend. We'd had it planned for a long time. They were going to go Christmas shopping at some of the big stores. Mildred had gone home for the weekend so they were able to stay and use her bed. I finally got in touch with Bob on Sunday evening, and we made a date for the following weekend.

I dated him pretty steady for the next four months. "Are you really serious about Bob?" Mildred asked as we walked home from the bus stop one December afternoon.

"I like him better than anybody I've dated for a long time," I admitted.

"He's too serious for you," Mildred continued. I agreed that he was a different type than I had ever dated before.

"I guess that's why I like him, because he is different. He's sophisticated and debonair," I said.

"He's a snob!" she responded. "Is he going home for Christmas?"

"I'm sure he will, but I am too." He did go home for Christmas in 1953 and I didn't see him again until mid-January.

By this time we had been in Nashville a little over 6 months at Christmas, and I was enjoying it more all the time. It was such a different life than I had known before. I guess, even though I argued with Mildred about Bob, I knew in my heart that he would never fit in with my family. I liked him very much, especially the way he treated me. He had such good manners, always going around opening the car door, being polite and kind, never telling off-color jokes. In fact, he was always the perfect gentleman. It was just when he talked about his family and his life in Minnesota that I knew how different our backgrounds were. This was the 1950's, but times were still really hard in rural areas, especially with big families.

I had always managed money well, and now was no exception. I had already paid back the money Daddy had borrowed for me, and I kept sending a small amount home just to help out. I continued to date Bob, hoping everything would work out.

One day Helen came into our room and plopped herself on the bed as usual. "How would you two like to get an apartment with Jean and me?" she asked.

"What are you talking about?" Mildred wanted to know.

"There's a two bedroom apartment available not far from Vanderbilt. We could actually save money if we split everything four ways."

"The big problem will be convincing Mama and Daddy," I said.

"You could try," she commented. Well, somehow we managed to get our parents to let us move into an apartment. We told Mrs. Boyce the following week and gave her a two-week notice, This gave us time to paint the apartment and get it in shape. It was furnished, but we rearranged the furniture before we moved in.

Our 1st Apartment

We moved in our apartment on February 24, 1954. It was such an exciting time in our lives, except for sadness about leaving the other girls. Mildred and I were to share a room, and that left Jean and Helen who were complete opposites. Jean was quite messy, so instead of sharing a room, Helen decided to sleep on the daybed in the living room. We stayed friends with the Boyces, especially Graham and Katherine. They had a little girl about three years old and had been looking for a place of their own for some time. Just before we moved, they bought a house and planned to move shortly after we did. "We'll call you and you can come over for dinner one night soon," Katherine said on our last night before we moved.

"We'll miss the rides to work and all the great talks," Mildred said. I agreed from the bottom of my heart.

I knew that Graham Boyce had been a profound influence on my self-esteem. Other than Mrs. Flynn Pickens, my 9th grade teacher, no one had been more of a positive role model to me than Graham Boyce. On more than one occasion, he had told me what a lovely girl I was, and to stand up straight and be proud of being tall. He told me all models are tall, and you look like a model, so wear your heels and don't let anyone intimidate you. This really made a difference because all my life I had been teased and called skinny and long legs. "How's the weather up there?" was a question my brothers and uncles were always asking. So to have someone build me up was one of the greatest things that had ever happened to me.

Graham and Katherine were true to their word and invited us to their new home in Bellemeade shortly after they got moved in. It was a great house, and they seemed so happy to be on their own. We, too, were happy to be on our own. For the first time in almost a year, we could make our own rules. The lady that owned the apartment house lived in an apartment across the hall, so if we got too loud with our music or such, she'd call us. She was a teacher and taught adult classes at Seward Air Force Base. (There were several other apartments in the old house.) Most of the occupants were students from Vanderbilt or Peabody College.

It was a real nice area on 16th Avenue South, just across the street from a rest home for nuns, called Little Sisters of the Poor. It was so neat because in the late afternoons if we were on the front porch, we could hear them singing or chanting prayers. It reminded you of the convent in *Sound of Music*.

We had only been in the apartment for a week or so when I got a call from Mrs. Boyce, saying I had a letter there. She said she could forward it or I might want to come and pick it up. After finding out it was from Bob, I decided I would go over after work the next day and pick it up. I was so glad I did because I was able to write him and let him know we had moved, so when he came the following weekend he could come to the right place.

We dated off and on until the end of March before he had to go to South Carolina for around 3 months. Just before he had to leave, he called and said to get dressed up because he was taking me someplace special on Saturday night. It was all a surprise, but it also turned out to be one of the most memorable dates I ever had. He had reserved a table at the Maxwell House Hotel Restaurant. After a wonderful dinner, we went to a special movie and then to a place in Bellemeade and danced. He left shortly after this, but we promised to keep close by letters and an occasional phone call. We never discussed not dating anyone else.

I missed him, but I also knew I could find someone else to help fill my time. I dated one of Jean's friends from college, but he was about the biggest bore I'd ever gone out with. "Opal, let's go have some fun again," Mildred said one Saturday morning.

"What do you suggest?" I asked.

"Let's go back to the Y dance tonight," she replied. We went out to eat and then to the Y dance. It had been a while since we'd been by ourselves. We had no trouble getting dance partners.

An hour or so had gone by when I glanced up to see this really tall boy, at least six feet seven inches tall, coming toward me. He asked me to dance and we hit it off so well we danced the rest of the time together. As they played the last dance, I had the surprise of my life. "Opal, how would you like to go to church with me tomorrow?" This was the very first time a boy had ever asked me to go to church, so needless to say, I was shocked.

My Place In Time

"What church?"

"The West End Methodist Church would be all right, if it's all right with you. I'll pick you up around 10:30 am" he said as Mildred and I grabbed our jackets.

After I got on the bus, I asked Mildred, "do you know where I'm going tomorrow?"

"No, I don't."

"I'm going to West End Methodist Church with Chuck Majors," I said smugly. "I've never gone to church with a boy before."

"Neither have I," she answered.

The next morning I awoke bright and early, wondering if Chuck would really show up to take me to church. "What are you going to wear?" asked Mildred as she sipped her second cup of coffee.

"Do you think it's too early for my new white dress?" I asked.

"No, it's after Easter so you can wear white, so go ahead. I hear it's going to be a nice warm day." Mama had made me a beautiful white dress a few weeks before.

I didn't have as good a tan as I'd had the year before, but it was still early for that. We had used suntan booths a few times on our lunch hour so after I put the dress on, I decided it didn't look too bad.

"Did you know there's a nice place to take your lunch and lie in the sun at National Life?" Mildred asked.

"Someone else told me that; she said it was just up the stairs from the indoor pool." We had used the pool several times the year before. It was absolutely great.

We had an hour for lunch so we could bring our things, including suit and bathing cap, swim for a short time, and then play cards in the lounge beside the pool. Both of us had real short hair, and styled very simply, so there wasn't any problem about messing up our hair. I doubt if anyone ever had a better place to work. We also stayed some afternoons and went swimming before we went home.

"How do I look?" I kept asking her.

"I told you, you look great!" she answered.

I was dressed and waiting by 10:00 a.m. "He probably won't show up," I commented as I dug out my camera Glen had given me. I thought of him when I looked at it but decided he was probably dating someone else too. I also thought of Bob, wondering if he had another girlfriend already. He had never asked me to go steady so I had nothing to feel guilty about. I did miss Bob and hoped I would get a letter the next week. I saw Glen occasionally when I went home, which was only about once a month now, I also dated other guys from Perry Co. Louise had dated a boy named Jim Stricklin for the past two years, but he was now in service, so at this point I knew it would never last. The last few times I had been home she was dating Frank Walker, one of Jim's close friends. I was really glad because I had never cared for Jim very much and Frank was really a nice guy.

"Opal, quit your daydreaming, I think he just drove up."

I looked outside and gasped, "Would you look at that car!" There was a brand-new yellow convertible in front of the apartment. I opened the door to his knock and there stood Chuck in his uniform. He was probably the most handsome guy I had ever dated. I loved tall men and he really fit that description.

"Would you like to go on a picnic after church?" he asked. "It's such a beautiful day and it's a shame to waste any of it."

"I'd love to, but I'll have to come back here and change clothes."

"I'll have to change too, but I threw some shorts in the car."

This was April 24th, but it felt more like late May or June; the weather was so warm. Bob had been gone since the last of March. It seemed much longer than three weeks and I did miss him, but I certainly wasn't one to sit around and mope. I had already dated several guys since he'd been gone. My friend, Louise Carlton, saw that I wasn't lonely. If we didn't have dates, we either went to the Y or one of the bases for U.S.O. dances. If all else failed, a bunch of us would go to Coopers, just to dance and have

My Place In Time

fun.

Well, anyway! Here I was on this beautiful Sunday on my way to church with probably the most handsome boy alive. "Mildred, come out and take a picture of us before we leave," I said as we left the apartment. By this time Mildred had changed clothes and was planning a leisurely time reading. She was an avid reader, and I was always accusing her of having her head stuck in a book. I didn't have time for reading right now in my life. She came out and took a couple of pictures and we proceeded to go to church.

I remember telling him what a great car he had as he opened the door after we got to the church. I remember feeling so chic and sophisticated as we entered the church. We went back to the apartment and changed clothes before going to the park for a Sunday afternoon picnic. We stopped at a corner market and Chuck bought all sorts of things for our picnic. We had ham and cheese sandwiches, chips, cookies, and, of course, Cokes. He had a radio, so we ate and listened to music and just talked all afternoon. "How about a movie tonight?" he asked later in the afternoon.

"I'd love it," I responded. We stopped at Krystal for hamburgers for supper before going to a drive-in movie close by.

When I walked in about 10:30 p.m., Mildred was still awake and I kept her awake for the next hour, telling her all about my day, and how enchanting Chuck was.

The next weekend I went home, but Chuck was waiting for me when I got to the apartment on Sunday afternoon. We had a date that night and then dated off and on for the next 2 months. I was keeping in contact with Bob through letters, and he had called me once in the past month. Mildred was always glad for me to date other people; she hoped that I would just forget about Bob.

The month of May went by in much the same routine, but I was beginning to get terrible migraine headaches. I knew I needed to rest more because every morning it seemed to get harder to get up and go to work. We had two other women that lived in one of the apartments in our building that we had become friends with. Barbara had a car, so she and Wanda drove to work.

One night they came over for coffee, and the subject of riding the bus came up. "Why don't you and Opal ride to work with us?" Wanda asked Mildred.

"We could pay you what we pay for the bus to help with gas," I chimed in."

That was the beginning of our having a ride to work in the morning, but we still had to catch the bus in the afternoon, because they worked later than we did.

These ladies were quite unusual neighbors. Barbara was in her mid-thirties and was having an affair with her boss, who was married. Wanda worked for the state, for someone close to the Governor. She had a great job but dated very seldom. She was in her late twenties.

One night we were at their place for coffee when she picked up her knitting. She was doing a shawl and it was absolutely beautiful. "Do you think you could teach me to knit?" I asked.

"Sure, I could." She told me what to buy and we planned to begin the following evening. "Let's start on a scarf instead of a shawl," she remarked. "We'll do a simple knit and pearl stitch, which will be easier to begin with."

I just about drove her crazy for the next month or so. I would mess up and she would have to get it straightened out. Eventually, I mastered it. I not only finished my red scarf; I knitted shawls for Christmas presents that upcoming year. I loved knitting and kept it up for the next thirty years or so of my life. I made mittens, sweaters, and eventually ski sweaters.

Life continued much the same for the next few weeks. I finally realized that Chuck was very much struck on himself. I really loved Nashville, my friends and my life in general. But, as I mentioned before, I was having headaches that seemed to be getting worse. We had a nurse and a small hospital area in the building where we worked. There were six or eight beds and you could go up, talk to the nurse, take safe medication and lie down for a few hours. This was an alternative to taking off sick and going home. I found myself doing this on the average of once a week. I didn't know then, but this was the beginning of a life of suffering from migraine headaches. I knew my dad had suffered terrible headaches and found out later that they are inherited. At least four of my siblings would suffer the same fate.

My Place In Time

The One!

On June 8th, 1954, we went to a Y dance as usual, but on this particular night I was destined to meet someone that would change the course of my life. I remember having on a new dress that Mama had just made for me. It was blue with a small design, made in a princess style, with no waistline. It just hung freely from your midriff. I felt really sharp and confident on this particular night.

I had danced several dances with other guys when this particular Air Force guy came over and asked me to dance and we danced the rest of the evening together. His name was Warren Johnson and he was also from Minnesota, but from Minneapolis. That was where the similarities ended with him and Bob. He was down to earth, easy to talk to, and a good dancer. We talked and danced and before we knew it they were playing the last dance. "Could my buddy and I drive you and Mildred home?" he asked as we finished the last dance. He seemed so nice and I felt as if I'd known him a long time already.

"I'll ask Mildred," I answered. She said it was all right with her, so they drove us home and came in for a cup of coffee before they started back to base.

Just before they left, I remember Warren asking "Do you have a phone?"

"Of course, we do. Do you want to use it?"

"No, smarty, I just want your telephone number. I thought I might call you if you don't mind."

"I don't mind" I said glibly.

Louise Carlton rode up the elevator with me on Monday morning. "I hear you had a new boyfriend Saturday night."

"Who told you?" I wanted to know. I think she knew everybody in Nashville and kept up with most of their lives.

"I talked to Dorothy, one of my friends that was there on Saturday night. You know he was engaged until about 2 weeks ago?" she continued.

"How do you know that?" I wanted to know.

"Dorothy knows Mae, the girl he was engaged to."

"Who broke it off?"

"She did and gave his ring back. She decided she didn't love him or just didn't want to get married right now, Dorothy said."

"I'll probably see him tomorrow night and then I'll ask him about it," I said as I headed for the bathroom. I was a little upset that he hadn't told me, but I reasoned that it wasn't something you just blurted out right away.

However, he called me on Monday night and we made a date for the following night to go to the Y's Tuesday night dance. I approached the subject of his recent engagement later in the evening, and he said he didn't think he really loved her either. I hoped he wasn't just on the rebound. I told him about Bob and that I really cared for him, and when he came back from South Carolina, it would probably be over with us. I would probably start dating Bob again. Thus began our whirlwind courtship.

About a week after we'd met, he was waiting for me when I got off work. It seems he had an accident on a forklift and had stitches in his head. They gave him the afternoon off and he had decided to come into town. He didn't have a car so he either had to hitchhike or catch the bus. We decided to go to a movie after we got something to eat. Later, he rode the bus with me back to the apartment. I saw him almost every night for the next couple of weeks. Sometimes he came in with one of his buddies from the base and we would double date, but most of the time he hitchhiked or caught the bus. We could walk across Vanderbilt campus and go to a movie on 21st Avenue.

I met Warren on the eighth of June, and my nineteenth birthday was ten days later. Mildred planned a wonderful birthday dinner, and Warren had made reservations at the V.F.W. club to go dancing afterwards. He came in with one of his buddies, named Ray, for Mildred's date. We had a wonderful time and just before he left, he gave me my present. It was the most unusual round tube box with a small drawer that opened up to reveal a beautiful string of pearls. "Oh, how beautiful!" I exclaimed. "I'll cherish them forever." I knew they weren't real, but on a serviceman's salary, who could afford real pearls?

"Opal, you have a letter from Bob," Mildred announced a few days later as she glanced through the mail. I opened it, knowing he was probably going to let me know exactly when he'd be coming back to Fort Campbell.

"He'll be coming back next week," I said to Mildred. "He wants us to have a special date next Saturday night," I continued.

"You don't seem overly excited?" Mildred remarked. "You know, Warren is a much nicer guy and I like him."

"I like him too," I admitted, "but I don't feel for him the way I do about Bob," I said.

"Bob is a snob and he'll never fit into your life. You're just fooling yourself," she continued.

"Nevertheless, I'll probably break it off with Warren this week."

Warren came in the next evening as I expected with one of his friends. We picked up his friend's girlfriend and went to a movie. We stopped at Centennial Park to feed the ducks before going back to the apartment. Warren and I walked around the park and stopped at one of the pavilions and sat down on a park bench. "It's such a beautiful evening," I commented. There was no air conditioning in our apartment, so it was nice to be outside in the cool breeze. He agreed but seemed to be in a more serious mood, I still had not told him about Bob coming back, and it really upset me to think about telling him.

What he said next made it even more difficult to have to tell him my news. "I've fallen in love with you," he said and he seemed dead serious.

"You're not serious," I responded. "You thought you were in love with someone else a month ago. How could you be in love with me now?"

"I've never felt about anyone else the way I feel about you," he said. I didn't say anything else, but I guess I also knew there was something special between us.

Needless to say, I didn't sleep much the next few nights. Warren was coming in on Thursday night, and I knew I couldn't postpone breaking our relationship off any longer. I cried when I thought about it and worked myself into a migraine headache. "Opal, go up to the nurse's desk," Louise announced on Wednesday. "You look terrible." I took her advice and took some medication and spent a couple of hours in sick bay. I had to be fair, I reasoned, so I decided to tell him early on Thursday evening.

We had just finished supper and were sitting drinking coffee when the doorbell rang. "Opal, it's Warren," Jean called from the living room.

"Tell him to come to the kitchen for coffee," Mildred yelled. "Want a sandwich?" she asked as he took a chair by the table.

"Of course," he answered, which wasn't a shock, since he'd never been known to turn down food. Mildred was always wondering how he could eat so much and stay so thin. He had a thirty-two inch waist and weighed about one hundred and sixty pounds. In those days we all smoked, which was probably a factor in keeping our weight down.

"Finish your sandwich and let's take our coffee and go sit on the glider," I commented. We went to the glider on the front porch with our coffee cups in hand. "Why are you so serious?" he wanted to know as we got comfortable.

"I've had a headache for two days. You know when we started dating a few weeks ago, I told you I had a serious boyfriend that was away for a few months?"

"I remember."

"Well, he's home," as I began to cry. "We have a date for Saturday night."

"Are you in love with him?" he wanted to know.

"I feel something for him, but I'm not sure it's love. I have to find out, so it's better if we break it off for a while," I said. I think I was more upset than he was. I cried and cried for the next hour or so.

"You need to go in and get some rest and try to get rid of your headache," he remarked as he got up to leave. "I'm going back to base early," he continued. "I'll call you in a few weeks and see how things are going," he said as he walked down the steps.

On Saturday night, as I dressed for my date with Bob, I kept trying to work up some excitement. After all, I hadn't seen him for over two months and I kept trying to think of his good points. He was such a perfect gentleman, such good manners, very well-educated, well-read, and could discuss anything intelligently. He was also very handsome. We made a good-looking couple, I kept telling myself.

But Warren, on the other hand, had his good qualities too. He was easy-going; nothing ever seemed to upset him. You could talk to him about anything that was bothering you, and he was just down to earth and sincere. I kept asking myself – *Was Mildred right? Was Bob just a phony?* I knew that even if I loved Bob, he would never fit in with my family while, on the other hand, I could see Warren getting along with them all.

I had finished dressing, in one of my best outfits, and was waiting in the living room when Bob arrived. We had our usual chit chat about how glad we were to see each other and how good we looked, before we proceeded on our date. He had not told me what we would be doing, only to dress up nicely. I thought maybe this is one of his good points: he loves to plan surprises. Then I remember thinking, he'd probably want to run everything, and I'd have no say in anything.

We went to a nice place to eat, and then to a place with quiet music where we could dance. "I've missed you, you know," he kept saying. I didn't tell him I'd been so busy that I'd hardly had time to think about him, let alone miss him. We made a date for the next Wednesday night to go to the movies.

The next couple of days were spent comparing and thinking about what I should do. Warren was true to his word, and I had not heard from him for almost two weeks. I heard through the grapevine that he was at the Y dance on Saturday night, and it looked like he had a date. Louise said he danced with the same girl all evening. I felt really jealous even though I knew I had no right to. I was not necessarily looking forward to my date with Bob on Wednesday because I kept thinking about Warren and comparing them.

I knew by the time our date rolled around on Wednesday evening that I was going to end my relationship with Bob. He had hinted at marriage and about our life together but had never come straight out and asked me to marry him. I didn't want it to come to that. I knew by this time that I probably was in love with Warren, and I thought to myself, it's too late for that now.

On the way home from the movie, I told Bob that I had met someone else while he was away. "Is it serious?" he asked.

"Not at the moment," I admitted, "because I broke it off with him, when I knew you were coming home."

He left, saying he would call me sometime in the future, but I knew that was probably the last I would see of him.

Well, you sure are smart, I thought to myself. *Now, you don't have either Bob or Warren.* I didn't know how to get in touch with Warren, but I knew he would be at the YWCA on Saturday night so I worked out a scheme.

On Friday night I said, "Mildred, let's go to the YWCA dance on Saturday night."

"I might be busy," she said, but it worked out so we could go to the dance. We got there early, hoping Warren would come by himself, but no such luck.

A little while later, Mildred announced, "Opal, look who's here!"

I looked over to see Warren come in with a girl holding on to his arm. "I'll get him to dump her and take me home," I whispered to Mildred.

"I'll just bet you don't!" she laughed.

Shortly afterwards, he saw me standing over by the refreshment stand and came over. "Where's Bob?" he asked.

"Probably at Fort Campbell. I'm not seeing him anymore. Who's the girl?" I asked. I think he said her name was Julie and a friend of Ray's girlfriend.

"Then, it's not serious?" I wanted to know.

"Of course not!" he answered.

"Then, you can take me home."

"No, I can't," he answered. "I'll have to go back with them."

I pouted for a few minutes, but he said he'd call me the next day. Mildred and I left shortly after that and I went home feeling better than I'd felt in weeks.

This was mid-July, hot and very humid, even for Tennessee. I got very little sleep during this period. Warren came over an average of three times a week. One night he came in very excited and said, "Guess what? I'm getting a car. My dad is sending me the money and I'll make payments on it."

I thought to myself, We'll never have any money to go any place now. I was excited about the car, but with payments and gas, it did seem to take all he made to keep it up. This began our time of playing cards. Mildred and Wanda liked to play, so if they didn't have dates, we would settle in for a night of pinochle or canasta.

New Friends

"Opal," Warren announced one evening, "would you like to meet one of my friends from the base? He just got married recently, and he and his wife Carol are living in a trailer not far from the base. They have asked if we would like to come out and play pinochle this weekend."

I thought that would be great for Saturday night, and I met Carol and Bill the next weekend. We had a great time, and that weekend began a friendship that lasted for the rest of our time in service. Carol was an unusual person and you couldn't help but like her. She had such an easy-going personality. Bill was also nice, so we spent a lot of time at their place, playing cards or just talking.

The Wreck

One night on our way home from Carol and Bill's, we had a very frightening experience. We were talking and listening to the radio in Warren's "new to him" Ford when a large trailer truck started to pass us in the left turning lane. We had our turn signal on and was almost in the left lane when this terrible crash sounded. This big truck had just sideswiped the left side of our car. "Are you all right?" I kept screaming at Warren. He was driving, so all the damage was on his side of the car. We stopped the car, and the driver of the truck got out - screaming to the top of his lungs.

The accident happened in front of Fisk University. There was a grocery store to the right of where the accident happened, and several people came out from the store. One gentleman, in particular, came over to us and introduced himself and said he would be glad to help us in any way he could. He was a black man, very well-dressed and well-educated. He stated he had seen the whole thing and would be glad to be a witness if we needed one. The driver of the truck had been drinking; you could smell it strongly on his breath.

The police came and we filed an accident report and got the truck driver's information. However, we found out in the next few weeks that the insurance company did not intend on paying to get Warren's car fixed. "I guess we'll have to go to court," Warren said one evening after he walked into our apartment. He said that one of the guys from the base thought we should get a lawyer and take the guy to court and try to get the car fixed. "Will it do any good?" I asked.

"It's our only hope. I'm now paying for a car with the whole side smashed in." We were able to drive the car by tying the driver's side door closed with wire.

The next day we contacted a lady lawyer that someone from work had recommended. She thought there was a good chance we could win and stated she would only get paid if we won the case. If we lost, she wouldn't get any money. We still had the business card of the eye witness, and she contacted him. He agreed to testify that he smelled liquor on the truck drivers breath and that he was passing on the wrong side at an intersection. We thought we had an airtight case.

"I'm scared to death," I said to Mildred as I dressed on the day of the trial because I had never been to court before, let alone on a witness stand.

"You'll do fine," she remarked. "Just try to stay calm."

Warren was about as nervous as I was. The lawyer was the only one that seemed in control of the situation. She called me as the second witness. The other lawyer had me in tears almost immediately. Our witness appeared and did a good job with his testimony, but to no avail. Our lawyer said the only thing she could figure out was that the judge must have been persuaded by the big truck line, and we could tell immediately the judge thought very little of servicemen. To make a long story short, we lost the case and Warren had to keep driving his Ford with the side smashed in and the door wired shut.

Going Steady

"When can I meet your family?" Warren kept asking me.

"Sometime soon," I would always say, but I would never set an exact time. It was now late September of 1954, and we had been dating about four months. He told me he loved me continually, but I had never said the words to him. I would tell him I cared for him, but I wasn't sure it was love and that's when I told him I wanted to be absolutely sure.

One night at the same pavilion in Centennial Park, he took his class ring off and asked if I would wear it and could he have mine to wear.

"What will this mean? I asked.

"Only that we're going steady."

"I'm not sure I want to go steady," I replied.

"You know I want to marry you," he said rather matter of factly.

"Maybe you just want to get married," I answered. We did exchange class rings, but I still wasn't sure I wanted to get married.

"Opal," Warren said about three weeks after he'd gotten my graduation ring, "I have bad news. I've lost your ring and I don't know what happened to it. I wore it on my little finger and it just slipped off someplace. I've looked everywhere I know to look. You just don't know how sorry I am."

I was really furious! "I don't think you know how hard I worked to earn that class ring," I cried. "It can never be replaced. What can I tell Mama? That I let some boy lose my ring." I pouted for a while but finally realized it didn't do any good.

Warren Meets the Phillips Clan

"Do you want to go meet my family next Sunday?" I asked Warren, when he came in the following week. I told him we could just get up on Sunday morning and drive down and eat dinner and come back in the evening. I dreaded it but I knew it had to be done. I loved my family and it wasn't that I was ashamed of them, but I guess I just hated it because we still did not have a bathroom in the house and there was a heater that furnished most of the heat. We did have wall heaters, but Daddy cut wood and heated most of the house with wood.

"That sounds wonderful!" Warren agreed. I had written Mama and Daddy and let them know we were coming.

The ride down seemed to take forever. I was very nervous and upset. I remember we stopped about ten miles from our house on the gravel road from Decaturville just to talk for a minute. "Daddy doesn't talk very much and neither do my brothers, Morris, and Sam," I said nervously. "Dan is only three years old so, of course, he just cries a lot. You know, six of us are three years apart in age," I added. "Louise, my older sister is five years older than me because Mama had two babies that died before I was born. I'm nineteen, Morris is sixteen, Joan just turned twelve, Pat is now nine, Sam is six and, of course, as I just told you, Dan the youngest is three. I'm not sure I have the ages right, so I don't expect you to even remember their names, let alone their ages," I remarked.

"You'll love Mama," I continued. "She's a great cook and I'm sure she'll have a really good dinner fixed today," I said just as Warren dropped his cigarette. I smelled something burning and looked to see the cigarette burning a hole in my new tapestry skirt. "Look what you've done!" I cried. "I don't even have this skirt paid for," I said through tears. "I just bought it last week at Palmers, and now it's ruined."

In my heart, I knew it wasn't just the skirt; I was just really scared about how the day would go, and a hole in my new skirt was just the icing on the cake, so to speak. "It'll be all right," Warren consoled me. "I promise to be on my best behavior."

I wasn't sure whether Louise would like him or not. At this point I remember just wanting the day to be over and wishing we could turn around and go back to Nashville. No such luck. Warren started the car and we drove our smashed-up car the rest of the way to Mt. Carmel, the community we lived in.

As we passed a little, white country church house, I

commented to Warren, "That's the Methodist Church, where I went to church and M. Y.F. when I was growing up. I also went to the Pentecostal Church down the road," I explained. "I didn't go all the time, only when my friends were going. My mother and dad aren't great church people," I remarked. "My dad's nickname is 'Preacher'," I said, "but it has nothing to do with his going to church or ever being a preacher. Daddy got the nickname when he was small and used to stand on a stump and pretend to preach to other kids, and I guess the name stuck for all these years.

My next comment took Warren by surprise. "I'd like to have a church wedding in that small white church when I get married someday," I said sincerely. "There's never been a wedding in it, as far as I know," I continued.

"That would be great with me," he said as we drove on past all the familiar places of my childhood. The old one-room schoolhouse was still there, even though it had not been used for school in many years. The Pentecostal Church had used it several years before building a building close by. At the moment it looked quite forlorn and deserted.

"We're almost there," I said as we drove up the schoolhouse hill where Mittie and Baxter's old house sat on the left at the top of the hill. Our neighbors, Mamie and Clay, lived on the left also, just before we turned up the gravel driveway to our house. We stopped in the driveway and sat there for a few minutes before getting out to begin our day. "Daddy just got the white siding on a few years ago," I commented. "It looks much better than it used to."

Mama met us on the front porch where my two brothers, Dan and Sam, sat staring at us like we were a strange sight from Mars. "This is Warren," I said to Mama, while Dan and Sam kinda snickered.

"We're glad you could come," she said and invited him to come inside, although it was much cooler on the porch.

There was a fan running in the kitchen, but it was still very hot because of all the cooking Mama had done for our Sunday dinner. Daddy was sitting in his usual brown chair by the door. Joan, Pat and Louise were seated on the new couch Louise and I had bought a few months before. Our living room ceiling was quite low, and I was afraid Warren would hit his head on the ceiling light when he came in. He didn't do any of the things I had imagined might happen.

The dinner was great and Warren had a good appetite as usual. Morris came back from hunting just before we sat down to eat. Dinner was the place of chatter with everyone trying to be heard. Daddy sat at the head, the only place he would ever eat. I guess I figured Warren would run from this country clan, but he said on the way back to Nashville that it was great and he liked a big family. He only had one brother and one sister, so this was all something different for him.

"Are you serious about Warren?" Mama asked the next weekend when I went home by myself.

"I'm not really sure yet," I answered. "I like him but I'm not sure I'm ready to get married."

"You're only nineteen years old," she continued, "so don't rush into anything."

I asked Louise, "Did you like him?"

"I guess he's all right," she said. "He seems to be easy-going, but it's what you think that's important," she continued. "You'll have to live with him the rest of your life."

"Yeah, I know."

I knew Mama didn't believe in divorce so I really wanted to be sure. Daddy wouldn't commit himself and said he'd have to get to know him a little longer.

"Are you going home for Thanksgiving?" I asked Mildred as we walked the block from the bus to our apartment the week before Thanksgiving. She said she knew her Mom and Nancy wanted her to. It's the same with me. I would have loved to stay here and cook dinner for Warren, but I knew Mama would have a fit.

We went home as usual for Thanksgiving, because unlike last year, National Life gave us the following Friday off from work. The year before, we were invited to eat dinner with Mildred's boss. It worked out great because we had to work on Friday, and we couldn't go home for just the one day. "I'll be bored to tears," I commented to Mildred, as we packed on Tuesday night. We took our bags with us so we wouldn't have to go back to the apartment the next afternoon after work.

Louise met me in Parsons as usual, but she was in a lousy mood so on the drive home we talked very little. I knew she had broken up with Jim completely, so I figured that was the main problem. "Maybe we can go to a movie on Friday or Saturday night?"

She snapped my head off and said, "Go by yourself, if you can't find somebody to take you."

"I just might," I added.

I missed Warren all weekend, and it seemed Louise and I fought more than usual. I was real excited when Sunday evening rolled around, but Louise was still in her rotten mood, so Mama had to get a neighbor to drive me to the bus. We still didn't have telephones at home, although there was a few people in the community that had party lines. In case of an emergency we could call the Crawleys, and they could deliver the message. I hadn't called Warren, but I'd told him what time my bus would get in on Sunday, so I wasn't surprised to see him at the station when we got there around 7:00 p.m. in the evening.

"This is great," Mildred remarked, "Now we have someone to help with all this luggage and junk." We always brought back as much food as possible.

"Don't leave for that long again," Warren said as we settled ourselves in his car, with the side smashed and the door wired shut.

"What about Christmas? You'll be gone for over a week then," I reminded him.

"Yes, but I'm going to be on a mission," he answered, smiling.

"I haven't agreed for sure yet," I said. "You said you would think about it while you were away for Thanksgiving," he pressed.

He had been bugging me to give him an answer for the past month or so about whether I would marry him or not. He said he would get the ring in December when he went home for Christmas. We would then be officially engaged and get married in June.

Jean, one of our roommates in the apartment, was dating a boy that lived in Bemidji, Minnesota, and she was going to ride up to Minneapolis with Warren, and Dutch would meet her there and drive her the other three hours to where he lived. The next few weeks flew by, buying Christmas gifts and just getting ready for the holidays.

"Will you accept my ring if I get it over Christmas?" Warren asked me again the week before he was to leave. I finally agreed but a few doubts lingered. I had never met his family and he thought we should move to Minneapolis after we got out of the Air Force. I finally decided I would deal with these things when I had to.

He left the next weekend, 4 days before Christmas and did not plan to come back until after New Year's Day.

I went home as usual for the Christmas holidays, although we only got off work three days for Christmas and one day for New Year's Day. We had the usual excitement about Christmas. It had been quite exciting for me the past two years to shop at the big department stores in Nashville. I loved Harvey's, Castner Knots and of course, Cain Sloans. This was before malls were around and downtown was wonderfully decorated and very festive. Everyone seemed to enjoy the gifts I'd found for them, carefully searching for them on my lunch hour and after work.

"What did you give Warren?" Mama asked as we ate breakfast on Christmas morning.

"Nothing elaborate," I answered, "just a sweater and scarf."

"Better still," Louise chimed in, "what did he get you?"

"Nothing yet," I said, "but he's bringing it back when he comes. I guess we're getting engaged. He's getting my ring," I continued.

"This is a big step," Mama responded. "I hope you've thoroughly thought it through."

"I have," I answered. "We'll probably get married in June. You know I've always wanted a church wedding, so I'll probably get Brother Nance to marry us at the Methodist Church."

Mama seemed quite sad for the rest of the day. "I guess you'll move away when he gets out of service," she said sadly.

"That's a long time off and I won't think about that now."

"He doesn't get out of service until October 1, 1956, and

that's a year and a half away," Louise commented.

"Opal, there's a strange car in the driveway," Morris said as he came into the kitchen where I was doing dishes. About that time someone knocked on the front door. I went to the door and was so startled I had to hold on to the door. I looked into the face of Glen, whom I had not seen for at least six months. Since I had been dating Warren, he had been pushed into the back of my mind. "Could you come out to the car and talk for just a minute?" he asked.

"Let me grab a sweater. Mama, I'll be right back and finish the dishes," I called over my shoulder.

"My brother is in the car," he explained as we walked to a brand new car parked in the driveway. "This is my brothers car," he explained. "I'm still driving my old one. Chris, my brother, has a girlfriend that lives in Franklin, and he wondered if we'd like to go along. We would drop him in Franklin, and you and I could take the car on to Nashville."

"I'm not sure Mama will let me go," I responded.

"I know it would be quite late when we get back, but you could at least ask her. I've kept in touch about you through the grapevine," he remarked.

"I've heard absolutely nothing about you," I said.

"Go and see if you can ride up with us, and then come and tell us," he concluded.

"Mama, Glen wants me to ride to Nashville with him and his brother. It'll be quite late when we get back, so I don't suppose you'd let me go?"

"How late are you talking about?" she asked.

"It's 6:00 p.m. now, and the drive up and back will take at least 5 hours, so a couple of hours there, and it would be at least 1:00 a.m. when we get back."

I certainly wasn't prepared for her answer. "I guess it'll be all right, don't you, Daddy? Tell them to drive carefully and certainly no drinking."

I figured out later why she was so quick to let me go; she thought it might stop my upcoming wedding. I reasoned that since I didn't have a ring, I wasn't officially engaged to Warren, so I decided it was all right to go. I went out and told them I could go, but I had to get dressed first.

Shortly afterwards, Glen and I were in the back seat of his brother's new car, being chauffeured to Franklin. "I heard you were dating some Air Force guy," he said almost immediately.

"That's true," I answered, "and I'm practically engaged. He's buying me an engagement ring in Minneapolis, while he's home on furlough. What have you been doing for all these months?"

"I've been on a boat most of the time. We were up in Canada for a while, so I picked up a souvenir for you," as he handed me a small package. I collected salt and pepper shakers, so he had bought me a most unusual set.

"I appreciate you thinking of me," I responded sarcastically, "but you could have taken time to write a letter now and then. I couldn't write to you because I had no idea where you were."

"I don't think you sat home pining away for me," he responded.

"We never agreed to go steady," I reminded him. We talked and argued most of the way to Franklin.

We dropped Chris at his girlfriend's house and promised to be back in a couple of hours. Chris's girlfriend had her own car, so they planned to go to a movie while we were gone. "You could show me your apartment," Glen said as we drove away. "Helen might be there, but I know Mildred and Jean are away for Christmas." We drove the twenty to thirty miles to Nashville and on to our apartment. It was now about 9:00 p.m., and we had promised Chris we would back in Franklin by 10:00 p.m.

Helen was gone for the holidays too so I took him on a tour of our apartment, which took all of five minutes. "You have a great place," he said as he seated himself in the living room.

I gathered up the mail, which had been shoved through the door. I noticed immediately I had a letter from Warren. "I've got to read this," I said casually. "I'll put some coffee on, and I think I might find something in a can for sandwiches." I walked on into the kitchen reading my letter as I went. In the second paragraph I gasped because he said they had wrecked his car someplace in Iowa. He had slid off the road in a snow storm. They had called his dad to come and pick them up, and he was going to have to deal with the car later. He said he'd probably sell it for scrap and that he and Jean would probably come back on a bus. He hadn't had time to get my ring but planned on doing that later. I was glad neither he nor Jean were hurt, although Jean had broken her glasses, which was a major problem for her because she was blind without them.

"When is that coffee going to be ready?" Glen called from the living room.

"Just a minute" I said, as I grabbed two cups from the cupboard. "It looks like we have some lunch meat that's still all right," I yelled. "Do you want a sandwich? I'm really hungry," I went on and he said anything to eat was fine with him.

"Is this your boyfriend's picture?" he said as I took the tray back into the living room.

"That's the one," I answered.

I sat our sandwiches, a tray of cookies and two cups of coffee on the coffee table. "You're really not going to marry this guy, are you?" he asked as he took my hand. "Somehow, I always thought it would work out for you and me," he said as he picked up his coffee cup.

"I did at one time," I agreed.

"You know, it's not too late. We could just up and get married; it happens all the time."

"I think it's too late," I responded. We talked a while longer and reminisced about what might have been. "This will probably be the last time I see you," I said as we got back in the car. "If I take Warren's ring, then I won't date or see anyone else and we'll probably set the date in June."

We picked up his brother in Franklin and they drove me straight home. We drove up in the driveway a little after 1:00 a.m.

"I wish you all the best," Glen said as he walked me to the door. "I just wish things had been different," he said sadly. I felt a little like crying myself because we went so many years back together.

"Opal, is that you?" Mama called from the bedroom.

"Yes, it's me; go back to sleep," I answered.

Warren came back, true to his word with my engagement ring and gave it to me a few days after he got back. "It's the most beautiful ring I've ever seen!" I exclaimed when he gave it to me. I really thought so at the time. It was 1/3 of a carat, set in a solitary setting. "I can't wait to show Louise Carlton and all the girls at work," I said, as I admired it on my finger.

Later when I showed it off to Mildred, she wasn't quite as excited, even though she liked Warren better than any other guy I had dated. "I guess you've set a date?" she asked.

"We decided to wait until June, but we haven't set the exact date yet. You'll be my maid of honor, won't you?" She said, "I would love to be your maid of honor, but I thought you might ask your sister, Louise."

"No, she can be a bridesmaid; I'd rather have you beside me. I thought I might ask Carol Pell to be the other bridesmaid, and I still want to have the wedding at Mt. Carmel Methodist Church."

When Warren came in the following weekend, I told him I thought it would be a good idea to talk things over with my parents before we set the date.

The following Sunday, we took off to the country to announce our wedding plans, hoping they would agree with everything. This time, it was quite a bit different than our first trip down. We had been several times in the past six months, so they were quite well acquainted with Warren. "I'm quite nervous," Warren announced as we drove into the driveway, just before noon. "Should I ask your Dad or just tell them our plans and see if it's all right with them?" he asked.

"We'll just work into it," I answered. Mama knew by now that Glen and I were through and I had gotten a ring from Warren so it wasn't coming as a total surprise.

After eating a wonderful Sunday dinner, Mama had spent her morning preparing, we were sitting in the living room around the heater, when I brought up the subject. "Warren and I are planning on getting married in June and I really want to have a church wedding," I said all at once.

Mama was the first to say something. "We have nothing against Warren, but you're both so young."

"I'll be twenty on June 18th," I was quick to point out.

Warren spoke from the other side of the room, "I'll be 21, and I really love Opal." Then he asked the wrong question of

Daddy. "Coy, would you stand up and give her away at our wedding?"

Daddy said quietly, "No, I won't. I have a big family, and I don't have a one I want to give away."

Mama cut in the conversation and said that that didn't mean he was against the wedding; he just meant that he would just stay at home and keep Sam and Dan out of the way.

"Then who will walk me down the aisle?" I asked almost in tears.

"Morris said he would," Mama continued.

"You have to be 21 in Tennessee to get married without your parents' signature," I remarked, so would you sign for us?" I asked Mama.

"If you still want to get married in June, I'll sign for you," she said sadly. "You'll be the first in our family to get married, let alone have a church wedding," she concluded.

"We'll pay for everything," Warren interjected. The rest of the afternoon was spent going over our plans for our great day in June.

"It was nice of Bill to let us borrow his car today," I commented on the way back to Nashville. Warren agreed and said that he had asked him to be best man at the wedding. That meant that he and Carol would both be in the wedding because I was planning on asking Carol to be a bridesmaid. "I'm not sure I'll be able to get a car before the wedding," he continued. "I'm still paying on the Ford I wrecked and sold for salvage. I thought we might go to Minneapolis on our honeymoon and buy a car and drive it back. My Dad said he would loan us the money in June when we come up after the wedding, and by that time I'll have the other one paid off." He went on to say that they would come for the wedding, and we could ride up there and stay for a week, look for a car and then drive it back to Nashville.

"That sounds real romantic," I commented. "There will be seven in the car, if your brother Bruce, his wife, Jeanette and your sister, Marlene comes," I concluded. "Maybe we could stay in a motel for a couple of days before we leave? They could stay at our apartment, and we could take Dad's car and have a little time to ourselves before we start that long trip to Minnesota."

"We'll have all the time in the world when we get back to Nashville," he added. It still didn't sound too great, but I guessed I'd have to go along with it.

The next few months seemed to fly by. I found a dress at Castner Knott and put it on layaway. It was waltz-length and so beautiful! I was very, very thin at this time in my life and I only wore a size nine. When I went for my physical around this time, the doctor insisted I was too thin and wanted me to go on a diet to gain weight. He told me to eat six times a day and to have my boyfriend take me for a milkshake before bedtime. Nothing seemed to help, mainly because I smoked and was running on nervous energy, and I had migraines quite frequently.

We decided to have pastels for the maid of honor and bridesmaids dresses. Mildred put hers on layaway too, and I found ones I thought would be great for Louise and Carol, so they also were put on hold. "I'll never get out of debt," I told Mildred sometime in March. We had credit cards at Harvey's and Castner Knott, but they had limits and mine were all maxed out. The flowers were going to be another big expense, but the Parsons florist agreed to let me pay them off by the month. I wanted invitations, personalized napkins, and thank-you notes. I ordered those in March, so they could be sent out in May. We had set the date for Saturday, June the 4th. I talked to the photographer in Parsons (there was only one) and he was available and agreed to be there. I decided to bring the cake down from a bakery in Nashville. This would be quite a feat, but Carol had agreed to hold it.

By Warren's birthday on March 17th, we seemed to have a handle on everything. Mildred and I cooked him a wonderful birthday dinner. Mildred had asked one of the boys she had been dating to have dinner with us and it was a great celebration. We went dancing afterwards at the Bellemeade restaurant and lounge. "This time next year, you'll have to have me over to your place for your birthday," Mildred commented.

"If everything works out, you'll only have to come across the hall," Warren remarked.

Mrs. Taylor had moved from the apartment across the hall from ours and that apartment was for rent. Things did work out and Jean got married in early spring, and then Helen moved out, so that only left Mildred and me for that two bedroom place, and we decided we just couldn't afford it. "Guess what?" Mildred asked that evening on the way home from work, "I heard the garage apartment out back is available."

"Let's call and find out about it," I said excitedly.

We called and it was much cheaper than the one we were in, so we simply moved out back to the garage. It was a unique place. Warren and I were able to put a hold on the apartment Mrs. Taylor had vacated. We agreed to keep the hall and stairways clean and vacuumed in exchange for lower rent.

Morris

"Opal," Mildred said one afternoon in late March, "you had a phone call from home and they said your brother Morris is very ill and you are to come home immediately. In fact, they said to not come home but to just catch the bus to Jackson and go to the new General Hospital."

"Did they say what the problem was?"

"No, just that it was serious."

I asked Mildred to call my team leader in the morning and started to pack my clothes in a small bag. I wasn't even sure I had enough money for the bus ticket and then a cab on to the hospital. After checking my finances, I realized I only had enough for the bus ticket with nothing left over. It was only a few days from payday and we were getting broke, as usual. Mildred remembered there was money in the grocery fund and said that I could borrow part of that and replace it when I got my check. I wasn't sure if I would be back by then, so I asked Mildred to pick up my check.

I was scared, not only about Morris, but whether I could find my way around Jackson late at night, or even if I could get a cab. I knew the last bus left Nashville around 8:00 p.m. and that meant it would be around midnight when I got into Jackson. When I arrived in Jackson, there was a nice gentleman who helped me find a cab at the bus station and I took the cab to the General Hospital, which was a couple of miles away. He let me out in front of the hospital and I grabbed my bag and headed for the reception desk to find out where my family was.

I had prayed almost continually that Morris would be all right and it would be nothing serious. I had no idea whether God heard my prayers, but I knew it felt better to pray. I knew I was not Christian, but I did believe in God, and I knew that he answered prayer. "Opal," I heard someone call from the waiting room across from the reception desk and I turned to see Louise there. After a quick hug, I asked what was wrong with Morris and why he was in the hospital. She told me they didn't know for sure yet but they suspected it was spinal meningitis and were taking him down shortly to do a bone marrow test. She said it was the only way they could know for sure.

"He's not going to die, is he?" I asked as I began to cry.

"All we can do is pray," she said, crying also. She said Mama was with him now in his room, and we can go up and wait outside the room until she comes out. They only let two people in with him at a time, and they said they preferred one person, if possible.

Mama came out of the room about that time, as a nurse went in to take his temperature. I asked when it had started and when did he get so terribly sick. She told me he had gone swimming earlier that day and had come home and said he had a bad headache. He laid down for a while and then later when she checked on him, he was burning up with fever. Morris was talking strange and looked wild-eyed so Mama had grabbed him up and told Daddy that they had to get him to a doctor right away. They had stopped to see Dr. Conger in Parsons, but he wanted Morris taken to Jackson right away because he suspected meningitis.

Mama was crying softly when they came to get him on a stretcher and take him to the x-ray department to check his bone marrow. As he lay there, Morris looked like he was near death. I had never seen anyone so sick. His temperature was over 105° and rising higher every hour or so. The nurses were cooling him as best they could with ice packs, but the doctors said they had to know immediately what they were dealing with. They had already placed a quarantine sign on his door and let only the immediate family inside and said he needed someone with him around the clock. It was a long wait before they came back and told us the results of his test and it wasn't good. It was bacterial meningitis as they had suspected. The nurse told the family that the next several hours would determine whether he lived or not. The doctors started him on strong antibiotics and kept putting ice packs on his head to lower his temperature. They also stated he might have some brain damage from such a high temperature. Because everyone had been exposed to him on the Saturday when he became ill, they told us we would all have to take sulfa drugs as a precaution.

    We all stayed the first night; Mama, Louise, Dorothy, who was Mama's sister, and J. C., Dorothy's husband, took turns sitting by his bedside through that long, long night. Sometime around mid-morning, his doctor came out and told us that he believed the worst was over and he believed he would live. He couldn't be absolutely sure about brain damage at this point, but he said he was hopeful that he would make a full recovery.

    Louise and I stayed the next night by ourselves. Mama felt she needed to be home with the other kids and, besides, she was completely worn out. We took turns sitting by his bedside just in case he needed something and couldn't get a nurse. I have never been one to stay awake easily. I can remember how hard it was to stay awake during my two hour shifts. Louise would come in and check to see if I was dozing and give me one of her lectures, if I was. I sat and looked out the window and counted the lights around Jackson. I did just about everything I could think of to keep myself awake, including drinking gallons of coffee. The night was finally over, and Morris was more alert by mid-morning, and Louise and I got to go home the following night. I was absolutely dead on my feet, and I knew I had to get some sleep before going back to Nashville to go to work.

    "Louise, your face looks weird," I said the next morning after we got up and were eating breakfast.

    She looked in a mirror and screamed, "What's happened to me?" Her face was red and swollen double. She looked at her hands and they were red with a rash. I told her, I bet she had a reaction to the sulfa drug. "What will I do?" she cried. "I can't go to work like this."

I told her the first thing to do is quit the sulfa drug and she should go to see Dr. Conger and see what he suggests. She followed my suggestion, and he gave her a shot to counteract the sulfa drug and told her never to take it again or she could die.

Morris continued to recover and was able to come home after about a week in the hospital, although it took literally months for him to get his strength back. I had gotten a couple of letters from Warren while I was away. When I arrived back in Nashville the following Wednesday after being gone for almost a week, he met me at the bus station and seemed really excited to see me.

We stayed busy the next few months getting ready for the wedding. Mildred had bought a portable sewing machine sometime earlier, so I set out to make my trousseau. One Saturday in April before the wedding, I told Mildred that I thought I would never get this all finished. Mama just didn't have time to sew for me very much, and I only had Saturdays and a little time at night. She reassured me that I would get it done.

The following evening Mildred told me that Wanda wanted to have me a lingerie shower, and I said that would be so much fun. She thought she would ask 8 to 10 of my closest friends, and we decided we would get a list together and decide on a time tonight after she got home. Mrs. Irene Lafferty, one of our neighbors in Mt. Carmel, is having me a shower in a couple of weeks on Saturday night. I told her how much fun all of this is and stated it was a shame our lives were going to change so dramatically. I'm certainly not sure I want to live in Minnesota when Warren gets out of service, but he always said we can make more money there. I guess I'll just have to face that in a year and a half. He doesn't get discharged until October of 1956.

I seemed to be living in a whirlwind of parties and excitement. The team I worked for announced they were having a lunch and shower for me the following week. Louise Carlton was still one of my best friends, so she had arranged it all. "This is all too much," I commented as I opened my gifts. We had a wonderful lunch at our favorite hangout, Zinnias. I got several small appliances like an iron, toaster, etc. I also remember getting a set of beautiful rugs.

I had very little time to actually think about Warren's family and the fact that I had never met them and wouldn't get to meet them until the night before the wedding at the rehearsal dinner. I also had a wonderful community shower in Mt. Carmel at Mrs. Lafferty's house. I remember getting like twenty sets of sheets and around forty towels. I told Mildred on our way back home that I was set for life.

Of course, the shower that was the most fun was the lingerie shower that Wanda Pruess gave for my closest friends. I got sexy panties, beautiful nightgowns, slippers, and, of course, a garter to throw. I had my wedding night negligee and gown on layaway at Harvey's. It was a beautiful Vanity Fair, also in a waltz-length.

I awoke early one Saturday morning and yelled to Mildred, "Do you realize I'm getting married two weeks from today?"

"I should," she answered. "That's all we've talked about for the past six months."

I told her I didn't want our friendship to change and that I hoped we could always be best friends. She said we have to face the fact that things will be different. I told her that Warren liked her so much and that he would never want to separate us. She said she realized he did, but she wasn't sure he would be pleased if she was there all the time.

Before I realized it, it was a week before the big day. I asked Carol a few days before we were to leave for Decaturville if she believed we could get the cake there in one piece, and she said yes and that she would hold it carefully. She stated that Bill would have to be careful not to make any sudden stops. We were going to Mt. Carmel on Thursday evening and I had taken Friday off work and then would be on vacation for the next two weeks. Bill Pell drove his car down, and Warren and I were planning to drive back to Nashville with his parents, brother, sister, and sister-in-law. They planned to stay at our apartment Saturday and Sunday nights, and then we planned to all drive to Minneapolis, where Warren and I would stay for a week. Warren's dad was planning on helping us find a car, and we would drive it back home to Nashville.

Opal Phillips Johnson

The Rehearsal

Mama had worked so hard getting everything spic and span for the reception to be held back at the house. She loved both Mildred and Carol, and we all had a great time the day before the wedding. Bill and Carol stayed at a motel on Thursday night. Mildred stayed at her home and came down early on Friday morning. Warren's family arrived in Parsons, where we had reserved their rooms for the night, around 12:00 p.m. on Friday. The rehearsal was to be held at the church around 6:30 p.m.

Everyone was there quite early. We did not have a rehearsal dinner, but most of us were going out afterwards. Mrs. Thelma Yarbro, our church pianist and a former Sunday school teacher of mine, was playing the piano. Her daughter Joy was our singer. Bill Crawley and another cousin, Buford Crawley, were the other two groomsmen. Bill Pell, of course, was Warren's best man.

The rehearsal went quite well. Joy practiced singing *I Love You Truly* and *Because*. Brother Nance went through the ceremony and helped us know where to stand and tried to reassure us. My sisters, Joan and Pat, were lighting the candles. Daddy had not changed his mind, so Morris was giving me away.

Warren seemed quite nervous as he introduced me to his mother, dad, then his brother Bruce, his wife Jeanette, and then his younger sister Marlene. I didn't remember too much else about that evening, Ma and Dad, Warren's parents, went back to the motel, but the rest of us went to some nightclub and ate and danced until quite late. Bruce was the life of the party and kept everyone laughing and at ease.

Warren and I had very little time alone that night, and before I knew it, I was lying in bed wondering, *what on earth am I doing.* This was the first time I had doubts about marrying someone from another part of the country. How would I fit in and would they accept me? I laid awake most of the night, thinking about it and wondering if there was any way I could get out of this wedding. I finally came to the conclusion that everything had gone too far, and it was inevitable that the wedding would take place.

The Wedding Day

I awoke with a headache from no sleep and stress like I had never known before. I was always an organized person and had always planned everything well in advance. I reasoned that I had done everything I could do, so if things went wrong on this most important day of days, there was nothing else I could do about it.

"What time are they coming with the flowers?" Louise asked as I grabbed a second cup of coffee.

"Around noon, they said," I answered.

Louise said that they would go to the church and be sure it's decorated the way we've told them. I told her that getting everything ready here at home for the reception was the big problem. Louise reassured me that Mama said she and Mamie would come back while we were taking pictures at the church and finish getting the punch and everything ready here. As I was finishing my second cup of coffee, I reminded her that not everyone from the wedding was invited to the reception and I hoped they knew that.

"I wish Daddy would reconsider and be there," I remarked as Mama came in the kitchen.

"You know how he is," she reasoned, "and, besides, he's promised to keep Dan and Sam out of our hair for a few hours." I decided I wasn't going to let it ruin my day.

The flowers looked beautiful, they had not forgotten the kneeling bench, and all the corsages were lovely. The wedding

ceremony was set for 4:00 p.m. but the music would begin at 3:30 p.m. Mrs. Thelma would play for thirty minutes while people were being seated.

"Mildred, your dress looks beautiful," I commented as she helped me with my wedding dress. Louise, Mildred, and Carol had put their dresses on at the house, but I had waited until we got to the church around 3:00 p.m. to get dressed. There was a very small Sunday school room in the back of the church where I was able to get everything together with a lot of help. It was June 4th in Tennessee and, of course, the church had no air conditioner. It rained a small shower on our way from the house, which only added to the steam and humidity.

Morris stood waiting outside the room in his new suit. He looked thin and drawn from his ordeal with meningitis. As I took his arm to start down the aisle, I was thankful for him just being alive. The music started after Mama had been seated and then the wedding party filed down the short aisle. First, Mildred, and Bill, Bill Crawley and Louise, then Buford and Carol. There was a pause, then Ms. Thelma started playing *Here Comes the Bride*. I looked at Morris and said, "This is it, let's go."

I looked around the church as we started down the aisle, and I could not believe how many people were there. The church was completely full with people standing outside. I guess the community just wanted to see its first church wedding.

I looked down the aisle and saw Warren standing there looking at me, and I became somewhat calmer. He had on a pale blue suit that he had picked out. All of the groomsmen's suits were different colors.

At that moment I didn't know if the photographer was there or not, and I only hoped he would take the list of pictures I had given him. His name was Mr. Jennings, and he was quite well known, not only for his pictures but for his drinking problem, too. I just hoped I would have some pictures! A flash bulb went off and I realized he had taken one as Morris and I were going down the aisle.

I think my knees were shaking, but we managed to make it to the front of the church. I remember very little about the actual ceremony. Joy sang two songs, which were quite beautiful. As I look back now, I realize what a pleasure it was to have known Joy.

She had polio as a child and died in an automobile accident when she was quite young.

The ceremony was over and Warren and I were walking back out of the church arm in arm. I was now Mrs. Warren Johnson, for better or for worse. The wedding party got back to the house about an hour later after taking pictures and finishing up at the church. Some of the crowd from the church had ventured up to the reception, but, on the whole, it had taken us so long to get there after taking pictures that most of the people had left.

Warren and I cut the cake that Carol had so lovingly held all the way down from Nashville. We took more pictures at the reception. At this time I realized the photographer was drinking, and I was a little nervous about how they would turn out. The reception was over by 6:00 p.m. and everyone was anxious to start back to Nashville.

Warren and I decided to ride back to Nashville with Carol and Bill. We decided to go with them so they could follow us back to the apartment. Warren's dad had a new Nash Rambler that we were going to borrow for the night to go to the motel. The drive back to Nashville was uneventful because everyone was so wiped out from the wedding.

"It was a beautiful wedding," Carol said for the third time.

"People will remember it, I'm sure," I answered. I said the biggest disaster was at the reception when Daddy brought my two dirty, little brothers back right in the middle of it.

Warren said, "They were fine and no one had paid any attention to them."

I told him I noticed them and they were either supposed to get cleaned up or stay away, but he said if that's the worst thing that happened, we're doing great."

We arrived at the apartment around 9:00 p.m. Warren's mother suggested we have coffee and talk for a while before we left for our honeymoon. She had brought all sorts of food so we had sandwiches along with the coffee. I kept getting more tired by the minute.

At around midnight, Warren announced, "I think we should go. We'll be back sometime tomorrow morning and all go sightseeing."

The Wedding Night

We left the apartment with our house guests intact and started off for our short honeymoon. "Where are we staying?" I asked matter-of-factly. He had taken that responsibility. The motel, having enough for the down payment on the car we were going to buy in Minneapolis, plus other spending was his responsibility. I had saved $200.00 that we hoped to use for expenses after we got home.

He looked at me rather calmly and said "I haven't decided yet. We'll just drive around and look for something we like and can afford."

"At this time of night, we may not find anything available," I answered, already annoyed. Needless to say, we could not find a motel that had a vacancy anywhere in Nashville or the surrounding areas because there was a convention in town, and the motels were more crowded than usual.

At two o'clock in the morning I was beginning to cry. I was so tired and we had no idea where we were going to spend our wedding night. In an effort to soothe me, Warren suggested trying some of the hotels downtown. We tried the Maxwell House but they were full. "There's the Sam Davis Hotel," I said crying and frustrated.

Warren went to check and see if they had any vacancies while I waited in the car for what seemed like an hour. He came back carrying a key and said we had a room for two nights. We took our bags inside and had to ride the elevator up to third floor to our room. The room wasn't too bad. The biggest problem was there was no air conditioning. It had a ceiling fan, and we opened the window a crack to get it cooled off. All I can say is it was a honeymoon wedding night I would never forget.

The Day After

We were back at the apartment around noon the next day after stopping to have breakfast. The family said they had slept well and were ready for a day of touring Nashville. Before we left to go sightseeing, I had a chat with my new sister-in-law, Jeanette. She filled me in on the family as a whole, especially my new mother-in-law. "She rules the roost," she informed me. "She has strong opinions on everything." I told her we'd be in Nashville for over a year, so I guess I can deal with her from a distance.

She said that she and Bruce had lived with them for short periods of time since they had been married. She went on to say that they lived with them until after David was born, and he was now 2 years old. They had lived in a small apartment since David had been born and that had been a lot better for them. The rest of the family came out of the front door, and we got up from the front porch glider and our conversation was ended.

"Where are we going first?" Bruce wanted to know.

"I thought we'd go out to Centennial Park and see the Parthenon, then on to Bellemeade Mansion," Warren commented. "If we have time, we might drive out to the Hermitage, where Andrew Jackson lived," he continued. We toured the park as planned, but the other places were closed by the time we got there.

We spent quite awhile at one of the places, drinking coffee and just getting to know each other. Ma said I should call her "Ma" because that's what everyone else did and suggested we have supper back at our apartment since she had brought so much food. Besides, we'd have to eat out on the long trip to Minneapolis. We were planning on cutting the trip in half by staying in a motel somewhere along the way. I was really dreading the trip; just thinking about seven adults being cramped in a car for two days made me sick to my stomach. I knew it would be even harder on Jeanette because she was now about six months pregnant.

Warren got up, stretched, and announced, "I think Opal and I will go back to the hotel earlier than last night since we're leaving so early."

"Oh, we understand," Bruce commented.

I felt rather embarrassed but agreed with Warren that I was tired. We left them at the apartment around 10:00 p.m. and checked back in at the Sam Davis Hotel downtown. It didn't seem quite as hot and humid the second night. We had a wake-up call at 5:30 a.m., and were back over to the apartment at 7:00 a.m. ready to leave on our journey.

"I'll take a second cup of your coffee," I told Ma, as she finished cleaning up the kitchen. "I'll rinse the cup and put it in the sink for when we get back," I said as I sipped the hot coffee. We had fixed the apartment up quite nice. It was furnished, but we had added our own special touches and moved the furniture around to suit us. I really looked forward to being back in our own place, even before we got started.

The Journey to Minnesota

The first day of travel was a series of shifting around, trying to help Jeanette be more comfortable. We caught up on a lot of things, and the fact that we had not known each other before seemed trivial. Jeanette and I hit it off from the beginning. She had a temperament a lot like mine. Later in life, we would become not only best friends, but neighbors.

About 5:00 p.m. that day, Jeannette asked that we not drive too late; she really needed to stretch out and rest.

"We've got to find a place and eat supper," Warren's dad answered. After we eat, then we'll start looking for a motel to spend the night."

I already knew by this time I was going to really like Dad. Everyone else was always teasing me about my accent and my southern drawl, but he always commented about how he loved to hear me talk and he hoped I'd never change. He always built me up and tried to make me feel good about myself. So in the 2 days I'd known him, I knew we would be friends and that I would have an ally. I was really nervous about Ma but just decided to try to make the best of it. Warren got along so great with my family that the least I could do was try to get along with his.

The second day of our trip was shorter because we had driven until about 9 hours before we were able to find a motel. We got up and left around 6:00 a.m. and drove a few hours before we stopped for breakfast. We arrived in Minneapolis around 2:00 p.m. in the afternoon.

"I've got to go to the grocery store before we get to the house," Ma announced. "We have no food in the house so I'll need to pick up some supplies to make something for supper."

When we stopped at the supermarket I said to Warren, "I think I'll go in; do you want to go?"

"I'll go," he said quite agreeably.

Jeannette looked up and said the first thing that put me on the defensive. She seem to laugh and said, "Why do you want to go; haven't you got supermarkets in Tennessee?"

I snapped back at her "We've got everything in Tennessee that you have in Minnesota and maybe more!" I also set them straight when they started making comments about the way I talked. I guess I handled it the right way because I never had to deal with that sort of thing again.

The two weeks we spent with the in-laws was not as bad as I had anticipated. Warren's dad helped us find a car right away.

My Place In Time

We found a 1949 Chrysler New Yorker. It was just a few hundred dollars and about what we thought we could afford. Warren still owed his parents for the Ford that he had wrecked and had to junk. We just added this to his account and planned to make payments along with interest.

This was my first glimpse into Ma's way of thinking. "I would never charge my own child interest," I kept saying to Warren.

"She says that they have to pay interest on the house, so we should do the same" was his answer. It still seemed odd to me, but I also knew I would get it paid off quickly and I hoped we would never have to borrow money from her again.

This rang true until Adrienne was born three years later, and we had to borrow fifty dollars to help pay the heat bill. As far as I can remember, that was the only money we ever borrowed from them. We took several loans from the bank, but I always thought there wasn't much advantage from borrowing from relatives if you still had to pay the going interest.

After getting our own car, we weren't as dependent on them for our transportation. We saw many of Warren's band buddies. Marlene, Warren's sister, had a banquet for her graduation so she invited us to go with her and that was great fun. She graduated from high school while we were there, so we got to attend that.

Jeanette called at the beginning of the second week and asked us, Warren and me, if we would like to eat at their apartment on Wednesday night, and I told her we would love to. She said maybe we could play cards afterwards. I told her I only play pinochle or canasta, and she said they could teach me to play 500. The supper was good, although she cooked more spaghetti than I've ever seen a person cook for four people. She said she would just put the sauce together with the pasta and have leftovers. We did play cards but decided on canasta since we all were familiar with that game. David, her two-year-old, was such a cutie, and took to us right away. She had no trouble getting him to bed, so we played cards quite late, even though Bruce had to get up and go to work the next morning.

Before we realized it, our two weeks were over and we were loading the car to head back to Tennessee. Ma packed us a lunch, and with all the presents from the other relatives, the car was loaded down. Ma had arranged for a reception for us with all the relatives coming for food and a look at Warren's new bride. I enjoyed it all except the hugging and kissing from all his aunts and uncles. Our family had never been very demonstrative in showing their affections, so it made me terribly uncomfortable. I endured and, besides, they had all bought wonderful presents.

Homeward Bound

"I'm so excited about going home to our new apartment," I said to Warren, as I snuggled up to him in our luxurious big car.

"Me too," he answered. "We'll have all the time we want - just to ourselves."

I said I was anxious to see Mildred too. "I hope you won't be upset about us spending time together now that we're married."

"Of course, I won't," he said; just don't overdo it.

We drove straight through from Minneapolis to Nashville and got there around two or three in the morning. Our money was running short, so we felt we couldn't afford another motel. After unloading most of the car, we sank into bed totally wiped out and grateful that the next day was Sunday and we could sleep late. This was actually the first night we were alone in our own place. It was so wonderful to be young and in love. I had just celebrated my 20th birthday a couple of days before, and Warren had turned 21 in March, so he felt quite mature.

As we ate breakfast the next morning, Warren asked, "Do we have to go to your mother's next week?"

"I suppose so." I answered, "they'll be expecting us, and besides, we just spent two weeks with your folks."

"I just wish we had the whole weekend together, that's all," he said sadly.

From that point on I never remember him objecting to going to my home. We went home at least once a month for the next year and a half. I had explained to him that since he insisted on moving to Minneapolis to get a job and live, that I needed to be with my folks and Mildred as much as possible. At this point in my ouldn't think about moving so far away from my family. I ~~ thinking I'll deal with it when it comes.

Mildred was living in an apartment out back, where she and I had lived before Warren and I had gotten married. It was sort of a garage apartment, but not really a bad place. Betty, a friend of hers from work, had moved in with her to share expenses. I felt a little bit jealous of their relationship, but I knew ours would be different from now on. Before we had finished breakfast, the phone rang and I answered it and told Warren that it was Mildred and asked if it was all right if she came over for a cup of coffee. He said it was all right with him, but we'd better get the bed made and our place picked up a little so she could walk.

We still hadn't unpacked from the night before and several of the presents were still in the car. What a car! We had no trouble and it was like riding in a Rolls Royce. The only problem was it took a lot of gas for such a big car.

A few minutes later there was a knock at the door and there was my best friend in the whole world! (other than my new husband Warren) We hugged and kept saying how glad we were to see each other. "Tell me all about your honeymoon!" she exclaimed, showing more enthusiasm than usual.

"Our so-called 'honeymoon' was great, I guess, but I think it should be better classified as a visiting trip." I told her that Warren had promised me a real honeymoon on our first anniversary. We're going to Chattanooga and to see Lookout Mountain, where you and I went on our class trip. She remembered our trip and said that should be a real neat honeymoon. I asked her what she and Betty had been up to and she told me that Betty was dating a really nice boy who was in the Air Force.

"What's his name?" Warren wanted to know. "I might know him."

"Fred, but I can't remember his last name," she said. She said he would have to ask Betty sometime. Betty was a beautiful girl with the prettiest reddish auburn hair I'd ever seen. She was the first girl that ever made me jealous.

"We're playing cards with Mildred and Betty at their place tonight," I informed Warren as he came in the door from the base.

"That's fine," he answered, "but I told Bill Pell that we would come out to their new trailer and play cards with them one night this week too."

"Let's do that on Friday night, so we won't have to drive home so late," I suggested. He agreed and said he would tell Bill the next day to ask Carol about Friday night.

Our First Fight

Our first really serious fight came the next night, when we went down to Mildred and Betty's apartment to play cards. Warren sat and talked to Betty the whole evening and seemed to ignore me. Fred, her boyfriend, was in the Air Force Academy, and she didn't get to see him very often but said it was quite serious.

Anyway, the longer we played cards the more upset I got until finally, I announced I had a headache and was going home. I left but Warren stayed for a few minutes after I left so I had even more time to fume before he came in. We had a bad argument and I pouted for the next couple of days before we made up. I don't remember being jealous very much after the first year of our marriage.

Our next episode occurred when his ex-fiancé called. She asked to speak to Warren when I answered the phone. I asked who was calling and told her that Warren had not gotten home from the base. She told me who she was. I asked her if she knew Warren was married and she said she did but still wanted to talk to him. "Well, I'm sure he doesn't want to talk to you," I said curtly, and "don't call here again."

Needless to say, when Warren got home I was in a rage. I accused him of talking to her before. He said he had not seen her or talked to her since our wedding. I finally believed him, even though she called again in a couple of weeks. He wasn't home at that time either so I said a few choice words, telling her there would be no communication between her and my husband and to not call again.

Life with the Newlyweds

Our life for the next few months centered around playing cards with Wanda Pruess, Mildred, Betty or friends from the base. I did see Louise Carlton on occasion. We went to see a movie on special occasions and went out to eat very rarely. We tried to budget our money where we could eat at this one place that had specials on Saturday for $2.00 each. We had to wash clothes at the Laundromat after we finished cleaning on Saturday morning. We would then buy groceries and if we could afford it, then we would eat out. We had very little extra money so most of our entertainment was playing cards with friends, or walking in the park, maybe feeding the ducks.

Grandpa Phillips

"This is our weekend to go to the country and see my folks," I told Warren on Thursday evening in early September. We had now spread our visits out to every 3 or 4 weeks. We just could not afford the gas after we paid all the payments on things from our wedding and the car. "It seems like we just went," he answered.

"It's been 4 weeks, and I know Mama would like us to come."

"All right, I'll get home as early as I can and we'll drive down Friday evening."

We left the apartment around 5:00 p.m. as planned and I said "Let's stop for a hamburger in Centerville because they'll have already eaten supper by the time we get there."

"I guess we can afford that, if we don't have to eat out any more this weekend."

"We won't," I assured him, "and you know how much food

Mama always sends back with us."

"Yeah," he agreed, "I guess that almost pays for the trip because it will help cut our grocery bill in half next week." We stopped for close to an hour and ate our supper. That made it about 8:30 p.m. by the time we got to Mt. Carmel community.

Just before we got to the bridge over White's Creek, we could see several car lights and what looked like a search light, and there was also a police car with the lights flashing. "What do you think is going on?" I asked Warren, as we drove up to the bridge. I saw Daddy's pickup just as we stopped. We walked over to where several people were standing, including Daddy, a couple of his brothers, along with my Grandmother Phillips.

"What's going on?" Warren wanted to know.

"We don't know for sure yet," Daddy answered. "Grandma is worried because Pa should have been home hours ago from fishing in the creek. She says he always gets home by 5:00 p.m. because he knows she has supper ready by then."

"Why are the police here?" I wanted to know.

"Kathleen called them to come and help search for him," Lynn, one of Daddy's brothers, volunteered.

"They've been looking for the last hour," Omer, Daddy's oldest brother, commented.

My Grandma was crying softly. "I know something bad is wrong," she sobbed.

Kitty, or Wallace, which was his real name, and his wife Kathleen came walking up the hill from the creek. "They've found his boat," she cried. "It drifted up one of the sloughs and was almost hidden in the brush."

"Is he in it?" everyone asked at once. The crowd had grown enormous in the last thirty minutes. My other two aunts had arrived. Alice, Wallace's twin sister, walked up with her husband Andrew and then the oldest girl Zoomer and her husband Arch came running up the road.

"News spreads fast doesn't it?" Kathleen commented. Someone said the search team should be back shortly.

"Look," Warren cried, "there's a boat and they are pulling

a fishing boat behind." The sheriff walked up the hill first. "The news is not good," he said sadly. "It appears as though he's been shot through the head."

Grandma started to scream, and chaos seemed to erupt. "Who would have done such a thing?" people kept asking over and over.

The sheriff informed us they would have to do an autopsy on the body and it would take a couple of days to get it done, so the body would not be ready for burial for at least three days.

Grandma was still screaming and crying. "I want to see him before they take him away," she begged. Kathleen reassured her that they'll see him when they bring him up to put him in the ambulance. She said it might be an hour or so since the sheriff had just now called for the ambulance and it'll take a while to get here.

"Warren, let's go on to the house and let Mama and them know what's going on," I reasoned. Daddy said he would stay until the sheriff came. "Who do you think did this?" I asked Warren as we drove the mile or so to our house. *Could it be someone we know?* I wondered out loud.

"It must have been someone he knew," Warren answered.

We drove up the driveway still totally in shock that something like this could happen, especially in our community. Mama came to the door, glad to see us, but wondering why we were so late. "Your daddy left some time ago to look for your Grandpa Phillips," she told us. "I hope they've found him by now." Warren told her that they had found him shot to death in his boat. "Don't they have any idea who did it?" she wanted to know.

"At this point, I'm sure they don't. They'll probably find out something tomorrow, if not tonight," Warren added.

"Grandma was really taking it hard," I told Mama.

"I guess Rodgers and Ethel will take her to their house tonight, don't you think?" she asked. Rodgers was another one of Daddy's brothers. In fact, he had yet another brother that lived in Perry County; his name was Jim Allen. He was better known as Derby. The oldest was Zoomer, then Omer, Daddy, Derby, Lynn, Rodgers, Kitty and Alice. We had never been very close as a family, but something like this certainly did draw you together.

"Will they bring the body back to someone's house?" Louise asked.

"I'm sure they will," Mama answered, "probably to Rodgers' or Kitty's." Warren told her the autopsy would take a few days.

"I just hope they find out who did it," I was quick to add.

"The whole community will be in an uproar," Louise added.

About an hour later we heard Daddy's truck pull up in the driveway, and it was now close to midnight. The smaller kids had been put to bed, but we knew they were probably not sleeping.

I was so exhausted I went to bed around 2:00 a.m. I awoke with a start a few hours later when I heard Mama and Daddy talking in the other room. "They took him to Nashville in the ambulance," he said as I came into the room. "They also think they know who killed him. One of the black kids that lived in the community had been fishing with Pa for the past couple of weeks, or at least that's what Rodgers said. Pa had given him fish a couple of times to take home for supper. It seems someone saw him with Pa this afternoon. He's only about thirteen years old," Daddy said sadly.

By midmorning, the 13-year-old kid had been arrested for murder. Pa had told him he would be getting his social security check the next day and his motive was for the money. Grandpa had cashed his check and left most of it with Grandma before he came fishing, He only had $13.00 in his pocket.

Needless to say, there was outrage throughout the whole community. The sheriff thought it best to move him to a different county, because there was talk of a lynching. I had never seen my daddy in such a state. He just couldn't seem to sit still; he kept pacing the floor, trying to understand how this terrible thing could have happened.

"Warren, I think we should drive back to Nashville and come back on Monday or Tuesday, don't you think?" I asked. It was now Saturday afternoon and we knew at the earliest it would be late Monday before the body was brought back.

"We'll go back in the morning, and I'll work on Monday. You can go into National Life if you feel up to it. We'll drive back on Monday night and then stay for a couple of days for the funeral," he added.

We drove back to Nashville as planned, made our

arrangements at work and were back in Mt. Carmel by 9:00 p.m. on Monday. We found out they did have the body back, and they would have him at Ethel and Rodgers house. In our community this was not uncommon and there was always an all night vigil. "Warren, I'm not going to stay all night," I said as we prepared to go down after we changed our clothes.

"I'll stay and you can ride home with Louise," he answered. It was really a hard few days, especially on Grandma.

"Did you watch the Nashville news?" someone asked, as I came out of the kitchen. We had now acquired a T.V. from one of our friends, Carol and Bill Pell. They got a new one and gave us their old one. I said that I had not watched the news before we left Nashville. They said this story is all over the news, and it would probably be on again tomorrow so we might could see it. Mama and Daddy didn't have a television, so I knew we would probably leave to go home after the funeral the next day, so I didn't figure I would get to see the news story. Warren stayed through the night but came back in time to sleep a few hours before we had to go to the funeral.

It was all such a nightmare. I remember feeling so sorry for my grandmother. There was some discussion after the funeral about where Ma would live now that Grandpa was gone. She was scared to stay by herself, so we knew she would have to live with one of her kids. Daddy had such a houseful of kids that he was ruled out. Her house was close to Rodgers and Kitty's so they were the logical ones that she would choose to stay with. "I guess Ma's decided she'll try to stay or at least sleep at Rodgers and Ethel's," Daddy said after we had gotten back from the funeral.

Grandpa's death destroyed Grandma also. She started having nightmares shortly afterwards. She slept very little and seemed to get worse as time went on. They took her to Western State to try to get help because they just didn't know what to do. Several of the children were against it, but it seemed the only solution at the time. They said she would have to stay for a short while until they could get her nerves settled.

Meanwhile, they put her in a room with a highly disturbed patient. A few months went by and the family got a call to come immediately. "It seems your mother was in an unfortunate accident," the doctor told them when they arrived. "Her roommate went into a rage one night a week or so ago and kicked her on the leg. We thought it was minor, but yesterday when she complained of leg pain, a specialist was called in, but he thinks it's too late to amputate her leg to save her life."

"What do you mean?" they all asked at once.

"Is she near death?" Daddy wanted to know.

"I'm afraid so," the doctor answered. "Blood poisoning has set in throughout the body, and she doesn't seem to be responding to any antibiotics."

The family stayed at the hospital for the rest of the night, and sometime the next morning they called them in just before Grandma Nell slipped away. It was all so sad that both their lives were taken because of such a senseless crime.

The trial was held in the upcoming months that followed, and most of the family attended whenever possible. The kid was only 13 but his 14th birthday was only a few months away and the judge decided he could be tried as an adult because it was such a heinous crime. The sentence was life without the possibility of parole. At least, that's what the family understood. "How could someone do this to someone who was a friend to them?" was the question everyone kept asking. There seemed to be no answer except maybe his environment and the examples set before him. His father was serving 99 years in prison at the time for poisoning his infant son with lye.

In later years we found out that there was some way the lawyers found a loop hole in the sentence he had received, and he was paroled in twenty years – so he was only 33 years old when he was released. The family protested the release but with no success. Sometimes the justice system just does not work for the victims. Everyone was bitter and angry for quite a long time but over his lifetime, I saw my dad make peace with it and let go of some of his hurt and pain.

My Place In Time

The Colons

Warren and I continued our life living in Nashville. He carpooled with several of the guys from the base, which helped our budget. Money was probably our biggest problem and continued throughout most of our married life. We had lots of friends from Seward Air Force Base and several of my friends from work, so we visited a lot and played cards mostly for our entertainment. Mildred and I continued to stay close. We usually ate lunch together at work and continued to keep our friendship close in spite of my newly married status.

"What are you doing for Thanksgiving this year?" I asked her one afternoon on the way home from work.

"I'd like to go home, but it's for such a short time since we have to work Friday." She usually rode with us when we went down. I told her I would ask Warren if he wanted to go and get back to her later that night. "That would be great, and at least we would have a great dinner without having to cook it."

I called Mildred back after Warren and I discussed our plans and told her we had decided we would go. I told her we would leave as soon as we got home from work on Wednesday, and that way it won't be so late when we get there. Warren said we'd leave to come home on Thursday around 7:00 p.m. and that should get us home before 10:00 p.m. We usually took Mildred home down near Clifton Bend and then drove on to Mama's through what was known as the colon. It was a densely populated forest with a gravel road that ran through it. It was quite a short cut but the roads weren't very good and they were gravel and sometimes in bad weather they were almost impassable.

It was a crisp, cool November day when we started out for our first Thanksgiving together. We were able to leave around 5:00 p.m. Mildred and I had both packed a picnic supper so we would not have to stop on the way. We had a great time, talking and singing all the way to Clifton Bend, where we dropped Mildred off. "I don't think we should go through the colon," I said to Warren after she got out.

"It'll be all right," he said. "I think we'll be able to get through."

"It's been raining all week, and there is no predicting what the roads will be like," I continued.

"It's so much quicker", he argued "so let's try it."

It was now around 7:45 p.m. and a dark, dreary night. There is no way to describe how dark it is in a forest with no street lights or houses anywhere in sight. The whole trail was about eight miles long. If we had gone the other way, it would be about fifteen miles. We drove for about 3 miles before we began to see that the roads were really not in great shape. We managed to maneuver our way through 2 or 3 really muddy areas before we came to a place that I knew we would never get through. "Please, Warren, let's turn around," I cried.

"I think we can make it," he kept saying. Before we knew what was happening we were stuck in the mud.

"What will we do now?" I asked as I began to cry.

"We'll have to try to push it out."

As I got out of the car, I got muddy up past my ankles. I was really angry and upset, but most of all I was scared. I had heard tales about these woods or forest all my life, and now I could just see things coming out of the dark woods and attacking us. I knew there were bobcats and wolves and other creatures that I certainly wanted no part of - probably all around us. "I'll find some brush and put it under the wheels and then we'll both push and maybe we can move it out," Warren reasoned. I kept crying and said I knew we'd be stuck here all night or we'd have to walk for miles in the dark.

But through all my anxiety, Warren stayed calm. He came back with some brush and placed it in the mud underneath the tires. "All right now, let's push it forward." We pushed and the first time it moved very little. "Let's keep rocking it, and then it'll move." Our Chrysler New Yorker was certainly not a light car. We pushed and rocked for what seemed like hours before it finally started inching out of the mud. "Let's try to go on," Warren commented. "Maybe there won't be any more spots as bad as this one. We only lack about 6 more miles on this road." We were both cold, wet with mud, and very irritated. I was so furious I wouldn't talk to him the rest of the way to Mama's house.

We got to the house around 9:00 p.m. I was never so glad to walk into a warm house and get my muddy clothes off. "Let Warren tell you what happened," I said angrily. I told your mother that I would bet you came through the colon. The trucks from the mill drive through there and after a lot of rain it gets really bad in spots. "We found that out!," I called from the bedroom. I knew we had to pick Mildred up the next day, and I was determined to convince Warren to take the long way back to her house.

Our First Thanksgiving

We had a great Thanksgiving dinner. Warren absolutely loved southern cooking and my mother was a great cook. She had chicken and dressing and had made her famous coconut cake. Her cakes were out of this world and she did not use a recipe, so we were never able to duplicate them. She always cooked a big southern breakfast, which Warren also loved because he said he had grown up having cereal for breakfast. Mama's breakfast consisted of country ham or maybe sausage and eggs. Sometimes she made fried potatoes, gravy, a chocolate syrup, and always loads of homemade biscuits.

She had taken to Warren right away. He was always more than willing to help her with her projects. He went with her to milk the two cows they kept in a pasture below the house. He helped out with all sorts of other chores she needed him to help with. He did a lot of wiring or plumbing. Later, he installed an attic fan that really helped to cool the whole house. I used to tell her I thought she loved Warren more than she did me.

Warren seemed to fit in with all the folks in the community. My uncle Omer, Daddy's brother that lived up the road was always coming out to get Warren to help him or give him advice on how to fix some problem. Mama taught him all her remedies. For instance, he was going to go blackberry picking with us, but no one had warned him about the chiggers. "I'm absolutely covered with bites," he told me after our first outing, picking wild blackberries. Mama put coal oil on him and fingernail polish over the bites. She also told him if he went again to rub coal oil around his ankles and arms, and the chiggers would not go past that. She also had a remedy for his finger when he almost cut it off helping her make sauerkraut. "Grab that bag of salt," she yelled to Louise. "Warren's got a bad cut." She poured the wound full of salt and wrapped it up in a cloth. He didn't go to the doctor and it healed fairly quick. She also doctored him for a severe sunburn one day after we had been swimming in the river too long. This time she grabbed the vinegar and rubbed it all over his back and arms. I was always so thankful that Warren and my family got along so well. I just kept hoping it would be the same with me and Warren's folks.

We had a wonderful first Thanksgiving together and before we realized it, we were getting ready to start back. We had told Mildred we would be at her house by 7:00 p.m. I told Warren as we loaded the car. Warren said the road was probably dried up on the short cut and we sure could save some time. "No way," I was quick to point out. "I do not want to ever go through what we did last night again." He finally agreed to go the long route to keep peace. We loaded the car down with canned vegetables and meats of all kinds. They had killed hogs recently so there was fresh sausage and other pork. The extra food always helped out so much and we were so appreciative, since our money was so scarce.

We got to Mildred's a little after 7:00 p.m. and asked her if she'd had a nice Thanksgiving, as we loaded her stuff in the car. Warren had to get out and go see Mildred's mother for a few minutes. She spoiled him rotten too. We had eaten with her several times, and she had introduced Warren to polk salad cooked with eggs. "You and Opal had better come to see me sometime soon," Mrs. Jimmie said as we drove off toward Clifton Bend. We had to get to the ferry that crossed over the Tennessee River at Clifton before 8:00 p.m. They closed the ferry down at 8:00 p.m. and you couldn't get across until the next morning. It saved us some time if we went from Clifton to Linden and then to Nashville. This was many years before there was a freeway from Nashville to Memphis. We only had a two lane road that went through several small towns, the largest being Centerville.

First Christmas Party

"Do you realize that Christmas is less than a month away?" Mildred asked as we were driving back.

"I sure do," I answered, "but we don't have a lot of money to start Christmas shopping."

"Maybe we could put them on layaway at Harvey's." I agreed that might be a good idea, especially since we've got so many to buy this year. I said I would love to have a Christmas party a week or so before Christmas.

I knew we'd have to spend Christmas Eve and Christmas day with my folks and then we're going to Minneapolis to see Warren's family a week or so after Christmas. He has a week's leave and I was taking off without pay. I was saving my vacation for our anniversary in June so we can have our real honeymoon. The rest of the trip back to Nashville, Mildred and I started planning our Christmas party. We had a good size apartment and it would be such fun, decorating and getting everything ready. We went over who we would invite and had about 20 people in mind before we got back to Nashville.

The next week we began inviting quests to our Christmas party; we were planning it two weeks before Christmas. Some we just called and others we had to mail invitations. Of course, we would invite Bill and Carol Pell, Wanda and Kathleen from upstairs, Betty, Mildred's roommate, and her boyfriend Fred. I had several friends from work, including Louise Carlton and her boyfriend that we invited. Warren had several buddies from the base he said he would like to invite. I had a cousin that was stationed at Seward, so I asked Mildred if he could be her date for that evening so he wouldn't feel left out. It was all right with her since she was between boyfriends at the time.

Our next project was to get the decorating done. Our apartment was a great place to decorate for Christmas. There was a fireplace in one room that we used as our living room. I think it had been a bedroom before, but the living room was a room off to itself with a door from the hallway, but no other doors connecting it to the rest of the house. All the other rooms had doors to the hallway too, but they had doors connecting them together. Every so often servicemen that were visiting us or Mildred's boyfriends would sleep in our living room on the couch, so it got to be a joke about who we would find in our living room the next morning. On this particular occasion my cousin, Junior, was planning on sleeping on the couch instead of driving back to base the Friday night after the party.

"Let's go look for our tree this weekend," I commented to Warren about midweek after Thanksgiving. He said it would dry out too much if we got one this early but said he thought in another week, it would be all right. I agreed but went ahead putting up lights and having a ball getting it decorated. I called Mildred as soon as I got home on Friday a week before the party and asked her if she would like to go with us to get a tree tomorrow. She said she'd love to and was all excited. I had taken her advice and gone Christmas shopping and put things on layaway so I would have them paid for by Christmas. We had such a little bit of money and so many bills that all the presents we bought had to be inexpensive. We were planning a trip to Minneapolis in early January so we had to buy gifts for all of Warren's family, plus my family, a few friends and, of course, each other.

I don't think I was ever as excited about Christmas as I was this particular year. The year before I had spent the holidays apart from Warren, but this year it was so different. We were so in love and enjoying being married so very much. The big department stores downtown were such a treat - just to stroll through, listen to the music, look at the beautiful decorations and just to feel a part of it all. We would also get in the car at night and just drive and look at the lights, especially to Centennial Park, where they had a live Nativity scene set up in front of the Parthenon.

"Are you and Warren going out to see lights tonight?" Mildred asked as we came home on the bus from work.

"Maybe. Do you want to go?" I asked.

"They say Mr. Harvey's house is fabulous," she continued. I asked her if that was the one that owns the store and she said it was. She went on to say the house was in Bellemeade and everyone says it's well worth seeing. I told her I would see what Warren had planned and get back to her. He agreed to go and we left right after supper.

The houses were absolutely breathtaking - they were so beautiful. We drove around admiring houses for about an hour and then went back to our apartment. "Do you want to come in for coffee?" I asked as we got out of the car.

"I want to see your tree and all your decorations again." She went in and looked around at all our hard work over the past week. "It sure looks great," she said, as she inspected every room. We had cut a cedar tree the weekend before by Percy Priest Park. With the decorations on and the lights lit, it did look great. I had even wrapped a few presents and put under the tree. I had draped greenery and lights around the fireplace and placed the tree in a corner beside the fireplace. I walked around admiring my handiwork and looking forward to our upcoming party.

Friday night finally arrived, and all we had left to do was get the food together after work. Mildred said she would change clothes and come right over to help get ready. We were making lots of little sandwiches, chips and dip, loads of cookies, and of course, punch. We had picked all the records we would need to dance to. There was Glenn Miller and lots of other big bands. Helen, one of our roommates, had once had a reel-to-reel player, and we had really enjoyed that, mainly because it would play for hours without having to change it. But since she had now moved away, we would have to settle for a simple record player.

"I sure hope we don't get a lot of complaints," Mildred announced while we were preparing the food.

"I've told all the neighbors in the other apartments," I commented.

"Most of them will be here," she laughed.

"We can't let it go on past midnight anyway," I remarked.

"Someone would complain if we did," Mildred added.

We finished all the food and did all the finishing touches before Mildred left to go home and get dressed. As she closed the door, I told her that Warren and I were going out for a burger and she stuck her head back in and yelled, "Can Betty and I come?"

"You know you can," I answered. "I'll call you when we're ready to go," I yelled back.

About that time Warren drove up and I asked him if he'd wanted to shower before we go get something to eat and he said he sure needed one. He said it'll only take a few minutes and, besides, no one is supposed to get here until 8:00 p.m.

A few minutes later Betty, Mildred, Warren and I loaded into our New Yorker to go to Green Hills to our favorite hamburger joint. They had great hamburgers there for fifty cents. You could get fries and a drink with it for less than $1.00. We ate quickly and returned to the apartment by 7:00 p.m. I had made a new Christmas dress and added a red velvet jacket from a suit I had bought the previous Christmas. "You look great!" Warren commented as I came out of the bedroom.

"No regrets then?" I asked.

"We should have gotten married sooner," he answered.

The party was a great success. Carol Pell was seven months pregnant, so she didn't feel too great, but everyone else seemed to have a ball. I went around taking pictures of everyone and everything. We danced to Glenn Miller music, sang, and ate everything in sight. I think we had around eighteen there, but some left early. Around midnight someone announced that we had better bring this party to a close or we'd be getting complaints from the neighbors.

After the last one had gone, I turned around and looked at the mess, knowing I was just too tired to do it tonight. I told Warren as I undressed for bed that Mildred said she would come and help me clean up the next day. "Maybe we'll all feel better then," he agreed.

The clean up was worse than the preparation for the party, We had used paper plates and cups, but there was still a lot to do. This was before anyone had dishwashers, so everything had to be washed by hand. After sleeping until after 9:00 a.m., we were still through cleaning up and ready to go do the laundry by noon. We were going to my parents for Christmas so we picked up all our presents from layaway a few days before that. We planned on going down to the country on Christmas Eve.

My Place In Time

A few days before the holiday, Mildred asked me when Warren and I were going to open our gifts to each other, and I told her probably the night before Christmas Eve. She told me to call her when we were through and she'd bring ours over. I had bought several small gifts for Warren, and I decided to take one down to my folks so he would have one to open from me while they were opening theirs.

We sat down by our tree and exchanged our gifts with such love that it makes my heart ache to think about it. I had managed to save enough money to buy him a leather suede jacket, and he had bought me silk lounging pajamas. It was such a wonderful, perfect time.

We called Mildred later on in the evening and took her present over and a small gift for Betty, her roommate. Mildred made coffee and dessert, and we talked late into the night before going home to our apartment to finish celebrating the last of our Christmas holiday together.

The next morning we slept late, and I called Mildred and told her we were leaving for the country at around noon, so to be ready. It's really sad when I look back now and realize that we both knew nothing about the real meaning of Christmas. Neither of us were Christians at the time, and when we did go to church, it was not for the right reasons. I always marvel at the goodness of God that we took so for granted. Warren was a member of a church in the north called Congregational. He told me it was something like Methodist, but when I pressed him further, he had no idea what they really believed. I reflected further on being a church member several times right after we were married. I remember telling Warren I had never joined a church, but when I did, I wanted it to make a difference in my life. When I was growing up, I had often attended the Pentecostal church in the community I lived in, but it always left me confused and scared. I went to the Methodist church quite often, but it seemed more like a social club. When I was a baby, Mama had me christened in the Methodist church. I knew this because Mrs. Dovie Vise kept telling me she was my godmother and all about when I was baptized.

It was now Christmas of 1955, and I was twenty years old and a married woman. I loved Warren with all my heart and everything seemed perfect. I tried not to think about moving away the following year. I just put it out of my mind and tried to believe life would go on much in the same manner as it was now.

Christmas at the Phillips

We arrived at my parents' home about mid-afternoon on Christmas Eve. The younger kids were really excited and, as usual, everyone was talking at the same time.
"We're opening our presents after supper," Pat announced. "Mama said we could," she continued. "We'll still put our stockings out for candy and other stuff." Pat was now eleven years old and such a cute, bubbly child. Joan, on the other hand, was known as the pretty one, but she was always quiet and sometimes seemed withdrawn. Pat, Louise and I had taken after Daddy and had brownish-blonde hair, while everyone said Joan had taken after Mamie and had her dark hair. My mother was now only forty-three, but her hair had been grey as early as I could remember. I already had some grey hair by the age of 20, so I knew I had this to look forward to. However, I also knew what I would do to keep my grey from showing. Louise had started coloring her hair a few years before, and the last time she had it done she had taken me with her. I had mine made a shade darker, which made me look 5 years older, but I didn't seem to care at the time.

We had a wonderful time opening gifts, and then on Christmas Day Mama cooked a wonderful Christmas dinner, including her famous cakes. We planned on getting up early the day after Christmas and driving back to Nashville because we all had to go back to work the following day.

Warren and I were planning a trip to Minneapolis on the 4th of January. Mama seemed a little worried and apprehensive about our upcoming trip. She said it was such a bad time of year to take a trip to that part of the country, and Daddy said that we would probably hit a lot of snow before we got there. I told them that Warren grew up with that kind of weather and he was used to driving in it. Warren told them they plowed the roads almost immediately after it snowed. They told us to try to be real careful when we left the next morning.

Minnesota – January 1956

Our winter trip to Minneapolis on January 4, 1956, came around quite suddenly. I dreaded the trip but I knew we had to go. Jeanette, Bruce's wife, had given birth to a baby girl in the fall and they had named her Dawn. I was excited about seeing them but also a bit worried about how things would go with the other in-laws.

Warren asked me if we had everything, as we finished loading the presents in the car. I told him I thought so because the car was almost full. I wished we could stop and spend the night, knowing full well that we couldn't. Warren said since we had such a little bit of money, he said we would just have to drive all the way. I had packed some sandwiches and coffee for lunch but guessed we would have to stop several times to eat anyway. This was such a bad time to go since we had spent everything we could get our hands on for Christmas a few weeks before, and now we barely had enough left to buy gas.

Anyway, we were young and carefree so we drove during the day, only stopping for gas and bathroom stops. We ate sandwiches and drank loads of coffee in the car. We knew if we drove straight through, we should be there around 12:00 or 1:00 a.m. We left Nashville at 5:00 or 5:30 and it usually took 17 to 18 hours. Between 7:00 p.m. and 8:00 p.m. I got so sleepy I couldn't stay awake any longer, and I asked Warren if he was going to be able to stay awake. He told me to pour him some more coffee and he could make it for a while longer. I knew I couldn't take turns driving with him anyway because I had never gotten a driver's license, although I knew I would have to get my license at some point in time. I curled up on the seat beside him and went sound asleep.

I must have been sleeping for several hours before I awoke with a start. I realized we had stopped and the engine was racing. "Where are we, and what time is it?" I asked trying to wake up. Warren told me it was about 11:00 o'clock and we slid off the road into a snow bank. He said he was going to get out and see how bad it was. After assessing the situation, he got back in the car and said it didn't look too good. I asked where we were and he said we were somewhere in Iowa. We got out and tried to push it out of the snow bank but it was to no avail. "Look, there's a truck coming; maybe he'll stop!" God was looking after us because he did stop.

"Looks like you need a little help."

"We sure do," Warren replied.

The man said he had a chain in the truck and he would hook it on and pull us out. I stayed in the car because by this time I realized I was not dressed for Iowa weather. Within a few minutes he had us safely back on the road. Warren asked him if we could pay him something because we were really grateful but he declined. We asked him how far we were out of Minneapolis and he advised us if all goes well 2 or 3 more hours.

The snow didn't let up so we had to drive really slow the rest of the way. It was after 3:00 a.m. when we pulled up in front of his parents' home. They had gone to sleep on the couches but awoke quickly when we rang the doorbell. We stayed up another hour or so talking and discussing our trip before we finally got to bed sometime after 4:00 a.m.

Slippin' an' a Slidin'

We slept until close to noon the next day before waking to the most snow I thought I had ever seen – there must have been two feet on the ground. As we were getting dressed, Warren said this would be a great day for tobogganing. I told him I didn't have any good boots, and he said he was sure Ma or Marlene had some extra ones that I could wear. He said they'd teach me to ice skate and maybe even to ski. I doubted that and told him that you've grown up with all this snow but I have never been on ice skates in my life. I went on to say that I couldn't even roller skate. Warren told me that I wasn't too old to learn.

True to his word, Warren and Ma took me ice skating at a rink in Loring Park. I never learned to skate, but I was able to stand up on the ice long enough for him to get some pictures. Our next adventure was tobogganing. On Saturday morning Marlene, Bruce, Jeanette, Warren and I took off for Glenwood Hills for our outing of tobogganing. Warren said they would put me towards the back so that way everyone wouldn't fall on me when we stopped and I would be less apt to get hurt. "Gee, thanks!, I laughed.

It was a lot of fun, but the only problem was I was absolutely freezing by the time we got back to the lodge to get something warm to drink. We went up and down the hill a few more times before deciding it was time to go home for lunch. On the way back Janette said that Dad was taking us all out to eat Chinese tonight. Everyone thought that was great, but I didn't say anything because I had never had Chinese food before. I sure wasn't going to tell them that, so I just said that sounded great too. I did enjoy the Chinese food but I never told anyone that it was my first time to try it. Later it would become one of my favorite kinds of food.

I always knew from the time I was in Minnesota the previous June that I would like Warren's dad. He was a lot like Warren, fairly quiet, easy-going and very kind. I don't know if I got off on the wrong foot with Ma, but for some reason she seemed to resent me at first.

Our two weeks were over quickly and before we knew it we were headed back to Tennessee. I told Warren it was nice of his Ma to send us sandwiches and all the groceries, and I still couldn't believe she left the Christmas tree up this late so we could see it. Warren said she just wanted us to be able to open presents together for our first Christmas. He went on to say that Bruce was afraid she would start a fire when she plugged the lights in because the tree was so dry. I told Warren it was all really nice and I enjoyed it but I was sure I would never make an ice skater and he would have to teach our kids someday. "That I will do," Warren agreed.

We left at 5:00 a.m. and got home to Nashville before midnight and had no unusual incidents on the way back. Warren said when we go back this summer, we'll take a few days and go through Wisconsin Dells. I told him I didn't know we were going back that summer and asked if he had forgotten he promised me a honeymoon in Chattanooga. He said he hadn't forgotten and he thought we could do both. With sadness I reminded him that he would be getting out of service in October and we would probably have to go then. Warren had told me that he would look for a job in Nashville but was sure it would be easier finding work in Minneapolis. He said that Ma and Dad were fixing up an apartment in the basement of the house they were moving to their empty lot across town. I asked him if that was where we were going to live, and he said we could live there for a few months until we got on our feet. I didn't say much, but it made me sad and unhappy just thinking about leaving Nashville.

Home Again

Nothing too eventful happened for the next few months. I had gotten several promotions at work and was now classified as a key puncher. I was excited about that because I knew I could get a job almost any place by doing key punching. Warren had gotten a couple of promotions too, so our finances were a little better. I had always been a smart money manager so we had gotten most of our wedding expenses paid off and had a little left over. Our dream was to trade cars before Warren got out of service.

Mildred called up one Saturday morning to inform us Betty was getting married. She went on to say it would have to be a quiet ceremony because Fred would get booted out of the Naval Academy if they found out. He had applied and been accepted for the academy a few months before, and he would be shipping out soon and wanted to take Betty with him. He wanted Warren to stand up with him and Mildred to stand up with Betty. She asked me to take some pictures and I told her I could manage that.

It was a nice ceremony at one of the local Baptist churches, and we all went out to eat before they left for a short honeymoon. On the way home I asked Mildred if she had someone lined up for a roommate. She said she thought so and said her name was Lori and she works at National Life. Later I found out that Lori wanted Mildred to move into a different apartment with her, and it was several miles from where we lived. I sure hated to see her move but I guess it was unavoidable. We helped Mildred relocate the following weekend to an upstairs apartment in a fairly small house. The only good thing about it was that it had an outside stairway. On the way home, I told Warren that I wasn't very fond of Mildred's new roommate and, for that matter, I wasn't very fond of their new place. He said that maybe it would be all right.

Moving Again & New Furniture

We found out the following week that Wanda Pruess was moving from her upstairs apartment in our building. That afternoon when Warren got home from the base I told him that maybe we should check into it, and he said to go ahead and find out if someone else had already rented it. I called Wanda first and asked her when she was moving, and she said it would be in about two weeks. She told us how much she paid for the apartment and even with our discount for cleaning the hall, we could still save $25.00 a month. Wanda said she was moving to a new apartment building off West End Avenue. Kathleen had moved several months before, so I think Wanda was kind of lonesome and she had gotten a good promotion at the State Department so she felt like she could afford a nicer place now. She told me if we were interested that we had better call Mrs. Taylor, the landlord, right away.

I called Mrs. Taylor and she was all for us moving upstairs. She said that she could rent our apartment easier because it's much larger and had two bedrooms. She said she would still take ten dollars off our rent if we vacuumed and cleaned the hall every week. I told her that would be great, and we already started planning how we would arrange the place upstairs. We asked if it was all right if we painted some of the rooms, and she said that it was okay to do any decorating that we liked, but just don't move the furniture from one apartment to the other.

In early March of 1956, we moved our belongings from our first home together upstairs to a really cozy apartment. There were only three rooms and a bath but there was a large kitchen with loads of windows, almost like a sunroom, The view wasn't great because it looked out over the top of the other buildings, but Wanda had told me you could open one of the windows and go out on the roof and sunbath. I was looking forward to that in a few months. The living room furniture left a lot to be desired. Shortly after we got our things, I asked Warren if we could paint the living room and kitchen, and he said he could probably get some paint from the base. I asked him what colors he would get, and he said he was sure he could get some grey, the color they use on the planes. I told him that might be all right because it would be better than the pea green color Mrs. Taylor had painted every room in all her apartments. I told Warren it was just too much of the same color.

I was excited because I knew we would have extra money from the apartment rent so I asked Warren if maybe we could go look at a living room suite and make a small payment on it. Warren said the Air Force would ship our furniture and belongings when we moved in October and would even come in and pack everything for us. I know that we would need furniture later anyway.

That very afternoon we took off and went downtown to the furniture stores on Broadway looking at living room furniture. After about the third store, I found one I just fell in love with. It was two pieces, a couch and chair, and he said if we bought the end tables, he would throw in two lamps free. The couch was a soft pink with a little black tweed in it. The chair was fairly comfortable and matched the couch. The end tables were blond wood, which was really popular in the 1950's. We talked terms, and he said we could pay $15.00 a month and finish paying it off if we wanted to when Warren got his mustering out pay in October. "I just love it," I kept telling Warren. "Please let's get it," and he agreed. They said they could deliver it in about three days, and I told Warren that would be great since we needed time to get the living room painted before they brought it.

When we got home, we spent the rest of the day moving the old couch from the living room to the bedroom since we knew everything had to stay. We had a large bedroom with a fireplace and 12 foot ceilings. We were able to fit part of the furniture in our bedroom and figured out how the rest could fit in with our new pieces. As soon as Warren walked in the door on Monday, I asked him if he had gotten the paint and he said he had but it was still in the car. He had also gotten some pans, rollers, and brushes at the hardware store on the way home. I guessed we were all set, but Warren said not quite because we needed a step ladder. He went on to say there was a guy that was moving into our old downstairs apartment that had one he could borrow. I told Warren they had been working down there since I got home from work, and she said they had worked most of the day and planned on moving in over the weekend.

"Did you see their cute little girl when you came in?" I asked.

"Yeah, she was playing on the front porch."

The little girl was about 3 years old and as cute as a bug. Jim, the father, was still in school but he worked part-time, his wife Linda told me. I asked them to come to dinner sometime after we get our remodeling done.

Warren brought the supplies in and borrowed Jim's ladder for the evening. We moved the balance of the living room furniture to the kitchen and put drop cloths over the floor. He said he would use the brush and do the woodwork and I could roll. He loaded the pan with paint and placed it on the top of the ladder, which was about 4 feet high. We worked for a couple of hours before I suggested stopping for a sandwich. Warren said that was a good idea because he was beginning to get a little hungry. We took our break and went back to our painting by 8:00 p.m. I said we could work for a couple more hours and at least get the part next to the ceiling done so we could return the ladder.

We had been working for about thirty minutes, when I heard a thump. I looked up and saw the paint pan coming down all over Warren. "Oh, my gosh, what a mess!" I screamed. He only had on a tee shirt and pants, but he was covered with grey metal paint from the top of his shoulders to his feet. He said this was oil base paint, and that meant it wouldn't come off with just soap and water. We had bought turpentine for clean up so I grabbed it and told him we would have to use that. I told him to strip his clothes off and that we would just throw them in the garbage because I knew they would never come clean. I took a garbage bag and scooped up his clothes and led him into the bathroom to try to get grey metal paint from almost his entire body.

He stood in the tub and I took the turpentine jug and began to pour it over him. All of a sudden he started dancing and screaming at the top of his lungs, "Stop, stop; it's going into places it shouldn't, and I'm burning like fire!" I told him to turn the water on in the tub and start washing it off, all the while trying to keep from laughing. He looked so funny and was acting like a complete lunatic. We proceeded to soap him down and got the burning stopped. The grey paint was another story; on certain parts of his body it was just going to have to wear off. When he finally stopped burning he was laughing too. We both sat and laughed for the next thirty minutes.

We didn't get the living room finished until later that week because we had spilled the paint and had to wait until the following Monday for him to get more. We had drop cloths on the floor, so the hardwood floors were not damaged, and we were able to call the furniture store and have them delay delivering our furniture for a few days. We both remember this as one of the funniest episodes in our lives.

Our new furniture looked beautiful, and with throw rugs on the floor and our newly painted walls, it looked like a whole new apartment. We even had air conditioning in our living room. Our friends, Carol and Bill Pell, got a new air conditioner in the mobile home they traded for so they gave us the old one they had. They also gave us a T. V. set that they weren't using. We were really uptown now. Very few people we knew had televisions, let alone air conditioning. As it began to get warmer in the spring, we moved the air conditioner into the bedroom.

Mildred

Mildred's new roommate didn't work out very well, and in a very short while she was looking for another place. This time she decided to just look for a room for rent since it was so hard to get a good roommate for an apartment. She called us early in the week to go with her to look at a place down from West End Methodist Church off West End Avenue. It was an old Victorian house but it looked like it was in good condition. She had driven by with a friend and looked at the house before she called for an appointment to see the room. Warren asked if there were other girls living there, and she said she thought there were a couple but didn't know how old they were.

We rang the door bell and waited several minutes before an elderly lady appeared at the door. Mildred explained that she was the one who had called about the room she had for rent and told her we were her friends that would like to look too. She led us up a winding stairway, and from the entrance hall, it looked a little dark and sinister since the heavy velvet drapes were drawn in the middle of the day. When we got to the second floor, she paused a minute before opening the second door on the right side of the large hallway. She explained that an elderly gentleman lived in that room and we continued down the hall. Two other ladies lived in the other two bedrooms on this floor, and Mildred wanted to know how old they were and she said she thought they were in their early thirties. She opened the door to the room Mildred was inquiring about and didn't turn the lights on. The drapes were drawn in this room and all you could see were shadows. Mildred reached over and turned the overhead light on and asked if she could open the curtains because she wanted to see the view. With a hint of annoyance in her voice, the lady said she could. The lady went on to say the sunshine fades the furniture.

We looked around the room, also inspecting the view. It was nice enough but different than anything I'd ever seen. It was as if you had stepped back in time. The bed was high off the floor and the rest of the furnishings were in the Victorian period. She stated the bathroom was down the hall and must be shared with the other three girls. The rent included an evening meal. She explained several other rules, like no parties, drinking or coming in after 11:00 p.m. on week nights.

Mildred told her she would call her later and let her know for sure, but at this point she was leaning toward taking it. She needed a place to move since Lori had moved out, and the rent was almost due at the other place and she could not afford it by herself. She asked us what we thought and Warren said it was all right, and I said it would do at least until she could find something else. She said she'd guessed she'd take it but said she thought it had an eerie feeling about it. I agreed that it did, but maybe it would be different when she put her personal touch to it.

Less than a week later, Mildred called early on Saturday morning to come over and get her out of that place for a while because she thought she was going crazy. She really believed the place was haunted because she woke up in the middle of the night hearing weird noises. I asked her what kind of noises and she said sometimes screaming or crying, and at other times it sounded like doors were slamming. She had asked the others if they heard the noises, and they said they didn't. She felt like the whole house was weird. I told her we were going to the Laundromat, but after that we would pick her up and go to lunch.

While we were eating lunch, she asked if I had talked to Mrs. Taylor lately because she was hoping she could rent a garage apartment if there was one available. She said she was taking out a loan to consolidate her bills and could afford more for rent. I told her I'd call Ms. Taylor that week and she said that would be great. Mildred had to use the house phone downstairs and thought they listened to everything she said on the phone and she didn't want them to know she was looking for another place until she had found one. I called Mrs. Taylor the following Monday to see if there was a vacancy in one of her apartments in the near future and she said, as a matter of fact, there was. The garage apartment Mildred and I had rented before I was married and where Mildred had lived with Betty until she married was going to be vacant in a little over two weeks. I told her I would get back to her very soon, but not to rent the apartment to anyone else until she heard from

Mildred. I called Mildred immediately and she asked me to tell Mrs. Taylor she definitely wanted the apartment. She had worked her finances out and felt sure she could afford it and even had enough money left over so she could buy a dinette table.

I told her we were going home that weekend, and if she wanted to come with us, we would drop her off. She remembered she would be able to start bringing food from home when the garden came in and remembered how that helped the grocery bill out. Just knowing she was getting out of that haunted place lifted Mildred's spirits tremendously. During the next two weeks until she was able to move, we visited her and had her over to our place much of the time. She says to this day she believed that place was really haunted, especially her room.

I was so glad to help her get moved and settled back in her own place, and it was great having her so close again. I'd pop over for a cup of coffee before Warren got home or early Saturday morning before we started cleaning. I knew she had gotten a pistol a few months before, but I guess I had forgotten about it. I knew where she kept an extra key in case we needed to get in when she wasn't home.

I popped in one Saturday morning before she was out of bed. On this particular Saturday, I yelled "Millie" a couple of times, but there was no answer so I figured she must be in the shower. I took the key, opened the door, and was almost to the bedroom, when she screamed, "Who's there?"

"It's me," I yelled back, looking at a pistol drawn two feet from my face.

She said you could have gotten yourself killed, and I said I had forgotten all about her gun. My knees were still shaking. Mildred said she slept with it under her pillow and so next time make sure I made my presence known. She said, in fact, it would be good if I called to let her know before I came over and I told her that sounded like a good idea to me.

The next few months went smoothly. We played cards with Mildred and Wanda Pruess, sometimes getting home as the sun was coming up on Sunday morning. Needless to say, we didn't go to church very often; however, we had all gone to church on Easter Sunday and went back to Mildred's and she cooked up a big breakfast.

Billy Graham Crusade

As we were having coffee one spring Saturday morning, Mildred asked if we had heard that Billy Graham was holding a Crusade at the Vanderbilt Stadium the next month. Warren wanted to know when it was, and she said she thought it was going to be the middle of May. He said he might consider signing up for the choir because they usually need a lot of people.

Mildred asked him if he had sung in the Air Force choir since he'd been in Tennessee and he said there hasn't been one available, but he sure had a good time when he was with the choir in Texas. He said they had done an album while he was there that included most of the music from the musical *South Pacific* and he jumped up to show us his records. Mildred asked him to put one of his records on because it had been a long time since we'd listened to it. He walked into the living room and put the record on the player, as we continued our conversation about choirs.

On the following Monday, Warren told me he had signed up to sing in the choir for the Billy Graham Crusade, and I guessed that meant we would have to go every night. He said I could sit with Mildred, and it was for only 4 nights. I told him I would ask Mildred if she would go because I didn't want to go and have to sit by myself.

The next day I asked Millie if she would go and she said she would be glad to; in fact, she was planning on it anyway. This was the biggest thing to hit Nashville since the Grand Ole Opry. She said everyone at work was planning on being there, and she thought Pat Boone was a special guest and would be singing. I thought that was great because he was one of my favorite singers. She had guessed that because I had met him last year at the radio station upstairs where I worked. She had gathered he made quite an impression on me. He was quite different from Elvis Presley, whom everyone was so taken with. I loved Pat Boone's latest album, *Love Letters in the Sand*.

My Place In Time

The crusade came quickly in mid-May on a Tuesday night, and we were seated fairly close to the speakers stand at Vanderbilt Stadium. We had gotten there quite early because Warren had to be there an hour before because of the choir. The weather was beautiful and a clear, starry night. I was really impressed, not only with Pat Boone but also with Billy Graham. I had never heard personal testimonies before and knew nothing about a personal relationship with Jesus Christ. Mildred and I both told Warren how great the music was, and he said he had really enjoyed singing with so many people. We asked him how many people were there and he said several thousand.

The next two nights were much the same: they had a personal testimony by some famous person, followed by special music, and then at the end there was always an invitation given. They always ended with the song *Just as I Am*.

The last night was Friday night and Warren seemed sad that it was ending, but he didn't discuss the messages or anything other than the music. I remember sitting there so sad with a feeling that something or someone was tugging at my heart. I didn't say anything to anyone but when the invitation was given, I could hardly stay in my seat, but somehow I did. It would take another 15 years before I truly responded to God's Spirit and, strangely enough, that would be in front of a television set in 1971.

As I mentioned before, we had talked very little about the messages we heard, but I pondered about them a lot after I went to bed at night. I wondered what would happen if I died - if I would go to hell or not, but somehow I managed to put it all out of my mind and think about other things. I prayed, but I also knew down deep that I was not a Christian. I was also terrified of death.

Mildred & Johnny

In late April, Mildred called me one night just after supper to see if I could run down to her apartment for a few minutes because she had something to tell me. I yelled to Warren that I would do the dishes when I got back. Walking in the apartment, I yelled, "Hey, Mildred, what's the great news?"

"Guess what?"she smiled, as she poured me a cup of coffee.

"What, what? What's the big news?"

She said she had just met the most wonderful sailor last night, and they had a date for Saturday night. I asked her if it was the guy she had a date with the previous night and she said he was my friend's date, but they had talked the whole evening and before she left the car, he whispered and asked her for a date. His name was Johnny Clary and he was just the greatest. She went on to say he was very intelligent and good-looking. I said he must be something fantastic to get you this excited. She dreamingly said that he was. She had never met anyone quite like him, and I have a real feeling this is the beginning of something big.

We talked for another hour or so when I jumped up and realized I hadn't done the dishes yet. Warren would be furious if I didn't get back and get them cleaned up. She said, "Oh, yeah, he'll probably beat you." I told her he wouldn't do that but we had made a deal that I would cook and do the dishes if he would let me sleep an extra half-hour in the morning while he fixed breakfast. Sometimes I didn't think it was such a great deal, but I knew how sleepy I was in the mornings. I left and went back to tell Warren all about Millie's new boyfriend.

Mama's Little Surprise

Just before Mother's Day the phone rang, and I yelled for Warren to get it because I was getting in the bathtub. Warren said it was Louise and she was calling from a Jackson hospital. I wrapped a towel around me and told him I was coming. Louise, half-crying, said that Mama was in the hospital. I asked what was wrong and she said they weren't sure but they thought her appendix might have ruptured. She said Mama had gone to Dr. Conger that afternoon but he wasn't sure what was going on and had sent her back home. She had gotten to feeling better for several hours,

My Place In Time

but the pain had started back and she was really sick. She asked if Warren and I could come to Jackson General Hospital that night. I told her I had no idea where it was and she said we could ask for directions when we got to Jackson.

After I hung up, I told Warren that my mother was in the hospital in Jackson and asked if he could call someone and get leave to go and he said that he probably couldn't that night. I knew if Warren could work it out for us to leave that night, Mildred could tell my team leader that I had to go home for a few days. Warren said that we couldn't leave until the following morning and told me to call Louise at the hospital and tell her we would be there as early in the morning as we could get there. I called her back and told her there was no way we could get there that night, but we would get there as soon as Warren got leave worked out. Needless to say, she wasn't very happy.

The following morning, I got dressed and packed while Warren went to the base to get his leave worked out. We left Nashville before 9:00 a.m. and were in Jackson at the hospital by 12:30 p.m. Louise met us in the hallway and said that Mama had already had her surgery and she was still in recovery. By the time they did the surgery, her appendix had ruptured but they said although she was very sick, she would probably be okay. I asked her if she had talked to the doctor and she said he had stuck his head out after the surgery was over and said she was all right and that he would talk to us later today. I asked when she would be out of recovery and the nurse said it should be any time.

In another thirty minutes or so, the nurse came out and told us we could go in and see her. She looked really pale and weak but was able to talk to us for a few minutes. The nurse told us that she really needed to rest. It scared me to think that something might possibly happen to Mama. I loved her so much, and it just seemed she would always be there. We took turns staying in the room with her until later that afternoon when the doctor came in. He said he would talk to us all outside after he finished examining her.

Several of us gathered together in the hallway waiting for him to come out. We were all silently praying that everything was going to be all right. As he stood looking over his notes, he told us that our mother would be fine and while still looking over his notes said "By the way, the baby will be all right too. It was touch and go for a while but I'm confident both of them will be fine."

"The baby?!" we all asked the question at once.

Dan, the youngest, was over five years old, and we all thought Mama had gone through the change of life. He went on to say that Mama was over three months pregnant. I told him I didn't think Mama knew she was pregnant. As he left the hallway, he said he would tell her later that day when she was more alert. We kept saying what a shock it was because Mama was 43 years old. Louise said she was too old to have a baby, and Warren made the comment, "I guess not; the Lord must have other plans."

When the doctor told Mama later that day, she was quite shocked but after the initial shock wore off seemed a little excited. She stayed in the hospital for close to a week. We went back to Nashville after the weekend was over. I was so worried about Mama; she just seemed too old to be having a baby. When you're twenty, forty-three seemed so old. I remember praying every night for the Lord to keep Mama safe and let her be all right. Her due date was around October 30th and we had planned on moving to Minneapolis in October. I told Warren I guessed we would have to delay going until after the baby is born. I think Warren agreed because he felt bad about us having to move in the first place. He had checked out a couple of places that might have job openings in the fall for airplane and engine mechanics, but nothing looked very promising. He had more connections in Minneapolis because his uncle worked for a Naval ordinance plant, and he was pretty sure he could get him on there. I was like Scarlett in *Gone with the Wind;* I would think about it later.

Mildred & Johnny - Again

Meanwhile, Mildred and her new boyfriend, Johnny, were getting quite serious. She called me to come over one day in mid-July and told me she had something exciting to tell me. "Guess what? Johnny has asked me to marry him!" I just stood there looking kind of shocked. "Aren't you happy for me?"

"Of course I am, but isn't it a little sudden? You only met him a couple of months ago."

She said she knew, but they felt like they had known each other all of their lives. "Besides that, I want you to be in the wedding as my matron of honor and you'll be leaving in the fall."

I told her we were going to wait until Mama's baby was born, even though Warren gets out officially the 15th of October. I went on to say it might be mid-November before we actually moved. Our furniture was being shipped the 20th of October, and we'd stay with Mama until we left.

Mildred said they had thought about the 3rd of November for their wedding, and I told her that would be great because the baby would surely be here by then. Mildred said her sister Nancy would also be in the wedding, and she thought Johnny's mother was coming from Idaho. I told her I knew what it was like meeting your mother-in-law on the day of the wedding.

The next few months seemed to go by so fast because there were so many things going on that I really didn't have time to think about moving away. The people I worked with were sad that I was leaving, especially Louise Carlton. She and I had remained close even after Warren and I were married. She married Fred a few months after we got married, and we would get together with them quite often and play cards. But most of all, I just couldn't face the fact that I would be leaving Mildred. She and I talked about everything. I felt like she probably knew me better than anybody else on earth. I guess I knew things would have to change, but I also knew that my years spent in Nashville would always be the most special years of my life.

New Car – 1955 Pontiac

By mid-1956, we had most of our bills paid off and were seriously thinking about trading our car for a newer one. We decided to look at Chevrolets and Pontiacs about a 1955 or even a demonstrator 1956. One Saturday morning Warren announced that Bill said we would get a good deal in Murfreesboro, and he suggested that we should go there and look and I agreed. We knew exactly how much we could afford for a car payment and about what we should get for our old Chrysler New Yorker. Warren would get a substantial amount of money as his mustering out pay from the Air Force in October, and I was also going to have a good amount from National Life. Warren had already promised I could buy a new portable sewing machine and I would buy a cabinet later. We went to Murfreesboro as planned but the deal they offered us wasn't too appealing. We went to several other dealers in Nashville, but it seemed they just wanted to take our car without giving us money for it. We had even looked in Parsons at Townsend Chevrolet, but they were higher than the dealers in Nashville.

As we left and feeling discouraged, I told Warren that one of the last places on our list was Beaman Pontiac on West End Avenue in Nashville and it would probably be the most expensive because it was one of the biggest dealerships in Nashville. We knew we'd just have to wait and see. When we got to Beaman's, one of the salesman said he thought he had just what we were looking for. He had a 1955 Pontiac, like new, with only a few thousand miles on it. We looked at each other, thinking that's great, but what kind of deal can we get? He took us inside the dealership and proceeded to show us exactly what he could do, giving us a certain amount on our old car, and keeping our payments to what we felt we could afford. We left the Beaman Pontiac dealership driving our almost new, 1955 green Pontiac! I kept telling Warren it was the most beautiful car in the world and he said that it drove great.

I didn't have a driver's license but I knew someday I would have to get one. I had driven Daddy's pickup off and on when I lived at home but after moving to Nashville, I guess I never felt the need to get a driver's license since I didn't have a car and after Warren and I were married, the subject never came up. For the first time in my life, I felt a little bit jealous because I couldn't drive our new car. The next weekend we went to Decaturville mainly to show off our new car. Everyone thought it was great and, of course, we had to drive Sam, Dan and Pat to town.

I was glad Mama was doing so well with her pregnancy, but she seemed terribly tired. I don't really know if the Lord heard me, but I prayed for her every night that she and the baby would be all right.

I told everyone we were going on a real vacation in a couple of weeks to Chattanooga. Our anniversary was on June 4th and we were going to Chattanooga for four or five days. I had a couple of weeks vacation time built up and Warren could get a leave. We didn't have much of a honeymoon, I reflected for the one hundredth time since we had been married. Mama said that meant we wouldn't be home for several weeks, but I told her that they'd get tired of us when we come in October. I told her we might be there a month before we left for Minneapolis.

I just hoped Mildred's wedding date didn't conflict with Mama's due date. Mama said she'd probably be early since she always had with the others. It seemed so strange to think I was going to have a tiny baby sister. Mildred was crocheting a beautiful little baby sweater, and I was knitting a blanket for the new arrival. Carol Pell was also planning something special. She was very fond of my mother, and the feeling was mutual.

We got back to Nashville late on Sunday night. I saw Millie's light was still on so I called her. She had stayed in Nashville for the weekend, but she very seldom went home since she and Johnny had become engaged. We talked until Warren yelled and told me he was going to bed and said I would never get up in the morning if I didn't do the same.

Chattanooga

Our trip to Chattanooga seemed to come more quickly than I had planned. There was so much going on, but I was very excited to get away from it all for a few days. I hadn't been to Chattanooga since our class trip when I graduated from high school. Warren had never been to Chattanooga, and I was planning on showing him all the great things and places I had seen a few years before. I had made reservations for a motel a month or so before. The fiasco of finding a motel room on our wedding night was ever before us, and he could not live it down. I told him this was to be our real honeymoon.

Chattanooga was only a three hour drive from Nashville, but on that Saturday morning in 1956, it seemed to take forever to get there. As we drove up the road, we could see the motel and were really excited because it looked like an elegant place and had a great swimming pool. We registered, changed clothes, and decided to look for a place to eat before we did any sightseeing. While we were driving around town, Warren asked if I wanted a hamburger and fries and I said, "That would probably do and then we could eat a heavier dinner." This was before you had to watch everything for fat grams. The days before cholesterol were wonderful!

The next morning we stopped for breakfast before heading out to Lookout Mountain to see Rock City. The following day we planned on seeing Ruby Falls. As we looked through a viewer on one of the cliffs, I asked Warren if he could believe that we could actually see seven states, and he commented on how great it was. We finished our tour and decided to spend time at the motel swimming in the afternoon. We had another few days so we planned to spread the activities out so we'd have something to do every day.

As we lay sunning by the pool, Warren asked if I was going to ride the incline down the mountain and I said I didn't think I would. He said he would sure like to and I told him *we'd think about that* as I jumped in the swimming pool. The next day we toured Ruby Falls, which is a cave that goes for miles back into the mountain. The guides used flashlights and at the end of the cave, there was a beautiful lake and waterfall. The guides turned the lights off and I had never seen such darkness. I grabbed Warren's hand, whispering, "I sure never wanted to be in this place by myself," and he agreed it was a little spooky.

Our second honeymoon was over before we were ready to leave, but our money was always in short supply so we took off back to Nashville. I told Warren how much I had enjoyed the Civil War park and asked him if he'd enjoyed it, and he said it was all right, but he would have rather ridden the Incline. I reminded Warren that my Great-Grandpa had fought in the Civil War and he said that was a long time ago, so let's not get into that stuff again. I told him we could ride the Incline Railroad when we came back again and maybe we would have more money.

"It looks like Johnny is at Mildred's again," I commented as Warren parked our new, slightly used Pontiac.

"I guess they have a lot to plan before the wedding," he answered.

Just as we were unpacking our last bag, the phone rang. "Would you like to come over for coffee?" Mildred asked.

"I would, but I'd better ask Warren first," I answered. He agreed to go for a little while but reminded me that we had no groceries in the apartment, so we would have to go to the grocery store sometime soon.

Mildred and I never seemed to run out of things to talk about, especially when we hadn't seen each other for almost a week. We discussed the upcoming wedding. "I've decided to get married up here," she remarked. "I thought we would see about the Belmont Baptist Church. It would just be easier for my folks to come here than to try to get everyone from up here down to Clifton Bend, don't you think so?" she wanted to know.

"I think that would be great," I answered.

"Everyone from work would be able to come, and some of Johnny's friends from the base," Warren added.

Johnny had decided to ask one of his buddies from the base to be best man. Nancy, Mildred's sister, and Betty, her ex-roommate, were to be bridesmaids, and she asked me to be her matron of honor.

"Are we planning on making the dresses?" I asked Millie, hoping we would because I knew it would be cheaper. I had been looking at patterns for the last couple of weeks and was hoping she and I could get together next week to see what she thought. "Maybe we could look together next week and see what you think."

"I'm sure I'll like them, and besides, it's your choice; it's your wedding," I said.

"Johnny's mom will get here a couple of days before the wedding, but I guess she will stay at a motel; I just don't have room in this small apartment."

"She could stay in ours, but we're only paying the rent through October, and I'm sure Mrs. Taylor will have it rented by the first of November."

We were really glad to have Bill and Carol's old air conditioner, because I believe it was one of the hottest summers we had ever had in Tennessee. We spent a lot of time at my folks' house in July, almost every weekend. We could go swimming in the creek and the river and, besides, I wanted to spend as much time with my family as I could before I moved away. We played cards a lot with friends, especially Carol and Bill, at their new mobile home. Mildred and I were also busy getting our dresses planned and finalizing all the other details of the wedding. Before we realized it, fall was upon us. Summer was wonderful, I guess, because we were still newlyweds and enjoyed being together so much. We loved to swim and had spent some time at Cascade Pool, but it was always so crowded. A couple of weekends in August, we went with friends to Montgomery Bell State Park, which was only about twenty-five miles west of Nashville. "It's only a little over a month until they will come to pack our things to move them to your mother's," I said.

"I know; it seems to have slipped up on us," Warren answered.

"My last day is the twentieth, considering all the leave I have built up. That means we have over a week before the movers pack our things, after you get out of service" I said. I was calculating how we could have a few days together for a short trip, before we went to my mother's for a few weeks. I had close to a week's vacation built up, so I figured maybe I should set my last day for the twentieth of October.

"Let's take off and go to Montgomery Bell for a few days in late October. Do we have enough money, and then get by until I find a job in Minneapolis?" Warren asked.

"I believe so, since it won't cost us anything at Mama's while we're there. We will have expenses when we come back to Nashville for the wedding, I guess," I answered. "We'll come up the night before the wedding and stay in a motel and go back to the country the next day. I've figured out a budget and I think we'll be all right money-wise. I just hope Mama doesn't have the baby on the third of November...that will sure put a kink in our plans."

"She says she's usually early and we'll just hope she is this time," Warren reminded me.

On the twentieth of October, Warren walked away from Seward Air Force Base for the last time. I think in some ways he would have liked to have stayed in. I noticed when he talked to Johnny sometimes he seemed a little sad to be leaving. Johnny and Mildred had decided sometime before that they would be career Navy people. They were looking forward to traveling around and seeing the world at Uncle Sam's expense.

I was excited about Warren being out, but I still was not thinking about the fact that I was moving away from my family and everything familiar to me. "The furniture should arrive at my parents' home in about a week," Warren announced. "Dad said they would just store it in the basement until we get up there. It sounds like they have a nice apartment fixed up in the basement. Bruce and Jan lived there for most of this past year, but they moved into their own place a few weeks ago, so it will be all ready for us when we get there in mid-November. They had just had a baby, less than a year before so it was getting a little crowded for them. We'll only live there until we get our own place. It'll help us save some money to get started," Warren reasoned.

"How much will we have to pay your mother?" I asked, knowing she would not let us live there for free.

"She only charged them enough to help with the utility bill, heat and water. I think it was around fifty dollars a month."

We had our weekend at Montgomery Bell State Park before going to my parents' for the next two weeks or so. The moving people came just before we left on Friday morning and packed everything, including our new pink couch. They packed all our dishes, etc. in barrels with heavy foam wrapping, but I still had a few things I would not trust them with, so I packed those and stored them in the trunk of the car. We also had to keep out enough clothes to do for a couple of weeks or so. My dress for the wedding was all finished, so I was able to just leave it in Nashville with Mildred.

"You know I'm going to miss you very, very much," I said to Mildred as we said our goodbyes before leaving for Decaturville.

"I'll miss you, too, but let's not get too teary before you really have to leave," she said.

"We'll see you on Friday, the second," I said, holding back tears.

"My family will be up on Friday also, so I guess we'll have very little time for just us before Johnny and I are married," Mildred replied. We hugged, and by then both of us were crying.

"Let's go," Warren said, "It'll be all right; we can visit later."

I got in the car knowing that my relationship with Millie would never be quite the same, but I also hoped in my heart that we could stay close through letters and occasional visits.

I was quiet and sad on our drive to the country. Warren tried several times to cheer me up, but to no avail. It was a little crowded, to say the least, at my mother's house. Sometimes Louise would give us her room, that is, if she was in a good mood. Lately she seemed to be quite happy. She had given up on Jim Stricklin and was dating one of his friends, Frank Walker. I liked Frank much better than Jim, and I kept telling her that every chance I got.

Mama and Daddy now had seven kids with another one due any day now. When Warren and I were there, that made ten people in the house. I guess we had all gotten so used to it that it didn't bother us, but I knew Warren wanted more privacy. Almost every night he would ask me if I wanted to go for a drive. All the kids, except Morris, who was now eighteen and thought he was pretty grownup, would jump up and down, crying, "Good! Let's go to the Dairy Queen!"

Joan was fifteen and beginning to blossom into a beautiful young lady. Pat was only twelve and cute as a button. Dan and Sam were little rascals, always at each other's throats. Sam was nine and Dan, almost six. We were all hoping the baby would be a girl. Sometimes Warren would give in and let them go, but most of the time, he'd say, "No, we're just going for a drive; we'll be back in a little while."

Sometimes we'd go to the gravel pit, where water had made a small lake, and Warren would jump in and take a swim. I was always such a scared cat, as he called me; I would stay in the car, just waiting for him. I could imagine snakes and all sorts of things in the water, and even scarier, you could not even see them!

"Do you feel like the baby will be here this week?" I asked Mama as she was cooking supper one evening.

"I hope so," she answered. "My feet are swelling, and I'm beginning to feel pretty miserable.

I had been really praying that the baby would come before we left to go to Nashville for the wedding, but it was now Tuesday before we were to leave on Friday, and still no baby. "There's nothing you can do anyway," Mama kept saying, "so just go and you can see it when you get back."

"Opal, do you want to make an appointment to get your hair colored this week?" Louise asked, as she came into the kitchen. "I can do it tomorrow on my lunch hour," she continued.

"That would be great," I answered. "I was going to do it myself, but I need to get it cut and styled before this weekend for Millie's wedding."

Louise was still working at the factory and made pretty good money, but she spent most of it on her car and clothes. "I'll try to get us one, right after I get off work and Warren can bring you to Parsons for yours, maybe right after mine. I know you're going back to Nashville on Friday, so I'll try to get it on Wednesday or Thursday."

True to her word, the next day, she announced that we both had appointments at the beauty shop at 4:30 p.m. and 5:00 p.m. on Thursday.

1956 was a beautiful year for fall colors. The area we lived in was very hilly with lots of trees and only about a mile or so from the Tennessee River. "Isn't it beautiful and just breathtaking?" I asked Warren on our way to the beauty shop on Thursday, November 1st.

"It really is," he agreed.

"I don't know if I can ever get used to all that flat farmland in Minnesota," I said sadly.

"We'll live in the city," he reminded me.

"I know, but I'm still dreading going."

I guess it was now beginning to hit me that this would be my first Christmas away from my family. I also knew there would be no way we could come back.

When we got to the beauty shop, Warren dropped me off and said he was going downtown for a while and would be back in about an hour. "It looks like you're about through," I said to Louise while they were putting curlers in her hair.

"It looks like I am almost done. I just have to dry after this, but it should only take you about an hour," she said.

"Maybe we'll get something to eat before we go home."

"Isn't Frank coming tonight?" I asked.

"No, he's coming tomorrow," she said.

They put the color on my hair, which had to stay for about thirty minutes. She gave me a magazine and told me she would check back in a few minutes.

I had only been sitting there for fifteen minutes or so when she came over and told me I had a phone call. It was Joan. "Mama's about to have the baby!" she cried. "Daddy drove her over here, but Dr. Conger said it could be a rough delivery. He thinks it's breach."

"We'll be there as soon as we can!" I said as I hung up.

Louise was now under the dryer. I walked over and shook her until she took her head out so she could hear. I told her what Joan had said. "Let's go!" she said.

"I can't go for another fifteen minutes!" I answered.

"Have her go ahead and wash yours out, and I'll put a scarf on, and we'll come back later and finish!"

"You have to leave it in for at least twenty minutes," the beautician told us, "or it want do any good at all."

"Okay, I'll wait another five minutes," I said.

Ten minutes later, we were on our way to the clinic. "Do you think she's had it yet?" Louise asked.

"Just be careful and don't drive so fast, or you'll get a ticket. I just pray Mama will be all right," I said for the tenth time.

"That looks like your Pontiac in the parking lot," Louise commented as she parked her car across the street, because the parking lot at the small clinic was full.

"It is," I answered.

When we got to the waiting room, Warren was there with Daddy and Joan. "How did you know she was here?" I asked Warren.

"I saw Preacher's truck and figured that he must be bringing Lemmie to the doctor. I came on over here and found out she's in labor." About that time Dr. Conger came out holding the most beautiful baby I think I had ever seen.

"Is Lemmie all right?" Daddy asked.

"She's doing fine, but she needs to rest several hours before you take her home and put her to bed. She had a pretty rough time for a while. Don't you all want to know whether it's a girl or boy?" Dr. Conger asked.

"Of course, we do!" we all said at once.

"It's a beautiful eight pound girl," he said proudly.

"Mama said Louise and I could name it if it was a girl. She said the middle name had to be Jane, but we could name her Cheryl, so her name is Cheryl Jane."

"That's a wonderful name for such a beautiful baby," the doctor agreed.

"She's certainly a gift from God," I commented, "and I'm very glad she's here."

"Can we see Mama for a minute?" Louise asked.

"For just a couple of minutes," he agreed.

We both went back to see Mama, before we headed back to the beauty shop to finish our hair.

We finished up at the beauty shop, drove home, and still got there before Warren did with Mama and Joan. Daddy came in the pickup and Warren brought Mama in the back seat of our car. "Get her right to bed," Warren said as they came in. "She's very weak and tired."

Mamie, our neighbor, was there by the time we got home, so she waited for Mama, in case there was something she could do. Louise and I had stopped for supper on the way. We knew someone would have to cook for the clan after we got home if we did not.

"I'm starved!" was the boys' first comment after they had seen the baby for a few minutes.

"We have supper, so just settle down," I snapped back.

We got Mama settled and fixed her something first. Everyone was so taken with the baby. She was like a little doll, so we all took turns holding her. The only one that looked a little forlorn and lost was Dan. He just sat in the corner of the couch, looking a little down. He was only six years old and had been the only baby for quite some time. I dreaded having to leave Mama and the baby the next day, but I knew I had to go.

We were getting together for lunch, then the rehearsal dinner on Friday night before the wedding on Saturday around 2:00 p.m. "Are you all packed, or have we forgotten something?" I asked as we loaded the car. We were planning on staying at the Days Inn, since we did not have an apartment any longer. "I'm thankful Mildred has found someone she loves; I really pray she'll be happy," I reflected. We told everyone goodbye and that we would see them Saturday night.

We planned on coming back right after the reception since Johnny and Mildred were leaving on their honeymoon. "I hope everything goes smooth but since she's not a member of this Baptist Church I'm sure we'll have to do everything."

"I thought she was paying the janitor to clean up," Warren said.

"I guess she is, but there's still all the preparation for the reception," I answered. "Several of her friends from work have volunteered to help, so it'll probably all work out. It usually does, and they'll be just as married, even if there are a few mistakes made."

We knew we could not check in at the motel before 3:00 p.m., so we drove into the drive at Mildred's apartment around noon. We were planning on going to lunch and then go over to the church to finish the details for the rehearsal. "We're here!" I yelled loudly as we knocked on the door.

Johnny came to the door. "Come on in," he announced, "Millie is in the shower. Grab yourselves some coffee and we'll be ready to go to lunch shortly."

I looked around at the familiar room with a touch of sadness, as I knew this was the beginning of a new phase in our lives. It would probably be sometime the next summer before I would get to see her. "When are you moving to the base?" I yelled to Johnny.

"It'll be a couple of months before something will open up," he answered. "I guess we'll stay in this lovely abode and I'll drive to Fort Campbell for a while."

"That's not so bad; I did it for over a year," Warren spoke up.

Mildred came out shortly, looking cool and collected in a bright cotton dress. "You look mighty cheerful," I said as I gave her a big hug.

"I am," she answered. "Weren't you happy and cheerful on your wedding day?"

I said, "It's hard to remember. I guess I was just so nervous and scared that I didn't remember to be cheerful."

"How many times do you think we've eaten at this place?" I asked, just after we were seated.

"Too many to count," Mildred answered, "but this may be the last for a while. My family will be here later this afternoon and Johnny's mother is already here."

The next thing I realized, we were rehearsing the wedding. Nancy stood in for the bride as we practiced marching down the aisle, etc. "I guess I can more or less relax now; everything is either done or it probably won't get done. The flowers will be delivered around ten in the morning," Betty commented.

Plans for the reception had been finalized. Mildred's family and future mother-in-law were in charge of the cake, punch, and all that. "You did make reservations for our dinner tonight?" Mildred said as she looked over at Johnny.

"Of course, I did," he answered.

The wedding party went out to eat, danced and had a great time. The party broke up around 11:00 p.m., mainly because everyone was about wiped out. "We'll see you tomorrow," I said as I gave Millie a peck on the cheek. "Sleep tight; it's all going to work out great."

Warren and I got back to the motel, after stopping for Krispy Creams on the way. We sat in bed, ate donuts, and reminisced about the past until after 1:00 in the morning. The wedding was to start at 2:00 p.m., but the music would start at 1:30 p.m. Everyone was to be at the church at 12:30 p.m.

Warren dressed at the motel since he was not in the wedding, but I had my dress in the back seat and was going to put it on a little later. I also had fairly high heels, which were quite hard to walk in. "There's Betty and Nancy already here," I said to

Warren as we walked up the drive to the fellowship hall. "How's Mildred doing?" I asked Nancy.

"I don't think she slept very much," she answered.

"You look so pretty," I said to Mildred's mother, while she kept busy working on things for the reception.

She replied, "I don't get this dressed up too often." She gave me a quick hug, "You know I'm going to miss you and Warren after you move away."

"We'll miss you, too," I answered. "No one else will fix him polk salad and eggs the way you do. He really gets into your cooking, you know."

About that time, Mildred came over and announced we needed to go to one of the Sunday School rooms and start getting dressed and that the music was starting in a few minutes. We helped each other with zippers, touched up our hair, made small talk, before someone knocked on the door to tell us the music had started.

The next thing I knew, I was walking down the aisle behind Nancy. We turned when the music played "Here Comes The Bride," and I could not keep my eyes dry. She looked so beautiful, and I knew at that moment I would never have another friend like Mildred. We had truly been soul mates, and I truly hoped we would be forever friends.

The minister had finished and now we proceeded out of the church. We all headed back to the fellowship hall for the reception. There were no formal pictures taken, but one of Johnny's friends took pictures with his camera. They only made slides, and I really never saw the pictures until many years later. I remember the cake and punch were great and everyone seemed to have a great time. We threw the rice, said our goodbyes, and it was over.

"Warren, don't you feel a little sad?" I asked.

"It's just that so much has been happening so fast for the past couple of weeks," he answered. "I'm glad we have almost two more weeks before we have to leave, but I'm beginning to realize how hard it is going to be. We'll try to come back as often as we can," Warren said, trying to soothe me.

"Do you realize Cheryl will be nine months old before we see her again?" I asked, wiping tears from my eyes.

My Place In Time

The next two weeks went by too quickly. The weather in Tennessee was beginning to get cold, so I knew there was probably very cold weather in Minnesota, probably even snow. On a cold November day, the twentieth of November 1956, we departed on a new phase of our life together.

Phase II –
November 1956 to August 1968

"What time do you think we'll get there?" I asked waking up from a short nap.

"It should take around eighteen hours, and since we left at six this morning, I think we should be there around midnight," Warren answered. "I sure hope we don't hit any blizzards or snow storms like we did last year."

"We shouldn't; it's still early in the year, even for Minnesota."

Warren was right on the money and we drove up in front of the house right around midnight. The lights were still on and Ma and Dad were waiting for us. Dad had just gotten home from work, since he worked 3:00 to 11:00 p.m., and it was usually around midnight when he got home. After we said our greetings, Ma asked if we were hungry, and we had something to drink and a sandwich. Later on I found out this was Dad's usual routine when he got home from work. He was a machine repairman for Munsingwear.

As I looked around I noticed our pink couch was upstairs, along with several other things scattered around. Ma told us they just hadn't had the help to move our living room furniture downstairs, and Warren said we would get it situated the next day. I told him I'd like to see the apartment, and I was shocked to see how much they had accomplished since we were here in January of last year. The kitchen had all the appliances; there was now a bathroom and a large room that could be divided into a living room/bedroom combination with a makeshift closet. I thought to myself that at least we would have some privacy. After the tour Warren suggested we bring the suitcases down and retire for the night.

We awoke the next morning, and I said, "I guess we would have to eat breakfast with them since we didn't have any groceries." Warren jumped out of bed and said all that he wanted right now was coffee. He said he'd run upstairs and bring us coffee downstairs as he threw on his pants and ran up the stairs. I thought to myself, *he's such a bundle of energy.* I'm still not a morning person; it seems to take me an hour or so to wake up. We had breakfast upstairs with Ma since Dad was still sleeping.

He was up shortly after we finished and with his usual good humor said he had talked to Floyd the day before, and they were hiring at the Northern Ordinance Navy Plant. Floyd was Dad's brother and Warren's uncle. He also said he would put in a good word for Warren since he'd been with them for many years. Warren said that sounded great and was very excited at the prospect of a job. Our money was just about gone, and we had a car payment due shortly. Warren had a job in less than a week and went to work for Northern Ordinance, but it also was a night job. They were supposed to work from 3:00 p.m. to 11:00 p.m., but they were working two hours overtime so they worked until 1:00 a.m., and he didn't get home most of the time until after 2:00 a.m.

Newlyweds

The apartment worked out quite well. We got our couch, tables, etc., downstairs, and I used a divider to separate the living room and bedroom. The main problem turned out to be that Ma's washing machine was in our kitchen area, and she would come down and start washing before we were awake sometimes. Warren had a talk with her and it got some better.

I remember how excited I was about his first pay check. We had very little left after we paid the car payment, groceries, and rent on the apartment. But it was a beginning and I knew it was only temporary We hoped to have our own place in the spring.

Bruce and Jan were over quite a bit and, of course, Marlene, Warren's younger sister, was still home. She graduated high school the prior year and was now working at an office job downtown. Bruce and Jeanette's little boy, David, was about three years old and Dawn was over a year old now. I was fortunate to have Marlene and Jan about my age because I found out very soon that this was the North and people up here were not as friendly and outgoing as they were down South.

We had left so many friends where I worked and from the Air Force base, and we suddenly found out that most of Warren's friends had moved away or just were not interested in doing things with other people. We didn't have a lot of time to get together with others except on weekends.

With me it was a different story. I found myself really getting bored. Marlene was dating, going skating, or just out with girlfriends. Ma and I played a lot of scrabble and watched a lot of old movies on television. I got to where I would always look forward to when Dad would get home from work. I would make sure he had coffee, and we would sit and eat Bongard's cheese and crackers. Ma was usually tired and would go ahead and go to bed. We would talk sometimes for hours about his job and just the world in general. He always treated me like I was so special and loved everything I cooked, or at least said he did. Warren got home a couple of hours after Dad did, so after Dad retired, I would go downstairs and watch television or read until Warren got home, and we would then sleep until at least ten the next morning.

I think Marlene began to notice how homesick I was getting, especially the closer it got to Christmas; and one night she asked if I would like to go on a hayride with her church group, and I told her I would see what Warren thought. He said it was fine with him, but I felt a little uncomfortable knowing I was married, especially because several guys made a play for me. I just usually hung around Marlene to avoid talking to most of the guys.

The next day I said to Warren, "Maybe I should get a job,"

He said, "Then we would never see each other." He went on to say that we agreed to try to have a baby after he had gotten a good job with good insurance. I told him we would have to have our own place before that happened. I even went as far as interviewing for Honeywell for a key punching position, but Warren talked me out of it. He said we would make it all right on what he made, especially with all the overtime, and that at least we could spend our days together. He said if I worked from 8:00 a.m. to 5:00 p.m., then he would be asleep when I left and gone when I got home.

The days were great because I would sleep until Warren got up and then we would run around or do things together. He tried again to teach me to ice skate but to no avail. We went bowling, met with some of his band buddies for lunch or just spent time together. But when he left to go to work around 3:00 p.m. or so, sometimes I would just sit and cry.

The next time Marlene asked if I would like to go roller skating with her and a friend, I readily agreed, even though I knew I couldn't skate. She said they would teach me and besides we can just sit and eat chips and sandwiches if I didn't want to skate. It was nice to get out and be with young people, but I knew I didn't belong with a group of unmarried kids. Guys were falling all over me, trying to help me learn to skate, and they loved my southern accent.

I told Warren all about it the following day, but he didn't seem the least bit jealous or concerned. He said that it got me out of the house for a while, and he could trust Marlene not to find me a date.

Thanksgiving

We had a big Thanksgiving dinner at Ma's. She not only invited Bruce and Jan but loads of other relatives and I felt like I was on display. Jan said I would get used to them as she changed her new baby's diaper. I said I didn't know if I ever would or not because they were so different than my family. I told Jan that Dawn was such a cute baby, and she said she was glad they had a girl but said that two children sure tie you down and said she never had time for anything but taking care of kids. I asked her how long she would be off work and she said that she had taken off for thrirteen months and it all depended if they could get Ma or her mother to keep the kids. She went on to say that it would be spring at least before she went back to work.

I told her I sure hoped we had our own apartment sometime in the early spring. We had to try to save some money before that could happen. She asked me if I was planning on going back to work, and I said that Warren and I had discussed it quite a bit but, for now, Warren had won. He wanted me to stay home so we can have some time together.

Christmas - 1956

The next month went by quickly because I was busy Christmas shopping and getting things ready to mail to my folks. I had never been away from home at Christmas, and I knew it was going to be difficult, but I knew I had Warren and he tried to keep me cheered up.

I wrote Mildred letters on a regular basis but I could begin to see things changing. She had new friends, and so did I, but we continued to write and share our new lives with each other as best we could on paper. I told her we would sure try to come to Fort Campbell and see them when we came home in July of the following year. Warren would not get a vacation until then so I knew, unless it was a dire emergency, we would not be in Tennessee until then.

Warren's mother and dad tried to make Christmas as festive as possible, but I was still very homesick. Warren and I opened our gifts from Tennessee on Christmas Eve and also our ones to each other. Warren said that I had gotten some wonderful presents and I agreed that they were just the right things for living in the cold climate. I had gotten boots for the snow, sweaters, etc. Warren had also given me lots of beautiful nightgowns and other sleeping apparel.

On Christmas Day in 1956, Ma had a huge Christmas dinner, and then everyone came over and opened gifts that afternoon. As Marlene got the coffee for second cups, she said that it was snowing and Jan said she couldn't imagine Christmas without snow. She said you get used to it and, besides, Christmas had nothing to do with the weather because it was being with family and loved ones that was important.

I took that the wrong way and went into the bedroom and cried. I came out later when Marlene said they were going to play Scrabble or canasta. I said I'd play canasta. The rest of the afternoon was spent playing cards and, of course, eating again. Looking out the window, Dad said he hoped they plowed the roads or Jan and Bruce might have to spend the night. We had gotten six or eight inches of fresh snow.

Jeannette said maybe we could go ice skating next week. I told Jeanette I had heard she was a really good skater and she wondered who had told me that and I said that Marlene and Ma said that she did great figure skating. Ma said that she also played the piano, and maybe she could play the organ for us. For the next hour or so, Jan played Ma and Dad's new organ and we sang Christmas carols.

When we were getting ready for bed later that night, Warren made the comment that he thought, all in all, it was a very nice Christmas. I said I guess it could have been worse, and I hoped that Bruce and Jan got home all right with those two babies in the car. Warren said that Bruce was used to driving on it and he would be careful. Warren had the next two days off, and I asked what we were going to do for the next two days while he was off and he said maybe we could go to some of the after-Christmas sales.

Winters in Minnesota go from bad to worse. January was so bitterly cold, and I barely stuck my head out except when Warren would go warm the car up for us to go out. We went ice skating a couple of times, and even though I was bundled up as much as possible (including a couple of pairs of wool socks), I still almost froze. Jeanette was a very good skater and so was Marlene and Ma. I fell down so many times, I finally decided you had to learn to skate when you were a child, and I had gone far beyond that.

The next two months were much the same. Sometimes it would get down to thirty below zero at night. There would be weeks at a time the temperature would not climb above zero during the day. I was really glad I was not working at this time.

Warren told me we would start looking for our own

apartment in the spring. He also talked me into trying to get pregnant. I skipped my first period in March and I told Warren a week or so later I thought this could be it, but I thought we should wait for a couple of weeks before I saw the doctor.

The Stork

"Hurry up!" Warren shouted. "We don't want to be late for your appointment." I told him it wasn't until 10:00 a.m., and we had plenty of time. It was now late April, and I figured I was about six weeks pregnant. We had made the appointment about two weeks before that morning, and I was quite nervous as I sat in the waiting room. I had been to very few doctors in my life, and when they called my name, Warren went with me. The doctor came in and talked to us for a few minutes and told Warren he had to leave and stay in the waiting room.

After the examination and specimen sample was collected, he came back in and announced, "Mrs. Johnson, you are indeed pregnant and I expect the baby to be here mid-December." I was very excited but I did remember to ask if I could travel in July, and he said that shouldn't be a problem.

We rushed home to tell Ma and Dad before Dad had to leave to go to work, and they were very excited too. Ma wanted to know if I was going to call Jan and Bruce, and I told her I would wait until later that night. I would have to wait to tell Marlene when she got home a little later. Warren said he wished Mama and Daddy had a phone so we could call them, but it would be some time before they got the lines finished. Sadly, I said I would write them after he went to work that night.

Marlene had just walked in the door around 5:00 p.m. when Judy, a neighbor that lived across the alley, rang the door bell. She said how beautiful the weather was and said how glad she was that winter is finally over. Ma said, "Opal has some news for you." At the same time Judy and Marlene said to hurry up and don't keep them in suspense. I told them proudly that Warren and I were having a baby in December. They both were so excited, and Judy said that they'd have me a baby shower that fall. Marlene asked Judy if she would be here in the fall and she said that she would and that Punch and her both would be around for the rest of this year.

Judy's parents were with the circus and traveled all over the United States. Judy and her brother, Punch, were twins and lived with their grandmother, Mrs. Fuller, most of the time. Warren had told me how sometimes when their parents came through, they brought their elephants with them. He said they all had so much fun riding the elephants in the street behind their house. I really liked Judy; she was cute and perky and always seemed to be as happy as a lark. I told her a shower would be wonderful since we would have to buy everything.

About a week after I had written home about being pregnant, I got a letter from Mama. She had written back in a hurry and she was very excited. Warren said to just think about it; her grandchild will be about a year younger than her daughter. They would be more like sisters. I said I can hardly wait to see Cheryl because she would be so grownup when we went in July.

First Apartment

A few weeks later, I told Warren there were a couple of apartments for rent in the paper. We didn't want one in an apartment building but were hoping to find one in an upstairs of a private home. Jeanette and Bruce had found a cute place and the rent was very reasonable. I told Warren there was one on Bryant Avenue and he said that wasn't a bad area. That apartment had its own outside entrance but also had stairs through the main house. She rented a room to a single girl across the hall, and we would have to share the bath with her. Warren said he didn't know about that, and I said at least let's go look at it. I guess I was just ready to get moved.

The lady's name was Mrs. Wall and she and her husband were around eighty years old but seemed very nice. The apartment was next door to the telephone company and it did, indeed, have an outside entrance. I loved the apartment, and the rooms had big high ceilings like our apartment in Nashville. We met Betty, and she seemed very nice, so we decided there would be no problem with the bathroom. She seemed like a really nice girl, and I thought how nice it would be to have someone to talk to. Besides, just knowing she was across the hall, somehow would make me feel safer. We decided to take the apartment and since it was vacant, we were able to move in the following weekend. We had almost enough furniture, and the stove and refrigerator were furnished.

"Jump up; let's get going!" I yelled to Warren quite early on Saturday. Bruce would be there soon and we needed to be ready to start loading the pickup. Warren crawled out of bed after only five hours of sleep and grabbed a cigarette and coffee to get him jump-started.

We had just finished a quick breakfast when we heard Bruce and Jan talking upstairs. Ma was going to keep David and Dawn so they could help Dad and us get moved into our own wonderful apartment. We finished getting all the furniture moved and in the place before noon. We had moved most of our clothes and personal items the night before, so it was just a matter of getting the boxes unpacked and everything organized. I loved the apartment so much and it was so nice to be out of that small, cramped basement.

I was now about three months pregnant and had morning sickness most of the time. Betty and I became fast friends right away. She worked at Sears during the day and was usually home around five, and this worked out great because Warren left for work around three in the afternoon. She had a steady boyfriend and, in fact, they were engaged and planned on being married later in the summer. She went out a lot at night but would usually knock on my door when she got in to see if I wanted to talk or have something to eat. Many nights we talked late into the night. I always felt bad because she had to get up early and go to work the next morning, and I could sleep late with Warren. I very seldom went to sleep before Warren got in around 2:30 a.m. or 3:00 a.m. I was always so scared.

It seemed when I would close my eyes or doze off, I would

hear the stairs creaking or noises that sounded like someone was coming up the back stairs. Warren told me that I had to get hold of myself because it wasn't good for the baby or for me to be so upset and scared. I sobbed and told him I had really heard someone walking up the stairs the night before. I read and watched television but I got so tired before Warren got home, but I still couldn't sleep. When I did fall asleep, I would wake up hearing terrible noises. Warren said all I would have to do is yell and Betty would hear me. I was always so glad when the weekend came, but then I couldn't enjoy Sunday because I was thinking about Warren going back to work on Monday night.

One night late in June, Betty asked me over for coffee later. As we sprawled out on the bed while the coffee was perking, I could tell she was very excited. She said they had set a wedding date and I asked when. She said it was going to be the first weekend in August, and I asked where they were going to get married and she said in northern Minnesota, where her parents lived. She said they were Swedish and it was very important that they have a family wedding. I told her I wished it were where I could go and she said she did too, but they would take a lot of pictures.

She said she guessed she was going to wear a suit or just a dressy dress because it was going to be a small wedding and they had very little money. I told her she could wear my dress and she looked up with tears in her eyes and asked if I really meant it. I told her, of course, she could wear it. I said I was never going to wear it again and I would love for her to wear it, if it fit her. She asked what size it was and I told her a size nine and it was about her size. It might be a little longer on her because she was shorter than I was, but that wouldn't make any difference since it was waltz-length. I told her I would go get it so she could try it on. I rushed next door and got the dress, hanging neatly in a bag in the back of my closet. I couldn't believe how good it fit her and told her it probably looked better on her than it did on me. She kept asking me if I was sure it was all right if she wore it, and I said that I would love to know I had a small part in her wedding. It was agreed she would wear the dress. She was so excited she could hardly wait to tell her mother.

Later, while we were talking, I told Betty we were going to Tennessee the first two weeks in July. This was the longest I had ever been away from home and I was really homesick. My baby sister, Cheryl, was almost seven months old and she would be eight months by the time we went in July. Betty said she would keep an eye on our place while we were gone. Mrs. Wall had given her an extra key so she could check on things periodically.

Home Again

A few weeks later while we were packing the car to leave the next morning, I said I couldn't believe we had two whole weeks together and I got to go home too. Warren said he hoped I felt all right for such a long trip. I told him the doctor said I would be fine since I was only four months along, and most of my morning sickness was gone. Besides, we were going to stop and sleep sometime. We were going to try to leave by eight the following morning if Warren could wake himself. I didn't know how he made it on only four or five hours of sleep since I slept twice that much and was still always tired. He laughed and said it could have something to do with my condition.

The next morning by eight o'clock, we were on the road, leaving Minneapolis for a two-week vacation with my family in Tennessee. We had been driving for about ten hours when Warren asked if I wanted to start looking for a motel. I told him, no, not that early, because I was so excited about getting there. I started thinking about not even stopping. As if reading my thoughts, Warren said that there was a lot less traffic at night and maybe we should just drive on. He said he was wide awake and used to being up that late, and we would be there by two or three in the morning. I made him promise if he got sleepy that he would pull over and stop. I slept part of the way, and the next thing I knew we were within an hour of Decaturville. Warren asked me to get him another cup of coffee from the thermos and said that he had been wanting one but hated to wake me up. I poured him about his tenth cup of coffee, hoping it would keep him awake the rest of the way. He said maybe they would let us sleep late in the morning, but I said I doubted they would.

We drove into the driveway a little before three o'clock in the morning, a little less than seventeen hours since we'd left Minneapolis. As I jumped out of the car, I told Warren to just take in the small bag we were going to use at the motel, and we would unpack the car in the morning. By the time we got through the back porch and into the kitchen, I heard Mama coming through the living room. She said, "Oh, you're here!" as we embraced. I told her we had decided to drive on and not stop, and she said she was glad we did and said we must be worn out, especially Warren. Shortly after that Lou, my oldest sister, appeared and then Daddy. The rest of the clan was dead to the world.

We talked for a while before Mama said it might be better if we went to bed and talked in the morning. Louise gave us her bedroom, and she would sleep in with Joan and Pat. As we collected our things for bed, I said to Warren that I guessed we would have to wait until morning to see Cheryl. It was a hot July night, but by that time of night, it had cooled down some so we decided we didn't need a fan. There was no air conditioning anywhere in the community. I was totally wiped out but so excited about being home.

The next morning at 8:00 a.m. I heard Daddy up. He always got up early in the morning and would take a walk in the woods before breakfast. He always said he thought he lived in the wrong era because he would like to have lived back when Daniel Bone lived. He loved to hunt, trap and fish and he used to make quite a bit of extra money when we were growing up, selling his fur pelts.

I heard a baby crying and then a lot of commotion. I told Warren that I was getting up because I couldn't wait any longer to see Cheryl. He had been snoring loudly, but by now I had him awake too. I told him he hadn't brought my robe in the night before, and I didn't want to put my dirty shorts back on and asked him to please get our suitcase. As he closed the door, I told him to not get sidetracked on the way.

In a very short while, I was sitting in the living room trying to make friends with my baby sister, Cheryl. She didn't take kindly to strangers and started crying for Mama. I said I would eat breakfast first and then maybe she'd get used to me.

Mama had cooked one of her famous breakfasts: biscuits, ham, eggs, and a chocolate gravy that was out of this world on homemade biscuits and butter. Everyone talked at once. Warren had grown up with one brother and one sister so this was all foreign, but it always amazed me how easily he seemed to fit in with the family.

"Do you still have your cows?" Warren asked Mama and she said that she sure did. She was going to milk after she finished breakfast. Warren told her he would go with her because he used to milk on his uncle's farm when he was younger and he got pretty good at it. Mama told him she would sure let him try since no one else around there was interested in learning. I had tried several times when I was younger, but to no avail; I just could never get any milk out. "I'll get dressed and stay here with Cheryl and maybe she'll warm up to me," I said.

We had two weeks but it went by so fast. We had fish frys and loads of family gatherings. Cheryl had just started to play with me and gotten used to me being around, and we would be leaving shortly. Everyone was so excited about the baby, but I knew none of them could be there with me. The baby was due in mid-December, and I knew it would be next summer before I would see them again. Cheryl would be another year older and would have surely forgotten me by then. It was one of the saddest days of my life.

Everyone was crying but my heart went out to my mother. Her first grandchild would be born a thousand miles away, and she knew there was no way she could be there and the baby would be six months old before she could see it. I told her we would write often and when the baby came, I would call Mary Ann and Grady and they could come and tell her. By this time there was now four or five phones in the community, all on one party line, and getting through with a long distance call would be a real feat.

Back to Minnesota

As we left Tennessee, I cried softly to myself for the next thirty minutes in the car. Warren kept saying he wished there was something he could do and promised we wouldn't spend our whole life, away from my family. This was a promise I would hold him to later in life, but for the time being I knew I had to go back to the apartment where I was scared most of the time.

I was so happy about the baby, and I guess that was the only way I got through it. I guess I was a little scared about my first baby, but I couldn't wait to hold her. I was reading every parenting book I could find, especially Dr. Spock. I remember telling Warren the only thing I was really concerned about was if the baby was going to have his nose. Warren had a great nose, especially right for his face. His dad had the same type nose, so I knew there was a chance that it could be passed on. I guess I should have worried about more serious things; I look back now and see how I took everything for granted.

A New Home

Betty was in the middle of her wedding plans and spent as much time as possible with her parents so I hardly ever got to see her, but she would still knock on my door a couple of times a week and catch me up on all the details. Betty would be moving in two weeks so I sat around depressed and brooding. The wedding was the first part of August, which was only a couple of weeks away. The thing I was most sad about was the fact that she would be moving away. I told Warren one night that it would be horrible to have a man rent that room, and I couldn't imagine sharing a bathroom with a strange man. However, things have a way of working out.

One night Warren yelled from the kitchen for me to answer the phone. I picked it up, knowing it was probably his mother or

My Place In Time

Jeannette on the other end. Ma told me there was a house next door to her sister Nellie for sale. I had met Nellie and Leonard several times before, and they seemed like nice people with a son named Genie, who was about Warren's age. My mind finally got back to what Ma was saying, and she said the house was out by Medicine Lake, almost in the country, about twelve miles out Highway 55.

I told her we couldn't afford a house then, especially with the baby coming. She went on to say she thought the man that owned it would carry a contract for deed with very little down payment. Nellie said the house isn't much to look at, but it had a beautiful wooded lot and you could probably remodel the house later. I told her to talk to Warren about it, and they talked for several minutes before he hung up. He said maybe we should look at it and that it wouldn't hurt to just look. I told him we didn't have any more than $200 that we could spare, and I was sure it would take more than that for a down payment. Warren said we could borrow money from Ma and Dad, but I said I didn't think so because we've just got his debts to them paid off and I didn't want to start over.

So we'd know where we were going, we drove over to Ma and Dad's and picked them up because they had visited Leonard and Nellie a few times. As we drove down Medicine Lake Drive, I made the comment that it was a nice day for a drive.

Nellie's house was painted pink and sat facing a cove street. Next to it was the most beautiful lot with huge oak trees, but the house left a lot to be desired. There was a small one-room stucco building that could be used for a guest house, but the main house wasn't much, just four small rooms and a bath. A man named Mr. May was there and showed us around and we found out he had sold Nellie and Leonard their house and was quite flexible. When we sat down to talk money, he said he wanted $5,500 for it and would carry the note himself. I told him we had very little money, and he said he would sell it for as little as $200 down. Warren told him we would think about it and get back with him the following day.

On our ride back to town, I asked if anything could be done with the house. They said we could live in it like it is for a short while. The back two rooms seemed quite solid and they were sure they could be saved. The two that had been added on would have to be torn down. Dad said a builder's loan was possible sometime down the road, and he thought we could make a nice house out of it. I felt he was pretty wise in these matters since they had moved their house from northeast Minneapolis a few years before. He went on to say that since Warren and he both worked nights, they could do most of the labor themselves. I said I guessed it was better than putting your money in an apartment month after month.

Warren and I talked late into the night, trying to decide if this was what we should do. "I really don't think I would be any more scared there than I was at the apartment," I commented. Nellie and Leonard were quite close and Gene was there most of the time. Warren also said he really liked the lot and the idea of being out of town. I asked him if he thought we could keep it warm enough for the baby, and he said he didn't see why not because we could buy a bigger heating unit.

Before we made our final decision, I said let's call and go back out one more time and look at the house. The next day was Sunday and since we weren't involved in church, we slept late, had a big breakfast, and then called to see if Mr. May would show us the house again and we set up an appointment for later that day. I kept asking Warren if he thought we should buy the house, and he said the big thing would be how much our monthly payments would be. He doubted they would be any more than what we paid at the apartment. I made the comment that I'd like for us to go look at the house by ourselves and he agreed. We took a picnic and stopped at one of the tables around Medicine Lake and ate lunch. The house wasn't on the lake but at certain times of the year when the leaves were off, we could see the lake from the kitchen window.

We toured the house again, seeing possible ways we could make it into something livable. We could put a heater in the little building and make the cutest extra room with a bed, couch, and one corner for an extra closet. There was an old well house that Warren could use for storage and tools. As we walked around the yard for the tenth time, Warren announced, "I think we should do it."

The next thing we knew we were sitting around their kitchen

table working out the details. He said if we could pay $55 dollars a month with a $200 down payment, he would write up the contract. We told him we would probably pay it off when we got a builder's loan to remodel. Mr. May said he would call us the next day after he'd had a lawyer draw up the papers, then we could get together and sign the paperwork in the next few days. I told him we had already paid our rent through August on the apartment, and we would need to give Ms. Wall a two week notice. He said they would be out and we could move in September 1st.

I was so excited I told Warren to call Ma and Dad as soon as we got home, or maybe we should just go by there and tell them. They were home and Ma put the coffee on, as usual. We sat around talking about the possibilities of our new property for the next couple of hours. I told Warren I was really worn out and had been on my feet too much today because my legs are swollen. Ma said I probably needed to lie down and rest for a awhile.

We left and went home but it was hard to unwind and relax. I knocked on Betty's door and told her we, too, would be moving the first of September and she seemed very excited for us. She asked if I had told Mrs. Wall and I told her I guessed we would do that the next day. She was such a nice lady and had been especially nice to me by letting me use her washing machine, etc. Betty said she was sure she'd understand. I told our landlady early the next morning that we would be leaving and she seemed sad to lose us but said she certainly understood.

I told her I would bring the baby to see her sometime later. I wrote long letters to Mama telling her all about our little house and what great plans we had for it. I wrote that maybe she'd be able to come up and visit sometime after we got the house going or maybe in the spring.

The next few weeks flew by so fast, and suddenly it was time to move. Warren had a buddy from work who had a pickup and agreed to help us move. Bruce and Dad were there, of course, and I tried not to lift anything too heavy.

I had a real scare the week before when we visited Warren's cousin, Dick. They lived in an upstairs apartment and when we started to leave, I caught my heel on a rug and fell down almost the whole flight of stairs. I called the doctor as soon as I got home and he said if I wasn't spotting, I would probably be all right, but he wanted me to come in the next day and let him check me. I went in the next day and he said everything looked good, but it scared me into being more careful. I certainly didn't want anything to happen to this baby. I was getting to the stage now where the baby was very active and you knew there was a life growing inside you. Warren treated me with kid gloves, mainly because he had the scare of his life too.

The house deal went through without a hitch, and suddenly we were living in our own little cottage out by Medicine Lake. I was extremely happy, especially on the weekends when Warren was home. He was working nights and I hated being by myself, but Nellie, Leonard and Genie, lived close yet it was still quite a change.

Labor Day

A few days after we had moved in, I told Warren that Nellie was having a Labor Day picnic and he said that sounded like fun to him. She said I didn't have to bring anything, but I later ended up making a macaroni salad and the picnic turned out great fun. The leaves were just beginning to turn and the weather was still extra nice, even for Minnesota. Of course, everyone had to tour our house while they were so close. I made it clear that we were planning on remodeling the following year and this was only temporary.

Adrienne

As we drove home from Ma's after Sunday dinner, Warren told me that one of his friends from band was having a Christmas party Saturday night. He said he ran into him at the hardware store and we were invited to come. Warren asked if I thought I'd feel up to going to the party, and I said I should because I wasn't due for another 3 weeks. He said to plan on going then.

On Saturday morning, the day of the party, I still felt great but by that afternoon, I was beginning to feel some discomfort. Warren said maybe we shouldn't go, and I said we could always leave if I was feeling bad. We had a great time at the party but on the way home, I began to get weird sensations in my stomach again. After we got home, Warren said maybe we should call the doctor and I said I really didn't know what to expect since I had never done this before. I told him we'd wait awhile and see if they stopped or at least had some pattern about them. I really thought it was only false labor. I went to bed and, sure enough, the pains stopped.

The next day was Sunday and I had pains off and on during the day but now decided it was nothing to be concerned about. The doctor says very few people's first child comes early.

This pain continued throughout the week until the following Wednesday around 5:00 p.m. when Warren had been gone a couple of hours. My little dog, Timmy, a little Chihuahua and Manchester, that Jan's parents had given me a few months before, kept barking and wanted to go outside. I took Timmy out and after I settled back to watch television, the strange sensations started again. I noticed a couple of hours later they were beginning to be about 30 minutes apart.

At 10:00 p.m. I called Warren and said I thought he should come home. By this time I was beginning to cry, and he said he would be there in a few minutes. I had packed my suitcase a couple of days before so when Warren drove in, I was ready to go. I told Warren as we drove to the hospital that Nellie was coming over to let Timmy out in the morning. I had called Dr. Nash before we left, and he said he would be there before I needed him.

When I arrived at the hospital, my contractions were ten minutes apart. The nurses said it could still be several hours, and Warren was able to stay with me and hold my hand. Around 5:00 a.m. the nurses told me I had dilated to about eight and it shouldn't be too much longer. I said I hoped not because the pain was almost unbearable. They gave me a shot that was supposed to relax me but absolutely did nothing more.

At 5:30 a.m. they took me in the delivery room, where Dr.

Nash finished washing up. As they wheeled me into delivery, I told Warren I wished he could be with me and he said he'd be right outside and he kissed me gently. I'm very thankful today there are epidural shots for childbirth, but back then they put a gas mask over your mouth and nose periodically. I kept telling them to not put the mask on me and that I'd rather not have it because it was making me sick.

"Push!" the doctor said it seemed for the tenth time. I pushed and heard the nurse say, "Here comes the head."

A few minutes later the doctor said, "It's a girl," and they held her up for me to see.

"Oh, how beautiful she is!" I cried and asked if she was all right and they said she was absolutely perfect.

She was born just before 6:00 a.m. the doctor told Warren, as they wheeled us into the hallway just before they took her in to clean her up. The nurse told me they would bring her in for me to feed a little later. I was so tired; all I wanted was to go to sleep.

After they got us in a room, I told Warren he should call Ma and Dad. He could do that from the hospital room, but he would have to call Mama after he got back home. Mary Ann and Grady Crawley said we could call them and they would go tell my folks. "I sure wish Mama and Daddy would get a phone," I said as I turned over to go to sleep.

We had decided on a name a few months before. I wanted to call the baby Kim if it was a girl, but Warren had seen the name Adrienne on television during the Miss Minnesota pageant. He kept telling me he really liked the name Adrienne. I agreed we would call her Adrienne Kim, but I would probably call her Kim.

"Did you finally wake up?" Warren asked around five in the afternoon, when he came back bringing me flowers. I told him I was feeling much better and sat up on the side of the bed. Dr. Nash said you will probably be here four or five days, and I asked Warren if he'd take care of my dog and he said he would and while he's at work, Nellie would come over and take care of him. I wondered how he would take to Kim, and Warren said he would be fine because Adrienne would be in her crib or bassinet.

A few minutes later, they brought this tiny little baby into my room and laid her in my arms. When I looked down at her, I had never felt such love for another human being. She was so tiny and so totally dependent and a part of Warren and me. I remember thinking to myself, I hope I can take care of her and be a good mother to her. No one thought of breast feeding in the fifties; it was just not done. A nurse then brought her bottle in for me to feed her. What a joy and a delight to hold her and take care of her. The next five days went by quickly. We had parenting classes in the morning, sitz baths in the afternoons, and long naps in between. The nurse kept saying, "Get all the rest and comfort you can before you get home."

I found out very quickly after I got home that the main problem would be lack of sleep. Kim was a good baby but I had read lots of baby books, especially Dr. Spock, and the big advice back then was to keep your baby on a schedule. They suggested you get a routine where the baby ate every three to four hours. If they were fussy in between, you could use a pacifier. Warren went back to work the next night, and there I was, all alone with a week old baby.

The first few nights I slept very little. I was never able to go to sleep until Warren got home and that was usually after 2:00 a.m.

Warren's mother and dad gave us a wonderful buggy that doubled as a cradle. We put it beside our bed and if she got fussy, we would rock the buggy instead of getting out of bed. Many times during the night, I would check her schedule to see if it was time for her bottle. If not, we would give her a pacifier and rock her. Sometimes it took an hour or so before she could eat.

"What in the world is that smell?" Warren yelled as he jumped out of bed early one Saturday morning. I jumped with a start when I realized the bottom of Kim's bottle had melted. We had a gas stove and warmed her bottles in a pan of water on the stove. On this particular night I was so tired that I went to sleep standing beside the stove, leaning on the counter. I told Warren I was glad he was there because if he hadn't been, I could have burned the house down.

The next few weeks flew by so quickly. I was totally wiped out from lack of sleep but still so overwhelmed by the demands of this tiny baby that seemed to rule our lives. I can remember laying

Kim on the couch beside me while Warren was at work and then most of my time was spent just watching her, or worrying that something was wrong. I would wake her up if I thought she had slept too long, or if it was time for her to eat. I loved her so much and thought she was the most perfect baby that had ever lived.

About 6 weeks later I said to Warren, "I can't believe she's six weeks old already and he said he couldn't either. Warren zipped her up in her baby bunting to go for her check-up at the doctor's office, and the doctor confirmed she was doing great. She had gained the right amount, and everything looked good. We stopped at Ma and Dad's to show her to them for a little while before Dad had to go to work. He worked nights too but left for work a little before Warren did. After we got Kim settled, Ma said we might as well stay for lunch and we were always glad to have lunch.

The only hitch in our perfect life was our finances. The heating bills were so high, and there were so many extra expenses with having a baby. One morning while we were eating breakfast I told Warren, "I don't think we're going to have enough money to pay our heat bill this month" and his answer was we could borrow from Dad and Ma. I told him I hated to do that, but maybe we can repay them the following month. We had never had to borrow money since we had been married, and it sure hurt to have to do it now. I told him I could get a part-time job in the spring after Kim got a little older. I told him if I could work in the mornings, then he could watch Kim until I got home. He said he would think about it. We borrowed $50 to pay our heat bill for the first January in our little house. It turned out to be the only money we would ever have to borrow from any of our relatives.

Part Time Job

In April, I brought back up the subject of finding a part-time job. I told Warren I had talked to Gene the day before, and he said I could ride to work with him and then Warren could pick me up around noon. Gene was Warren's cousin who lived next door with his mother, Nellie and his dad, Leonard. I knew I could ride the bus if for some reason Gene didn't go to work or had to go in early.

Warren finally agreed and the following week Ma kept Kim and, I went looking for a part-time job. I interviewed for a key punching position at National Auto Parts Association (NAPA for short.) They were hiring for two part-time positions - one girl to work in the morning and another to work in the afternoon. I guess that way they didn't have to pay for benefits, like insurance, etc. It was a small office and the key punch department only had three people in it: the computer operator, manager, and two others. The pay was pretty good and the hours were great. I would go to work at 8:00 a.m. and work until 12:30 p.m.

On the way home I told Warren I hoped I got this job because Kim usually slept until eight or nine and then he could bring her with him to pick me up. At this point in time, I hadn't learned to drive, or at least I did not have a driver's license, though I had driven off and on when I was in high school.

The phone rang the next day just before Warren left for work and it was the man from NAPA. "Mrs. Johnson, when can you start work?" I asked if Monday would be all right, and he said that would be great. I was so excited I yelled to Warren that I had the job and I was going to work on Monday.

I really hated to leave Kim, but I knew she would be with Warren and I also knew we really needed the money. It just seemed to take so much more money now that we had a baby. We were also talking about enlarging our house as soon as we could get it all together. Warren said that we wouldn't have any time together, but I argued that we would. I told him I would wait up for him sometimes, but he said I wouldn't be able to get up and go to work. He finally agreed I should take the job and see how it worked out.

On Monday morning when I left, I had such mixed emotions. I was excited to be going but very sad to have to leave Kim. It was now the first of April, so she was only about five months old. I met Gene around 7:30 a.m. and he got me to work a little before 8:00 a.m. I felt a little apprehensive at first but that soon diminished. I met my coworkers and they eased my fears immediately. George, the boss in our department, was very nice. He was quiet, young, in his thirties, with an easy-going personality. Sharon, the one girl who did all the clerical work, was super. She was unmarried, in her early twenties, very smart, and she made me feel right at home.

When Warren picked me up the first day of work around 12:30 p.m., I told him I thought it was going to work great. He said he didn't make it so great and that Kim cried most of the morning and he guessed she missed me. I told him she would get used to him in a few days.

Changing the subject, I said I'd like to stop on the way home and have lunch. He shot back with "you know we can't afford to eat out." I told him let's celebrate and I wouldn't make it a habit. We stopped and ate at Warren's favorite place in Crystal, called the Sweden House. They had a great "all you can eat buffet" and Warren never suffered from a lack of appetite.

After Warren left for work around 2:30 p.m., I put Kim down for a nap and sat down with a cup of coffee. I thought about my day and all the work I had to do now that I was home. Kim was such a good baby and she played a lot when she wasn't sleeping so I was able to do all the housework before I sat down to rest, watch television and wait for Warren to come home. He was supposed to get off at 11:30 p.m. but they worked at least two hours overtime so it was usually around 1:30 a.m. or 2:00 a.m. before he got home. I tried to stay up, but most of the time I was asleep on the couch before he came in. My little dog, Timmy, would curl up beside me and keep me company. She was a great little watchdog and would bark if she heard strange noises. She got along well with Kim, even though sometimes she seemed a little jealous.

About a month or so into our routine, I was bone-tired after having a very hard day key punching. I was having to stay later because the other girl that was supposed to come in at one in the afternoon was calling quite frequently saying she had to be late.

For most of the week I had worked until 1:00 p.m., and it was really hard to get home and have Warren ready to leave by 2:30 p.m. I had to wash and fold diapers and I was a fanatic about keeping everything in perfect order. We had a washing machine but had not been able to afford a dryer.

In Minnesota the weather is very unpredictable and it was

really hard the first few months after Kim was born. In January and February it was twenty or thirty below zero. I would hang diapers all around the house when it was absolutely so cold you could not hang them out. Most of the time I managed to hang them on the line, even if they froze.

That particular night I was almost asleep when Timmy jumped up and started barking. I yelled at her to be quiet or she would wake up Kim. She stopped barking, but then I heard something at the back door. I was petrified - I absolutely could not move. I looked toward the door and could see the handle turning. Timmy continued to bark, but I still could not move. In a few minutes the handle stopped turning on the door, but then I thought I heard someone walking around the side of the house. I managed to get my bearings and grabbed the phone. I looked at my watch and realized it wasn't quite 11:00 p.m. I peeked out the window to see if Bruce was still awake, and I could see his lights were still on. Bruce was a police officer with the Village of Plymouth Police Department. With my hand shaking, I dialed his number, praying he would be there. Jan answered the phone and kept asking who it was. I realized I wasn't getting any words out. I finally managed to tell her it was me, and I thought someone was trying to break into the house. She said Bruce was still home and she would send him over to check things out.

In a couple of minutes, Timmy started to barking again, but this time I felt sure it was Bruce. He knocked on the door telling me it was him and to let him in. I was still shaking but managed to open the door. He asked if I really thought someone was there, and I told him I was certain because they turned the door knob. He said it could have been Gene trying to scare me, but I told him I didn't think so and I wouldn't believe he would turn the door knob. There was another time when Gene was coming home from Bruce's house, he tapped on my window but he let me know it was him.

Bruce said he had checked all around the house, and there wasn't anyone there now. He said if I heard anything else to give him a call. Needless to say, for the rest of the night, I didn't go to sleep until Warren got home around 1:30 a.m. I couldn't go to sleep for several hours even after Warren got home and we went to bed. He tried to reassure me, but from that point on I was miserable staying by myself while he worked nights.

Springtime

The weather was warming up nicely, even for Minnesota. It was about mid-May and the temperature was in the 80s. Kim was almost six months old and was beginning to sit up and make sounds as though she was trying to talk. I was still so fascinated with her. She loved to be outside and after Warren left for work in the afternoons, I took her for long walks.

One week I asked Warren if he realized that Kim would be seven months old before Mama and Daddy got to see her for the first time. He said it couldn't be helped, and he wished we could go more than once a year. I said I felt like they were missing out on so much of their only grandchild. I reminded him that our agreement was we didn't intend on spending our lives in Minnesota. Warren said he couldn't find a job there, but he would try and find a job when we went home in July. He said we would get Mama to keep Kim and go to Memphis or Nashville and look for a job. This had always been part of our deal - we would not spend our whole life away from my family.

I thought I had adjusted well, but I still hadn't made many friends. I was very thankful for Jeanette because she and I did all sorts of things together. We both loved sewing and we spent many hours at Minnesota Mills, looking at fabric and patterns. I was always outgoing and I was shocked that it was so hard to make friends. Neighbors did not want to be neighborly so I gave up and enjoyed Kim and my dog, Timmy.

Timmy

One night in early June, I was watching television with Kim lying on the couch beside me, when Timmy decided he had to go out. I looked out to be sure there were no dogs hanging around outside. I knew there were a couple of female dogs in season in the neighborhood, and Timmy liked to wander off when this was the case. I decided at the last minute I had better put his chain on and hook him to the outside door. I told him to stay put and went back inside to check on Kim and watch the rest of the show I was watching. I didn't hear anything for the next few minutes so I waited for around fifteen minutes and opened the door and looked around for Timmy but he wasn't there. The collar and chain had separated and he was gone. I called for him at the top of my lungs and then ran back in the house and put Kim in her crib and went back to look for him. I ran all around the house and every place I could see but had no luck. I was frantic; Timmy was nowhere to be found.

About that time the phone rang, and I knew it would be Warren calling to check on us because he usually called on his last break around 11:00 p.m. I started crying immediately and told him that Timmy had run off. I told him "I had Timmy tied up but the leash had come undone and I had no idea where he was."

Warren tried to calm me down and told me "he is probably all right."

I told him, "I can't leave Kim alone and go look for Timmy,"

Then he said, "I'll go as soon as I get home."

I waited frantically until Warren got home around 1:30 a.m., all the while looking outside every few minutes to see if Timmy was at the door or if I could see him. By the time Warren walked in, I was reconciled to the fact that something terrible had happened to Timmy. Warren put his things away, grabbed a big flashlight and went outside to look for him.

About 30 minutes later, he came in and said he couldn't find him and he guessed we would have to wait until morning because there was nothing more we can do that night. This happened on a Friday night, and I knew I wouldn't have to go to work the next day. I finally agreed and we went to bed, but I slept very little.

We were up at the crack of dawn, and I fed Kim and took her outside with us. We looked all around our house and Bruce's before we started looking on the next street. I kept saying he was such a little dog, and I was sure something bad had happened.

Warren tried to be optimistic and said, "We don't know yet."

We looked for an hour or so before we ran into some kids playing, and they told us to go look at the end of the street because there was a big Labrador Retriever in a fenced-in area that was a really mean dog. She went on to say that her mom told her the dog had killed a cat last week. I told Warren that Timmy was probably dead and he said let's go find out. We walked around to the side yard where the dog was barking like crazy, and I could see Timmy's body near the gate of the fence and I screamed, "There he is." Warren walked over so he could see and by this time Kim was very upset and was crying and very frightened.

We went to the house and rang the doorbell and a man came to the door looking like he had just gotten out of bed. "Your dog killed my little Timmy," I cried. He asked if he had gotten out of the fence, and Warren said he hadn't but Timmy must have wandered under the fence. The man asked what Timmy was doing at his house, and I told him that was beside the point. By this time I was getting very angry and I told him that some children had told us that his dog had killed a cat last week. Warren asked him what if it had been a child that had gotten into that pen. Warren went on to say that no one should have a dog that vicious in our neighborhood. The man finally said he was very sorry about our dog and Warren asked him what he intended to do about his dog. Warren told him if his dog was not out of our neighborhood in two or three days, we were going to call Animal Control. I asked the man if he had something we could put Timmy's body in, and he found a small cardboard box so we placed what was left of him in it and started walking home. Warren told him we would be checking back in a couple of days. We took Timmy home and buried him in the backyard. Up to this time in my life, I had never experienced such pain and hurt, and I cried for several days. I said I would never have another dog for the rest of my life and ,of course, sometime later I would eat those words.

About a week later Warren visited our neighbor again, and the man said he had taken his dog to his brother's farm in southern Minnesota. I moped around for several weeks over Timmy, but I was beginning to get excited about going to Tennessee on vacation. I had already informed everyone at work that I needed to be off work the first two weeks in July, and I was looking forward to seeing everyone, especially Cheryl. She was only seven months old when we were there a year ago and now she would be around nineteen months old. Mama and Daddy had never seen Kim and I was really excited about showing her off.

Tennessee Bound

When Warren picked me up on July 1st, I could hardly contain myself. I couldn't believe we would be leaving the next day. Warren said we should leave that night because he wasn't going to work overtime that night and would be home around 11:30 p.m. and we could leave by 12:00 a.m. or 1:00 a.m. I asked him if he thought he could stay awake and he said he could and, if not, we could pull over and sleep for a little while. I told him that Kim would probably sleep better during the night anyway. We packed most of the car before Warren left for work so all I had to do was pack us a lunch, make coffee, bathe myself and Kim, and then sit and wait for Warren to get home. I got Kim to bed by eight and then time seemed to drag by.

At last I heard Warren's car drive up and I met him at the door. He said he needed to take a shower and have a cup of coffee, before we headed out, and by 12:30 a.m. we were on the road. I told him if we didn't have to stop too much, we would probably be there by 8:00 or 9:00 p.m. the next night. At that time it took about eighteen hours to drive from Minnesota because we had to go through Chicago, and most of the driving was two lanes. The bridge on Highway 55 near Dyersburg, Tennessee, was not built yet.

I had loads of coffee and sandwiches with us and kept pouring it to Warren to keep him awake. About six hours into our trip, I could tell he was getting tired. At this time I did not have a driver's license so I couldn't help with the driving. I told him we needed to pull over and sleep for a while, and it was just beginning to get light so I felt safer than if it were still really dark. He finally agreed and we pulled over.

Kim had been so good and was still fast asleep. I dozed a little, but Warren seemed to sleep fairly sound for a couple of hours. He woke up chipper and ready to go and told me he was ready for more coffee. I told him that was the last cup and we would have to have the thermos refilled when we stopped for breakfast. He said there was a good-sized town up ahead and we'd find a restaurant there. I was really glad we had a fairly new car. This was in July of 1958, and our 1955 Pontiac was only three years old and only had a few months left to pay on it. We stopped and ate breakfast and was on our way for several more hours, driving with an uneventful trip the rest of the way.

We drove into Mama and Daddy's driveway around 9:30 p.m. on Saturday, and we had been on the road for twenty-one hours. When we drove up, I grabbed Kim from the back seat and told Warren I bet Daddy had gone to bed. The lights were on all through the house but I could see Joan, Pat, Morris, Sam and Dan on the porch. Mama opened the door and came out about the time I got to the steps. She was crying and I started to cry, so this scared Kim and she started to cry. Mama took her and started talking to her, and she calmed down almost immediately, but you could tell she still didn't understand what was going on. Cheryl walked out rubbing her eyes and she started crying because Mama was holding Kim, and she did not want her Mama holding any other baby.

I asked where Daddy was, and Sam said he had laid down around 9:00 p.m. but he thought he was up now. What a wonderful reunion we had for the next few hours. Daddy did get up and was really taken with Kim. As I started getting ready for bed, I told them we would have two weeks to catch up and I was dead-tired and I knew Warren was wiped out.

Louise and Frank came up just before we went to bed. She married Frank Walker in January of 1956, and Daddy had helped them build a house across the road from the family home. I was really glad she had married Frank instead of Jim. She had dated Jim for 3 or 4 years but after he got home from the Army, he had changed and they broke up a few months later. Frank had been Jim's best friend, and he and Louise had been friends for many years and they seemed really happy at the time. I knew

Louise was having some problems and was thinking about having a hysterectomy, but we all hoped it didn't come to that. Mama said in the meantime she and Frank were spoiling Cheryl rotten.

The next morning I knew I was home when I smelled the country ham frying in the kitchen. Warren stirred and I knew he smelled it too. In the three years we had been married, Warren had really gotten into southern cooking, especially those big breakfasts. He just assumed everyone had bacon, eggs and biscuits every day. For the last three years I had gotten up and made a big breakfast for him, even though a lot of the time I didn't eat. I had to admit: there was nothing like Mama's big breakfasts. She had huge pans of homemade biscuits, country ham or sausage, eggs, fried potatoes, fruit and that wonderful chocolate gravy she made.

We jumped up and realized how famished we were. I fed Kim her baby food while Mama was finishing cooking breakfast, and when I got Kim's bottle out, Cheryl decided she wanted one too. Mama let her have one, saying it couldn't hurt her. I agreed with her that a lot of kids her age still took a bottle. Cheryl was having a hard time with another baby in the house getting part of her attention. The breakfast was better than I had remembered.

Mama said she had to go milk and asked if anyone would like to go. I told her I wouldn't be much help because she knew I had never learned how to milk a cow. Warren spoke up and said he would go. I looked at him ever so doubtful and Mama gathered up the pails and left.

I couldn't get over how grownup Joan was, and I suddenly realized she was almost sixteen years old and my little sister, Pat, was going on thirteen. They had changed so much in the three years I had been married. Morris was so grownup too and had his own car and I'm sure several girlfriends. Sam and Dan were still little boys, eleven and eight, and getting into all sorts of mischief. Dan kept asking when we were going swimming and I told him maybe that afternoon. Swimming in the river was a favorite pastime in July. Pat said, "The road is opened to Vise's Landing," and I told her we would talk to Warren when he got back.

Warren and Mama came back from milking and both of them were hot and sweaty. Warren said he was going to clean up and then we'd talk about plans for the afternoon. I asked Mama how Warren did milking, and she said he was pretty good and he sure wasn't afraid to try anything. I was so pleased with how Mama and Daddy had taken to Warren and made him feel such a part of the family.

The next two weeks flew by. We had picnics, made sauerkraut, picked blackberries, and ate a lot of wonderful meals.

As we put Kim to bed early the night before we planned to leave to go back, I told Warren I couldn't believe it had already been two weeks, and he said it seemed like we had just gotten there. I told Warren we should leave as early as we could so we wouldn't miss a whole night's sleep, and we decided we would get on the road as early as possible. Mama said they would be up by 5:00 a.m. and then we can leave by 6:00 a.m. We had one last big breakfast at five in the morning before we piled in the car for another long trip home. We had packed the car the night before so we had only ourselves and Kim to load in the car.

We hugged and cried for ten minutes before we finally got started. We had such a close-knit family and every time I had to leave, knowing I would be gone for another year, it tore my heart out. Warren seemed to understand. He promised we would eventually move back to Tennessee and live. Though this didn't help me leaving my family - I always seemed to cry the first fifty miles after we started home.

Home Again

The trip was fairly uneventful on the way back, and we drove into our driveway around 2:30 the next morning. We knew it was Sunday and we could sleep until Kim woke us up. She was usually pretty good and would play in her crib, especially if one of us got up and got her a bottle. She slept until about eight and was ready to eat breakfast. I let Warren sleep a few more hours while I fed Kim. After letting Ma, Dad, Bruce, Jeanette, and Warren's buddy from work know we had gotten back, we decided to have a lazy afternoon.

I really dreaded going back to work, but I figured I needed to work for a while longer because Warren and I were already discussing our plans for remodeling our house. We had books with plans, and Warren had drawn out the floor plan we were going to use. We planned on getting a builder's loan to work on the house and after we finished remodeling, get a mortgage large enough to pay off Mr. May, the one that carried the contract for deed. If everything went all right, we would be able to start in the spring of the following year because our car would be paid off and Warren should have time to work by then.

We looked at other houses but always decided we liked the lot where we lived and it seemed too expensive to buy a house. We spent many hours dreaming about remodeling and putting on a large addition to our little cottage near Medicine Lake.

Back to Work

I went back to work at NAPA the following Monday. The girl who worked the afternoon shift was getting more and more unreliable. Some days she would come to work at 1:00 p.m., sometimes at 2:00 p.m., and other days she'd just call and say she couldn't come in at all. I was working harder and harder and staying later and later in the afternoon trying to get the work done. When she didn't come in at all, the work would pile up for me to do the next morning. Needless to say, I was getting more and more frustrated.

One Friday afternoon one of the girls I worked with, Sharon, told me I should go talk to Mr. Hickman, the personnel manager, and ask for a raise and I told her I had thought the same thing. She said I was doing the work of a full-time employee, and I should get paid accordingly for full-time work. I agreed with her but told her I was going to think about it over the weekend and talk it over with Warren.

Warren said he wished I would just quit because we never saw each other, especially since I was staying later at work and riding the bus home. He went on to say that he didn't like having to cook too. Some days I would fix something the night before and all he had to do was warm it up. I also put things in the crock pot before I would leave. I agreed it was hard on all of us, especially Kim, who started taking her afternoon nap at Nellie's. I told Warren we would wait and see how it went about getting a raise. I told him I'd like to try to continue to work until the car was paid off the last of November. Warren reminded me that he would have his yearly raise in December.

On Monday morning I mustered up enough courage to go to the personnel manager's office. I called him before I went, and I suspect he thought I was going to give my notice. I laid out the work situation that I felt I was having to work too many hours, and the work load was too heavy for a part-time employee. He agreed the other girl wasn't working out, and he said he would talk to her and tell her if she couldn't carry her work load, he was going to look for someone else. I went on to tell him I had been there almost six months and felt I should have a raise. I knew George, my supervisor, would give me an excellent recommendation. He told me he would look into a replacement for the other girl and would consider my request.

I was shocked the following week when I got a raise on my pay check; however, my working conditions did not improve. In late September the other girl gave her notice and quit completely, and I now I had the whole work load. Sometimes it took until 3:00 p.m. or 4:00 p.m. to get everything where I could leave. I knew I would probably never last until the end of the year.

George, my supervisor, had a little girl too and he was always talking about her and how smart she was. I knew no one had a baby near as smart or as cute as Kim. I just listened to him, but I knew Kim was probably a whole lot smarter. His little girl, Cindy, was three months older than Kim and she was one year old in September. One day in October he said that Cindy was completely potty trained by the time she turned a year old. Sharon and I thought that seemed a little young, but he said it was a matter of discipline and spending time with it. I kept thinking about what he said for the next few weeks.

The last week in October, I approached Warren with my idea. I told him with my last two checks we could get caught up with all the bills and he would have his raise by then. We wouldn't have a car payment in December so we should make it all right. Warren was excited and said if I thought we could make it, then let's go for it. Warren never worried about money anyway. I went on to say that I would be able to potty train Kim and have her trained by the time she was a year old. Warren said Kim might not potty train as easily as I thought, but I told him she would and was ecstatic to think I wouldn't have to wash any more diapers.

    I gave my notice the following Monday and quit the next Friday. He had interviewed several girls for a full-time position so I guess he decided no one else would do the amount of work I was doing in a part-time job. I hated to leave Sharon and George, but I was elated to be going home with my baby again and also to have more time with Warren.

Stay at Home Mom

    True to my word, my first week home I started on my quest to potty train Kim. She thought it was a big game for a while and we had a few setbacks, but by the time she was a year old, she was going in her little potty most of the time. It was wonderful to be home again. I sewed most of my clothes and loads of beautiful little dresses for Kim. Every spare minute I spent sewing and when I sat down to watch television, I knitted.

    One of my friends in Nashville had taught me to knit and it was really relaxing and I thoroughly enjoyed it. Warren's grandmother had taught me to crochet and one night as I was finishing a sweater I was knitting, I told Warren I thought I would crochet a tablecloth like his mother's. Warren said that was a big undertaking but he knew someday it would be an heirloom. I told him I'd have to buy all the thread I would need in the beginning because if I didn't, the dye lots may not match. He asked if we had enough money for that and I told him we never seem to have enough, but maybe I could save it from the grocery money. He reminded me that Christmas was just around the corner and he would be working more overtime and maybe we could save some money from that. I bought the crochet thread and started on my quest to make a tablecloth. Ma had given me directions, but I still spent a lot of time the first two weeks trying to understand them. It was crocheted in small squares and when you finished around ten squares, you put them together.

Adrienne's First Birthday

December the 5th rolled around before I realized it. I couldn't believe our baby was now one year old. She was walking and holding on to furniture but just wouldn't let go and walk by herself. We had her a birthday party with all her cousins, aunts and uncles. I made a cake just for her, and Warren asked me if I was sure I wanted to do that. I told him when I put the cake in front of her to just take a picture. I gave her a spoon but she took her hands and ended up with cake and frosting all over her. We all had a good laugh before I took her in and cleaned her up. We let her open her presents, but she seemed more interested in the bows and ribbons than she did with the gifts. Jan laughed and said she would play with them later.

After everyone left to go home, I told Warren it had been a great time and he said it was hard to believe she was a year old already. I said I knew that she'd be walking soon and then she wouldn't be a baby any longer. I felt like crying because she was such joy in my life. I knew we would have other children, but we would never have another first one. I just never knew you could love someone so much.

Christmas 1958

Christmas came three weeks later and I was sad because I couldn't be in Tennessee, but I wasn't as sad as the year before. It was so much fun having a baby to buy Christmas toys for. Marlene had gotten married earlier in the summer, so she and

Scott, her husband, were there. She was a few months pregnant with their first child. Marlene and Jeanette took turns playing the organ so we could sing Christmas carols. After a huge Christmas dinner, Ma announced we should play canasta or some other game. David, Dawn, and Kim played with their toys, that is, until Kim got so tired she had to be put down for a nap. We played cards until it was time to eat again. Ma prepared supper again and we all ate before we started home. Warren said on the way home that, all in all, it was a good Christmas. I agreed that it was, even though I had missed being with my family. He said that having Kim made us a family.

Kim was exactly thirteen months old when she let go and started walking at Ma and Dad's one Sunday night. We were there for Sunday dinner, the first week in January, and she just suddenly decided she didn't have to hold on to tables anymore. She let go, held out her hands to balance herself, walked through the kitchen into the hallway and back into the living room. I yelled for Warren to look at her and he told me to be careful or I would scare her. We were clapping our hands but nothing stopped her. She walked around in circles until we left, and from that day forward she never went back to crawling.

One day in February I made the comment to Warren that I didn't think I would ever get used to the cold winters, and he said it would be over soon. I told him that two or three more months was a long winter, and he said we would probably need to get a bigger space heater. I told him I knew, but could we afford it that year. He said that he had talked to a guy at work, and we could get one with the bottle gas company and pay a little each month on our bill. I told him we needed to check into it, and he went on to say that even if we added on to the house, we would need a better heater the rest of that year and possibly the next. He said we could sell it after that and get a forced air furnace. I told him that was one of my biggest dreams: to have the same heat in every room. He told me to be patient and it would happen.

We got a new space heater the following week and the difference was like daylight and dark. It kept the whole house nice and warm. I liked it almost as much as my new apartment-size gas cookstove. We both agreed it paid to look through the shopper want ads.

We had bought very little since we moved into our house. The car was now paid off, but it seemed to take all our extra money for high heat bills or extra expenses for Kim. I told Warren I wasn't complaining and I told him we would get by rather than me planning on going back to work. I told him the one thing I would really like more than any other would be to seriously think about adding on to our house. Warren said he hoped we could think about that in the summertime. I asked Warren if that meant we couldn't look at other houses to get some ideas, but it would be impossible to make a really big house payment.

The next week we decided to go to some of the open houses on Sunday afternoon. The first week we went to Coon Rapids to look at Owen Thompson's homes, three bedroom houses with thirty year mortgages. On the way home, I commented to Warren that I thought they were too crowded and he agreed and said they certainly didn't have an acre lot. I really wanted a lot with trees and we had about the perfect lot but just needed a better house on it.

Even though we had basically agreed to stay where we were, the rest of that spring we looked at open houses to see if possibly we could find that perfect place we could afford. We always went back to the fact that we really liked to live where we were. I decided to seriously consider staying where we were and looking into getting a builder's loan to remodel our house.

We spent the next few weeks working on our budget, trying to figure out if we could afford to add another payment to our other expenses. We could eventually consolidate the builder's loan and the payment we paid to Mr. May, and that would be six months to a year after we got it all finished. In the meantime, we would have enough to live on and make our monthly bills. Warren said we would probably need to talk to the bank to make sure it was feasible.

Remodeling

The following week we made an appointment and talked to the loan officer at our local bank. They were very nice and informed us there was no reason we could not get a loan to remodel our house and later a larger loan to pay off our contract for deed and our builder's loan.

When Ma and Dad stopped over later that afternoon we told them we were so excited and we would be able to start remodeling in mid to late April. Dad said he would be able to help some in the mornings. We laid out plans Warren had been working on for the last two weeks. Dad asked why not go ahead and put in a full basement, but Warren told him we had considered that but it would be much less expensive just to put a half-basement with room for our furnace.

Our plans were short-lived for the spring of 1959. In early April, I woke up one morning feeling really nauseated, and I told Warren I must have picked up a bug over the weekend. Warren said he would run to the store and get me some Pepto Bismol and take Kim with him and let me stay in bed. Kim was excited as usual about getting to go for a ride.

After they left, I lay in bed thinking something was not quite right. The nausea went on for the next few mornings, and I was feeling tired and run down. About a week later I told Warren I thought I had better see a doctor because my period was late and I could be pregnant. Warren said that must be impossible and I agreed because I knew I hadn't skipped a pill the whole month, but I figured it wouldn't hurt to go and find out.

I called the doctor that afternoon and made an appointment a few days later. Warren went with me and kept Kim in the waiting room. I explained to the doctor all my symptoms, including the fact that I didn't see how I could be pregnant unless my birth control hadn't worked. He said he would run a test, but I might not be far enough along for it to be conclusive.

When he came back in, I immediately knew the results from the look on his face. He said I was right and my birth control pills must not have worked. As I gathered my things, I told him we had wanted another baby sometime anyway. I wasn't necessarily disappointed, just shocked. Warren knew the results before I told him. I wasn't a Christian at the time but I remember saying to Warren that the Lord had different plans for our next year.

The first few months were difficult, to say the least. I was sick every morning until noon. Warren always wanted a big breakfast when we got up around 9:00 a.m. or 10:00 a.m. I cooked him breakfast but I had to quit eating anything but crackers for several hours after I got out of bed. I told him I sure hoped I got to feeling better before summertime and our vacation. Warren said that was over two months away, and he was sure I would be feeling good by then.

My morning sickness continued well into June but by the time we were ready to go to Tennessee in July, I was feeling much better. Kim was now a year and a half old. She talked extremely well and was completely potty-trained. "Mommy, when do we leave?" Kim kept asking most of the day before our trip. Warren was still working nights, so we decided to leave on Friday night after he got home. Warren said he could take off an hour or so early and we could leave by 11:00 p.m. or so.

Kim was so excited about the trip and I couldn't get her to go to sleep before we left. I told Warren that was probably good because then she would sleep most of the night. Kim did sleep all night once we got going. We only had to stop once for Warren to sleep for an hour or so. As usual we were excited to be there, and Cheryl and Kim played together quite well. I told Mama and Louise at breakfast the day before we were to leave to go home that I sure wished they could come up and see us sometime next year. Louise said, "Who knows? We might surprise you and bring a car load up." I told her that would be great, never dreaming it might actually happen.

After we left the following day, I was sad and cried for hours. Over and over Kim kept asking why I was crying, and I told her I was just so sad because I'll miss Grandma and everyone so much. Warren tried to cheer me up and said they may surprise us and come to Minnesota for a visit.

My Place In Time

Summer of 1959

  The rest of the summer of 1959 was uneventful except for our efforts to remodel a garage cabin on our property one Saturday morning. It had a very high-pitched roof, and I just knew that Warren or Bruce would slide off the roof before they got the new one on. By the end of the day on Sunday, the new roof was completed. Jeanette said it looked great, and now all we had to do was remodel the inside and we would have a wonderful guest house. I told Warren that Jan had a point, about the guest house and since we weren't going to start working on the house until next year, we could make a place for guests to sleep. Heaven knew we didn't have any room inside our small house. Warren said he thought it was possible and we could get some new sheet rock, put ceiling tile up, and maybe some new floor tile. I told him it would be great to have one corner for a closet to store winter clothes. I thought we would find a used bed and couch at Goodwill or a rummage sale. I was getting excited about the whole idea! I asked Warren what we could do about heat and he said there was a flue so he guessed we could get a wood stove or a kerosene heater. It was settled and we agreed to do it.

  We spent August and September remodeling our cabin, or guest house, and by late September we were out looking for furniture for our new project. By this time I was almost six months pregnant, but it was so amazing you could hardly tell I was pregnant. I felt pretty good, most of the time, but I knew I needed to start taking it easy.

  One night in early October as Warren walked in the door I said, "Guess what, guess what?" He said he didn't know and to just tell him. I told him I had gotten a letter today from Mama, and they were thinking about coming up for Thanksgiving. Warren said that was great and he hoped it worked out.

Thanksgiving 1959

We went to Ma and Dad's for Sunday dinner the next day and Jan and Bruce, their kids, David and Dawn, and Marlene, Scott, and Phil were all there. I was looking forward to making my announcement, but Warren said maybe you shouldn't tell anyone until we were absolutely sure they were coming. I just knew they would come, but Warren said he hoped I wasn't disappointed.

I made my big announcement almost immediately. Ma seemed genuinely excited and offered to have Thanksgiving dinner at their house. She said she would set up the ping pong table in the basement and have plenty of room for everyone. Now I was even more excited. I wrote Mama and told her that Ma planned to have Thanksgiving dinner at their house and we had it all worked out for the sleeping arrangements. I planned on borrowing a roll-a-way bed to put in the cabin with the couch and the double bed. I told Warren the men could sleep in the guest house, and then we would have plenty of room for the rest of us in the house. I told them I thought there would be seven people coming altogether.

The closer it got to Thanksgiving the more excited I seemed to get. I still was not getting very big, and the baby was due the first of January. I was still wearing my jeans and Warren's shirts a little over a month before the due date. In my last letter from Mama, she stated they would arrive the day before Thanksgiving, on Wednesday, and would probably stay until the following Tuesday.

When I awoke on Wednesday, the day before Thanksgiving I still couldn't believe they were actually coming, but I had heard nothing to the contrary. Around 10:00 a.m. I told Warren to get up and he asked why did he have to get up so early because they probably wouldn't get here until late that afternoon. I told him I had to finish getting the house straightened up and supper finished. Warren said I was a little wound up and I had to agree that I was.

Around four o'clock the phone rang and Louise snapped, "I think we're lost." I asked where they were and she said there was a shopping center that had a sign that said "Golden Valley

Shopping Center." I told her they were only a few miles away, and we would come and meet them and to just stay put.

We drove the few miles or so to meet them. They were all very worn-out and tired to the bone after being on the road for twenty-one hours. I told them we would go home and have supper and then they could rest. Louise said, "I thought you were pregnant but you sure don't look much like it now." I told her I felt like I was.

We had such a wonderful week. The next day was Thanksgiving and Ma outdid herself on the Thanksgiving meal. There were about thirty people there because she invited some aunts and uncles besides the immediate family. It was just so great to have my family see where my life was now and to share it with me. We shopped, cooked big meals, ate out, and just enjoyed visiting.

On the third night they were there, Warren came running into the house about one o'clock in the morning and I asked him what was wrong. He said we've overheated our cabin, and he would take the box fan out and open the door for a while. He figured he had the kerosene heater on too high. I went out with him to check the cabin. Frank was still asleep but woke up when we opened the door and asked what was wrong. Morris jumped up, awakened by all the commotion. They turned the heater down and left the door cracked for the rest of the night.

The six day visit went by ever so quickly. Tuesday arrived before I was ready for our visit to end. The weather was cold, but we had very little snow for as late in the year as it was. Mama, Joan, Pat, Cheryl, Louise, Frank and Morris loaded in their car around six in the morning to head back to Tennessee. As I looked at my brothers and sisters, I realized how quickly time was going by. Pat was now fourteen years old, Joan was seventeen, Morris was twenty and Cheryl was three years old. Four years had passed.

I was sad for the next few days, but I also knew I had to prepare for the upcoming Christmas season and also for a new baby. The next few weeks Kim and I Christmas shopped. She was almost two years old but acted more like she was six. She was well-behaved, very seldom cried, and such a joy to have around. She walked beside me when I shopped and would hold on to my skirt. I loved her with all my heart.

I was very glad that I had gotten my driver's license back in the summer. It was an absolute must. I needed to take Kim to the doctor on several occasions when Warren was still at work. Warren had very little patience with me when it came to helping me learn to drive so Bruce volunteered to teach me. We lived on a dead end street so we spent hours driving back and forth learning to stop on a dime and to park. I was so excited when I passed my test on the first try, especially after Warren had to go two times to get his.

Kim celebrated her second birthday a few days after the family left, and she really enjoyed her toys and had a wonderful time. A few weeks later it was Christmas again. This was my third Christmas away from my family, and I started out being a little down and out, but before it was over, I was real upbeat about all the exciting things about to happen.

Warren worked the night shift at Northern Ordinance and I called him one night and told him he should come home early. He asked what was wrong and I told him I was bleeding and I was really scared. I had called the doctor and he said to wait awhile, and the labor pains would probably start but it still scared me. Warren said he'd see if Rollie could get a ride with someone else and would be home as soon as possible. It was about 10:00 p.m. on the twenty-ninth of December. I called Jeannette and Bruce and told them to come over and get Kim before they went to bed. I was so very grateful they lived next door.

Tammy

Warren was home before midnight, and my labor pains had started but were very irregular. The doctor had told me to come to the hospital some time after my pains started and some were around ten minutes apart. We drove into North Memorial Hospital's parking lot around 1:00 a.m. on the thirtieth of December. I called Dr. Nash again and he said he'd leave when the nurses called and told him I was close to delivery. Warren helped me settle in the labor room, and I told the nurses the pains were much harder now. They were five minutes apart and very intense. They said they would give me something to relax me, and she left Warren and me alone in the labor room. I told Warren I knew he would have to leave soon, but I really wished he could stay and hold my hand. By the time the nurse came back in, the labor was almost unbearable and she said she would get me a Valium. She brought me the shot and told Warren he would have to leave. The shot did no good at all but instead made me very sick to my stomach. I rang for the nurse and told her I was going to be sick.

For the next thirty minutes, I not only had the most intense labor possible, but I vomited continually. The nurse came back in and told me I had dilated to eight, but she didn't think Dr. Nash was there yet. She told me not to push even if I had the urge. By this time it was about 11:00 a.m. and I knew the delivery would have to be soon or I would never make it. When the nurse came back in the door, I screamed to her that I had to push. She said she'd see if the doctor was ready and ran to the delivery room. She said he was washing up and would be ready in just a few minutes, but to please don't push. I was very sick to my stomach and vomited every few minutes, all the while trying not to push when I had severe contractions. I felt as though each one would be the last I could possibly endure. I cried for Warren, but they wouldn't let him come back in so I endured it all alone.

After what seemed like an eternity, she started wheeling me into the delivery room. She said they were giving me a whiff of gas and pushed the mask over my face. I fought with all my might to get it off because I had to vomit again. I screamed loudly, and they took the mask off and I was violently sick. I decided to push as the doctor walked into the room. As he sat down on his stool, he said he saw the head and a few minutes later it was finally over. Smiling, he told me I had a beautiful, healthy, baby girl. I was so tired and drained I could hardly look at my baby. The nurse said she would bring her into you a little later and took her out to clean her up. My only thought was, *it's over, it's over.*

When they brought my baby to my room later, I was feeling some better but still totally wiped out. As Warren and I looked at her together, we thought how beautiful she was. She had lots of dark hair and was perfect in every way. She weighed seven pounds and two ounces, and was 19 ½ inches long. Warren asked if we were still going to name her Tammy Lynn, and I said that's what we agreed upon since you wouldn't go with the name "Amy." We had seen the movie "Tammy" some months before and Warren was taken with the name Tammy. "Tammy Lynn, it will be," I said softly as I drifted off to sleep.

After spending five days in the hospital away from Kim, I was really ready to go home. As we gathered up my things to leave the hospital, I told Warren I really needed the rest, but it would be good to be home. He said he had tried to clean up the house as much as he could and went on to say he knew it would be very crowded, but we'd begin remodeling in the spring. We had put Tammy's crib in Kim's small bedroom so there was very little room to turn around. Warren said we'd start getting the paperwork in order so when the ground thawed, we would dig our basement. That may be late April but I guessed Tammy will be more ready by then.

Kim was so excited about having a baby sister, she couldn't seem to keep her eyes off her. I still was not completely confident about leaving her in the same room alone for any length of time. I was afraid she might try to pick her up, thinking she was like one of her dolls. It was hard to remember sometimes that she was only two years old. I was really glad Warren was home to help for a couple of days before he had to go back to work on Monday afternoon.

The weekend went by quickly with very few problems. Tammy was very fussy, but I thought that was probably normal for a week old baby. The problem seemed to be worse right after she had her bottle. She would cry and cry and nothing seemed to help. I carried her around, patting her on the back, rocking her, just doing everything I thought would possibly help, but to no avail; she just kept crying. When Warren called on Monday to check on us, I was in tears myself. She'd cried continually for the last two hours, and I told him I was taking her to the doctor tomorrow and try to find out why she cried so much.

The next morning I called Dr. Nash to see if we could come

in and see him that day. He said he could work us in and to come on in about an hour. I fed Tammy her morning bottle just before we left and by the time we got there, she was screaming to the top of her lungs. He said he hated to tell me, but he thought I had a colicky baby.

There were several things we could try but many times they just have to outgrow it. We changed her formula, got different size nipples and I also had drops we put in her milk to soothe her tummy. He went on to say it would be a hit or miss situation for a while. He was right. We tried everything for the next few months, but nothing seemed to help. She just kept crying. She grew and seemed to be very healthy, but somehow we could not find the exact formula to stop the colic. It was usually after Warren left for work and I was at home alone with her. Sometimes she would cry from six in the evening until after midnight. I think I cried almost as much as she did. I was so tired I walked around like a zombie. I guess I was unprepared, since I had not dealt with colic in our first baby. I coped as best I could under the circumstances. Sometimes when Warren was home, I would leave the two babies with him and take off and go look for material and patterns. I still loved to sew, and my hobby was probably what kept me sane.

In mid-March, we left the kids with Jan and went to the bank to fill out papers for our loan to remodel our house. I sure hoped it went through, and Warren said he didn't see any reason why it wouldn't. He said it was going to be tough with the kids being so small, but he thought we could do it. We didn't have a time table, but I hoped it wouldn't take us over six months to finish it. Everything went well at the bank and they were optimistic we would have our money by April first. This was to be a home improvement type loan, and later we would combine the two notes and only have one payment.

Tammy was growing and developing normally. In fact, she seemed ahead of schedule on most of her development. She still had colic but she seemed to go longer periods of time without it. One Saturday morning as I was giving her a bath I told Warren that she was a beautiful child and he agreed. He went on to say that he had a feeling she's going to be an active little bugger. She wasn't quite like her sister, but Mama said all eight of us were different, and I guessed we just have to learn to treat them differently.

Remodeling Begins

On Monday, the last weekend in March of 1960, First American Bank called and told us our loan had been approved and we could sign the papers at our convenience. I told them I would call my husband at work and get back to them shortly. Barely able to contain my excitement, I called Warren at work. As soon as he came to the phone, I told him we were approved for the loan. He was so excited and wanted to know when we could sign the papers, and I told him I was supposed to call them back and set the time. We decided to go the next morning, if possible, and I called Ma to see if she could keep the girls. I then called the bank and made the appointment for the next morning.

Everything went smoothly at the bank and when we left, we had money in our checking account to begin work on our remodeling project. I asked Warren when he thought we could start, and he said he would start checking on getting someone to do the dozer work within the week. We would have to have the bedrooms torn down and everything moved around and ready before we could get them there to dig the basement. This was the part I dreaded most, being crowded with two kids into three rooms. We put the crib in our room and Adrienne's bed in the living room. Our clothes would have to be stored in the guest house, along with the rest of the furniture.

The next day we started a project that consumed our lives for the next nine months. Warren was still working nights, so he would get up around 8:00 a.m. and be ready to go to work on the house by 9:00 a.m. We would eat around 1:00 p.m. and he left before 3:00 p.m. This gave us about a half-day to spend on building our dream. We spent about four months getting it framed up and ready to close up the doors and windows. The girls were good, most of the time. Ma and Dad came out almost every day to help. Ma watched the kids and I helped right along with Warren and

My Place In Time

Dad. I helped nail shingles on the roof, sheetrock on the walls and painted most of the inside walls and woodwork. We also put down hardwood floors that would have been the envy of the whole neighborhood. One Saturday morning I asked Warren if we were ever going to finish the house. I was so tired. He tried to encourage me and said we would and just look at what we would have. We always got more done on weekends, since we could work as late as we wanted.

Trap Door

One Monday, I stopped to fix lunch about 12:30 p.m. Tammy was in her Butler, a child's chair with a table around it, waiting for her lunch. Ma was busy with some other chore, so I stopped to heat her baby food. "Are you hungry, sweetie?" and she looked up and stopped crying as I started feeding her. I told Ma she certainly had a good appetite today, and she never seemed to know when she was full. Ma said she was just healthy and said both of her boys were chubby, but they usually grew out of it when they started walking. I finished feeding Tammy her lunch and put her in her walker so she could explore while we finished eating our lunch.

About that time Warren and Dad came up from the basement. We had a trap door but the steps had not been built yet. They walked over to wash up for lunch and left the trap door open. The next thing I heard was a loud scream. "Warren, where's Tammy?" I screamed at the top of my lungs. I didn't give him time to answer but ran from the stove to the trap door. My worst fears were recognized. There she lay on the dirt floor of our basement - walker and all. In a flash, Warren's dad was down in the basement handing her back to Warren. I asked if she was all right, and Warren said that nothing seemed to be broken. She had several small bruises but nothing major.

Later as we were eating lunch Ma said the walker probably protected her. I asked Warren if we should take her in to the doctor and he said we'd just wait a bit and see how she was. An hour or so later, she still seemed to be fine, so the consensus was that she was all right. I was grateful and vowed to watch her a lot closer. She was only about six months old, but she could move in her walker like she was two. This was the beginning of an accident-prone child. No matter how closely I watched her, she seemed to always be getting hurt.

We continued to work on our house every spare minute for the next few months. Meanwhile, Adrienne and Tammy were growing into two adorable toddlers. Tammy went from her walker straight to walking, skipping the crawling stage completely.

As we were having a coffee break one Sunday afternoon I yelled for everyone to look at Tammy. Warren came running from the other room and we all stood and stared. She was actually walking by herself and she was only nine months old. Warren's dad had started calling her his "Dennis the Menace." I kept saying I couldn't believe she was walking.

Finished Remodeling

Ma and I finished our drapes just before Thanksgiving,

My Place In Time

1960. We got our drapes up on our huge picture window, brought our furniture in from the guest house, and just stood and admired our handiwork for the longest time. I simply could not believe we were almost through. I looked around and took in all that we had accomplished in the past eight months. There were still several odds and ends to complete, but Warren said we could do them as we could afford to and to look at all the room we had.

As I looked around it was hard to believe we had done all this ourselves. Our old living room was now Warren's and my bedroom and the kitchen was the girls' room. We had another bedroom but decided to use it as a den for the time being. We would get a hide-a-bed as soon as we could find one we could afford through the paper. It was so great to really begin to enjoy our newly remodeled home and to have room for the kids to play. Our den was paneled and had a huge walk-in closet. I told the girls there was no excuse to have toys all over the floor so we put their toy box in the corner of the closet. It was an old white trunk with animals painted all over it. It was quite cute, even if we had picked it up at a garage sale.

Plymouth Fire Department

Warren had been discussing joining the Plymouth Volunteer Fire Department for some time. Now that the house was livable and we had more time, he said he thought he would join up the following week. Rollie said they were a great bunch of guys and I might like to join the ladies auxiliary. I had talked to Jan about the women's group because she had been a couple of times since Bruce joined. She said they had a good time and did lots of things together. I agreed it would be all right, since they said it would take very little of their time, and, besides, they got paid a set fee for each fire they attended.

I was so glad Bruce and Jan had moved next door to us. We were the only two houses on a cove. About six months after we moved, they bought the lot next door, thinking they might remodel the cabin that was there. They later decided to buy a house that had to be moved, and moved it on to their lot. They put a full basement and completely remodeled the whole house. We stripped wallpaper and worked for months, before they actually moved in. David and Dawn were a little older than Kim and Tammy, but they loved to play together.

One Monday night after Warren got home, I told him we were invited to a picnic at Don and Gladie Otness's on Saturday night. I usually waited up for Warren even though sometimes it was 1:00 a.m. when he got home. Rollie, the guy he rode with, would sometimes stop and have coffee. I remember many times putting a frozen pie or other treat in the oven for when they got in. We later met his wife, Marcie, through the fire department get-togethers.

We went to the picnic at Don and Gladie's and began a long and fruitful friendship with them as well as many other couples. We met Carol and Butch Evenson, a young couple that had just joined the fire department. They were five or six years younger than we were, but the Otnesses were at least that much older. We had couples of various ages but we all got to be very good friends. I was very excited about having friends and a social life with other people than just family. In Nashville we had gotten together and played cards with friends almost every weekend and I had really missed that. I had tried very hard to make friends with neighbors and such, but I learned very quickly that people up north are not as quick to accept you and be your friend as they are down south.

The women's auxiliary was planning a Christmas party the early part of December and it should be a lot of fun. "Carl and Doris Rosaland have a daughter around fourteen years old and maybe we could use her as a babysitter," I said and Warren agreed that sounded like a good idea. Most of the time we took the girls with us everywhere we went. Virgina Rosaland become our steady baby sitter from that time on.

The Christmas party was a great success and became an annual affair. We had such a great Christmas, having our house finished, and the girls being old enough to really enjoy their toys. I believe it was the best Christmas since we'd been in Minneapolis.

One day when Carol stopped over for coffee, I said, "Let's start a dinner club."

She said, "We could go to the places in our coupon book that have the buy one and get one free." The books had been sold for a fund raiser for the Fire Department, so just about all the guys had one.

I asked her how many couples should we ask. If we went back to the homes for dessert afterwards, we could play cards or other games, but we would probably have to limit it to about four couples. She said we could ask Don and Gladie and maybe Carl and Doris. We discussed how often should we go and we both agreed upon once a month. We got it all set up and started our dinner club the following week. We had such fun together and continued to meet and developed friendships that were to last well into the future.

1961 came in with everything calm and peaceful. We were still enjoying our house and Warren was having fun being on the Fire Department. Bruce had joined the Plymouth Police Department full time. He stayed on the Fire Department for a while but eventually had to give it up because the demands of the Police Department were too great.

Hot Coffee

The girls were growing and developing their own personalities. Adrienne was a quiet, independent, loving child. Tammy, on the other hand, was always striving for attention. One Sunday afternoon Ma and Dad stopped over and I put on the coffee pot and, as usual, everyone gathered around the kitchen table. Tammy was sitting in her Butler, having milk and cookies. Somehow it was too close to Dad's hot cup of coffee. The next thing we knew, she had reached over and grabbed his cup and spilled it all over her chest and legs. Warren yelled to get her out and cover her up and Ma said to let her rub butter on it. She rubbed her down with butter and I covered her in a blanket and we took off for the emergency room. The doctor said he thought she'd be all right in a few days, and she didn't seem to have any third degree burns. He gave us medication and told us to put ice on her. Dad was so upset that it was his coffee she spilled. It wasn't your fault, I told him over and over. I shouldn't have had her Butler so close to the table.

Pat's Visit

Joan had graduated from high school and started working at the shirt factory in Parsons. Louise and I had helped to pay for several remodeling projects for Mama and Daddy before I got married. Now Joan decided to help them pay for adding on a new living room and a new bathroom and they had also gotten a telephone installed. It was nice to be able to call, but many times you could not get through since it was a party line.

One Saturday late in April, Warren yelled for me to answer the phone and when I answered, it was Pat. I asked her if anything was wrong and she said no and that she had been thinking about what I said to her about coming to visit me when school was out. She said she would be out the tenth of May, and she could stay until we came back to Tennessee the first week in July. I told her that would be wonderful and we'd try to get her a job as a waitress and she could work for about six weeks to save money to buy her clothes for fall. Pat was now sixteen years old and would be a junior in high school in the fall. She said she'd probably come on the train unless she got a ride to Chicago with one of our cousins that worked there. Before we hung up the phone, I told her it was going to be such fun.

Warren talked to one of his buddies on the fire department about Pat getting a job at a little restaurant next door to a hardware store they owned. She was all set to go to work a few days after she arrived. She rode up to Chicago with our cousin and spent the night with them. It was a bad experience from the time she got there because it was a bad neighborhood and she was quite scared most of the time.

"Hurry up or the train will be in before we get there!" I yelled for the third time. Warren said he was getting Tammy's jacket on and told me not to get so excited. Adrienne and Tammy were just about as excited as I was. "We've never had someone visit for that long," Adrienne commented. "It'll be fun, having her sleep in the den. She'll probably play toys with us all the time," Adrienne said.

The train was late as usual and it pulled into Milwaukee Station over an hour late. "I'm so glad you're here," I said as I ran to meet her.

"I'm glad to be here," she responded. "I've had quite a trip. I'm sure glad I'll be going home with you and Warren."

We heard all the details on our ride back to Medicine Lake Drive. The girls were both up a couple of hours past their bedtimes so they said goodnight and went to bed almost immediately after we got to the house.

Warren, Pat and I sat in the kitchen, drinking coffee and eating snacks until Pat said she simply had to go to bed. "We've got a long time to catch up," I added happily.

We took her on a tour around Plymouth Village, the next day; we also showed her the restaurant, where she would be working on Monday. Adrienne and Tammy hung on to every word she said. She spent time playing games or watching T. V. with them and, of course, they were happy with that.

The time went by very quickly. Pat made good money for the six weeks she worked and she also made very good tips. Everyone loved her southern accent and they kidded her a lot, but they also tipped her well. "You've bought some beautiful clothes," I told her one night as we were packing to go to Tennessee.

The plant where Warren worked was always closed the first two weeks in July so this was always our vacation.

"I wish I could have saved more money, but I guess I did all right," she concluded. "I think you did great, and the kids and I loved having you up here. Maybe you can do it again before you graduate and go away to college?" I added.

When we got to Tennessee, everyone was as glad to see Pat, as they were us. Joan had missed her terribly. "Hasn't Cheryl gotten to be a big girl?" I asked.

"She's four years old and will be five her next birthday," Mama added.

Times seems to fly by, we concluded. Dan and Sam were

also growing up. Dan was ten and Sam was thirteen years old. Daddy taught them both to hunt at an early age, so they were always out squirrel hunting. Morris was now twenty-three and a man about town with his own car and lots of girlfriends.

Routines

After we got back to Minneapolis, everything was depressing. Warren went back to working nights and seemed to be gone most of his days doing something with the Fire Department. Bruce gave up the fire department and joined the Plymouth Police Department full time. It seemed every time you turned around Warren had taken on another job. He taught first aid classes and was also involved in civil defense.

When he came in one day and said he and Carl Rosaland were going to be doing fire inspections, I just about hit the ceiling. "Don't you want to spend time with us"? I cried. He made excuses and I pouted. We never seemed to see each other except sometimes on weekends. We bought a tent and took up camping. Several couples from the fire department camped together. We had a lot of fun, but it was no substitute for spending time as a family.

Train Ride

We were in this routine in the fall of 1961, when I got a phone call from Louise. "Mama's going into the hospital to have lumps removed from her breast" she said crying.

"Does the doctor think they are cancer?" I asked.

"He won't know until they operate," she continued. "You need to come if you possibly can," she went on.

"I know Warren can't get off work, but I might could bring the girls on the train," I reasoned. "I'll call you back after I talk to Warren," I told her before I hung up.

After Warren got home, we discussed it at length. The biggest problem, as always, was where we would get the money. "We have enough for tickets in our savings and you could mail me some spending money after we get there, or else I could write a check later."

"Do you think you can handle the girls by yourself?" he asked. "That's a long trip, and you would have to change trains in Chicago."

"I think I would even have to change train stations," I added. Pat said you have to catch a shuttle bus to a different station". "I could do it, I'm sure," I concluded.

I called Louise the next morning and told her I would come. She said she would get someone to meet me in Nashville. I also arranged for the tickets to be picked up the following morning. It cost less than I figured. Adrienne was half-price and Tammy could go for free. I was sure I would be fine with Adrienne, but Tammy was less than two years old and a real handful. I would ship most of my luggage and if I had to, at certain times I could carry Tammy. I tried not to worry about it. When you are young, you tackle things you would not dream of doing when you get older.

We left the following Saturday, two days from the time I'd started thinking about going. "I'm sure going to miss you," Warren commented on the way to the station.

"I'll miss you, too, but I'm sure you'll be so busy you'll hardly know I'm gone."

We left Minneapolis about noon on Wednesday, the first part of October, and we were scheduled to arrive in Nashville around noon on Thursday. I knew I had a long twenty-four hours ahead. We were in coach but were fairly close to the club car and the scenic car upstairs. We spent some time enjoying the scenery from the dome car upstairs. The girls bored easily so there was a lot of time spent going to bathrooms, etc. I brought a sack lunch, but we ate dinner in the Diners' car.

"Tammy, please don't spill anything," I said for the third time as the porter seated us next to a window. A small vibration occurred just as the porter placed our drinks on the table and the next thing we knew, Coke and water were all over the table.

"That wasn't our fault! both girls piped in at the same time.

"I know it wasn't, but let's just let them clean it up," I agreed.

We ordered sandwiches and french fries. "Do you want a bag?" the waiter asked, since neither girl had finished her supper. I told him that would be great since they would probably get hungry before they went to sleep. I still had some snacks in my bag but knew I would need all I could get before I got there. The seats reclined, and we were very fortunate to have extra seats so they could stretch out.

By 11:00 p.m. they were both asleep. I read for several hours before dozing a few minutes before daybreak.

Mommie, Mommie, when will we be there? was asked over and over. We went back to the diner car to get cereal for breakfast somewhere around 6:00 a.m. I knew we had to eat early before our stop in Chicago. From the beginning I had been dreading this part of the trip. I was not afraid to ask questions, so everything went much better than I had dreamed possible. I carried my bags over my shoulder with Tammy in the same arm and held Adrienne's hand with the other.

"Mommie, please let me walk," Tammy kept crying over and over. I finally gave in and told her to not let go of my hand for any reason. We were just getting ready to load the train when she broke loose from my hand and started running toward the stairs that went several floors down to the trains below.

"Tammy, Tammy!" I screamed, to the top of my lungs. "Stop, stop!" I was dragging Adrienne as fast as I could, but I couldn't seem to catch her. She was within ten feet of the stairs when I noticed a man running towards her. He grabbed her just before she reached the first step. In another few seconds, she would have fallen down thirty feet of steps and been killed for sure. I was shaking and crying so hard I couldn't speak when we reached them. The man was holding her in his arms, talking calmly to her. "Oh, thank you, thank you!" I cried.

"Can I put her on the train for you? he asked. "You seem to have your hands full," he continued.

"Oh, that would be wonderful," I replied.

In a few minutes this stranger had safely deposited my child beside me on the train headed for Nashville. I said, "Thank you, again."

"You are more than welcome," he answered as he turned and walked away.

I looked out the window to watch him go up the stairs but he had totally disappeared. I never saw him again. As I reflected over the incident, especially after I became a Christian, I knew without a doubt, that he was an angel that protected my child.

We were met in Nashville by my aunt and uncle, J. C. and Dorothy. Louise was also with them. "How's Mama, and when is she having surgery?"

"She's going in to the hospital in Jackson tomorrow, but her surgery isn't until the next day."

"I'm so glad you got to come," Louise continued.

"I am too," I answered, "but it wasn't a very fun trip." I proceeded to tell them about the near accident with Tammy.

We had an uneventful trip on the ride from Nashville. The family was waiting and very excited we were there. Mama was quite worried about the upcoming surgery but still very happy about seeing us. We left the kids with an aunt and went to Jackson with Mama the following day. Louise and I stayed with her, even though she would have been fine the night before her surgery. We were all terrified the doctor would tell her he had found cancer. But to the contrary, everything was benign. With such good news we proceeded to enjoy our vacation. I called Warren a few times, but most of the time I sat down at night to write letters.

We decided to stay an extra week since we got to come so seldom. Everyone was happy, except Warren. His letters were much longer than mine and I could tell he missed us very much. The two weeks ended quickly, the train trip back went smoothly and now we were stepping off the train in Minneapolis.

"Look, Mommie, there's Daddy," Adrienne yelled. I looked and there he was, looking so happy and excited. I suddenly realized how much I had missed him.

"I don't think I'll ever let you go without me again," he said as we were driving home. "I have a surprise for you, when we get home."

Even before we went inside, he took me out back to show me his handiwork while I was gone. He had installed clothes poles in the back yard. I was really excited.

"You know I've wanted these for a long time," I said.

"These should last, not like the others we've had."

"Mommie, can I be an angel for Halloween?" Adrienne asked the next morning.

"I want to be a witch," Tammy put in.

"We've got a couple of weeks before that time, so just be patient."

Bruce's Accident

We bought costumes and took the kids to Ma's to go trick or treating. The houses were much closer together there so they only had to walk a few blocks before their bags were full. Jan always took David and Dawn with us. The kids had a great time with their candy at Ma's before we left around 10:00 p.m. Warren was still working nights and Bruce was also on duty with the police department. I had no trouble getting the girls to bed after we got home. They were totally wiped out.

I was lying on the couch watching a movie when Warren opened the door. "You're late," I called to him as he came in the back door. "I thought you were going to quit stopping for coffee."

"I didn't stop for coffee. Rollie decided to drive a different way tonight, and we came through Golden Valley and chanced upon a terrible accident." I could tell he was about to cry. "It was Bruce, and the guy with him was killed. They've taken him to the hospital and they're not sure if he's going to make it or not."

I started to cry and asked if anyone had told Jeanette.

"One of the officers came over a little while ago and they took her to the hospital, but we need to go and be with her."

"I'll call Ma and Dad," I answered.

After finding someone to stay with the girls, we took off for the hospital. We found Jan in the waiting room, completely distraught. "Have they told you anything yet?" Warren asked.

"They said it was too soon to tell and they would get back with us later."

It was a long night. We waited, hoping and praying he was

going to live.

Sometime around 6:00 a.m. the doctor came in and said, "I think he may make it. He's broken all over his body, but he's strong and young. The nurse will take you up to see him in a few minutes," he continued.

We were not prepared for how badly he would look. His face was swollen double and most of it was black and blue. He could barely open one eye, but he seemed to be conscious. After talking to the doctor again, we found out one leg was completely crushed, along with a broken pelvis and several other broken bones. "He'll be in traction for several months, but we're hopeful he will walk again," he assured us.

The next few months were very difficult for Bruce and Jan. She took off work as much as possible to be with him but could not stay with him as much as he wanted. Ma and I baby sat the kids continually so she could go to the hospital directly after work. The nurses usually ordered her a tray at night so she could eat with him.

One leg was in traction, so he was very uncomfortable. His emotional state got pretty bad a couple of times, mainly because he could not remember anything about the accident.

Thanksgiving was quite unusual that year. We all went to the hospital to try to cheer Bruce up. "Do the doctors think he'll get to go home by Christmas"? I asked Jan.

"I think so, but he doesn't know that," she added.

I knew I would not get to go to Tennessee for Christmas, but I never dreamed we would have such a depressing one. They told Bruce he would still be in the hospital. We all tried to be cheerful, but it was a hard time on everyone.

After opening our presents on Christmas Eve, we all went to the hospital and took presents for Bruce. He tried to be upbeat, but everyone could tell he was depressed. I had my hands full the first part of 1962. Jan was still working, trying to make ends meet, so we tried to help out all we could by babysitting when necessary.

Bruce continued to improve, but it was very slow-going. He had to undergo numerous operations on his leg. They would remove bone from other parts of his body and do grafting on the leg that was crushed. Everyone tried very hard to keep him cheered up, but after months in the hospital he was emotionally drained.

More Remodeling

Warren had also started working on our kitchen again. We had desperately wanted new birch cabinets before but had decided we just could not afford them at the time. Now we really wanted to finish the things we did not do before. "I'm so glad Sears had a big cabinet sale," I said to Warren, while he was working one Saturday.

"The copper tile between them looks great," he agreed. "Now all we need to get is that wagon wheel light we looked at to go over our table." I agreed that would be the finishing touch.

I wallpapered one wall, made new kitchen curtains and did all sorts of decorating, but there was still something missing. "It's the light fixture, " Warren commented. "We simply must buy that copper wagon wheel light." I agreed that maybe we could afford it.

On Saturday, Warren finished installing the light. "I think we have the most beautiful kitchen in the world."

"It really shows off my copper collection."

"You would think that," Warren laughed.

"Honey, I think we should get carpet for the living room," I announced one morning.

"You've got to be kidding," he answered. "We spent a fortune on hardwood floors and now you want to cover them up."

"We won't tack it down, just let it come to about a foot from the edge so the wood will still show."

"Let me think about it", he answered. I knew he did not like a cold floor, so I figured he would agree. The following day, Warren announced he was ready to look for a rug for the living room, and we spent the day looking at carpet and rugs, trying to get a bargain. We finally found just the color we wanted at a good price. We decided to pick it up ourselves the next day and save delivery charges. Warren borrowed a pickup truck from a buddy and was up bright and early the next morning to go down and pick up our carpet.

"I'll stay here with the kids and have everything ready to put it down when you get back," I commented.

Dad

He was back in a couple of hours ready to get started. "I guess we'll just try to move the furniture into the kitchen," he said.

"We sure can't put it out in the snow," I answered.

"Get the phone!" he yelled, just as we moved the last piece of furniture into the kitchen. I jumped over the couch to get the phone.

"No, that's impossible!" I screamed.

"What is it?" Warren wanted to know.

"Dad just had a cerebral hemorrhage and they say it's very bad. They said for us to come to the hospital as soon as possible."

"Get the kids ready while I get this rug laid so we can at least walk."

"Do you think it's really serious?'" I asked.

"I hope not, but he's been having bad headaches lately and his blood pressure has been running very high. He was supposed to go into the hospital last week to get it down, Ma said."

"I know; she said he wouldn't go because one of the other employees was on vacation, and he thought they couldn't do without him."

We had just finished moving the couch out of the doorway when the phone rang again. This time Warren answered it and he just stood there, white as a ghost, saying nothing.

"Who is it?" I kept asking.

He finally handed me the phone. Ma was crying on the other end. "He's gone, she said. "They just called back and said he had died."

We found out later that he had died immediately, but they thought the shock would be too much for Ma so they hoped to soften the blow by not telling her the first time.

Opal Phillips Johnson

It was Thursday, February 15, 1962, and one of the saddest days of my life. It seemed impossible he was at our house just two days before, helping Warren with something. He had been as good to me for the past six years as if I had been his own daughter. I loved him with all my heart. My own dad had never been very open with us when we were growing up. I knew he loved us, and he was a good provider, but he never talked to us. I guess he felt that was Mama's job.

Warren's dad had made me feel very special and he seemed very happy that I had married Warren. I simply could not conceive that he was gone. I had never experienced death this close to home before. I cried all the way over to Ma's. Adrienne and Tammy could not understand what was going on. I tried to explain as best I could, but to a three-year-old, it was really an impossible task. Adrienne was five and could understand a little better,

"Are you all right?" I kept asking Warren. He was very stoic and looked like he was in shock.

"I'm fine," he kept assuring me.

Marlene, Scott and her two kids were already there when we got there. Jan, David and Dawn drove up shortly. "What are we going to do about Bruce?" Jan asked, crying.

"Maybe they will let him come to the funeral," I answered.

"Speaking of a funeral, we have to make a lot of arrangements," Warren added.

The rest of the day, Warren spent making arrangements and calling relatives. I knew he was hurting, but I know he felt this was the last thing he could do for his dad. We went home sometime after midnight to try to get some rest. I remember dozing off, but sometime later I awoke to the most heart-wrenching sounds I had ever heard. Warren was sobbing his heart out. He had not cried all day. He felt he had to be strong for his mom and for everyone else, but now he had finally been able to vent his emotions. I tried very hard to comfort him, but at the time neither of us really knew the Lord. I know now that only God can give real comfort.

The doctors kept insisting that Bruce could not go to the funeral but to no avail. He simply said he was going. His leg was still in traction after three months in the hospital. They finally agreed he could be taken on a stretcher but just to the service and not to the funeral home. I don't think there was a dry eye in the room when they brought him in to see his dad for the last time. It was very hard and made his depression much worse. It would be another month before he was able to go home in a wheelchair to finish his recuperation.

The next few months were very difficult, especially for Ma. She was only fifty-six years old. The house was paid for but there was no money for her to live on. She sold their car and proceeded to look for a job.

Several months later she found a job working in a toy factory. I really admired her for her strong will and perseverance. She worked for six years until she could draw social security. She also started taking painting classes. She enjoyed it very much and was quite good at it.

Morris and Janice

One day in mid-April, we got a phone call from Mama. "You'll never believe who got married?" she said.

"I have no idea," I answered.

"Morris. He got married on the seventh to Janice Houston."

"I knew they were serious, but I didn't think they would get married right away."

"She's a very nice girl and I think everybody will really like her."

"She's a little younger than Morris."

I knew Morris would be twenty-four in June and I guessed Janice would be eighteen or nineteen. "I can't wait to meet her; maybe we can come home for Christmas this year."

"I know everyone would enjoy that," she concluded.

"You are still coming in July?" she wanted to know.

"I'm sure we will." Warren and I have been discussing going to the Smoky Mountains for a few days while we are there." "Maybe Pat and Dan could go with us and you could keep Adrienne and Tammy for a few days?" I added hopefully.

We had a tent and went camping almost every weekend with friends from the fire department. We had decided to pull a trailer and bring our camping supplies and go camping in the mountains. It sounded like quite an adventure.

Smoky Mountains

Our July vacation seemed to arrive quickly, since we stayed so busy most of the time. "Are you sure this trailer is safe?" I asked Warren for the third time.

"It's really secured," he assured me. He had built the complete trailer with a back that dropped down and could be used as a table. We had a camp stove, large cooler, lanterns, sleeping bags and, of course, loads of food.

"Are we still going to stop and cook breakfast on the way down?" I asked.

"If we can find a park with picnic tables, it would be a break for the girls."

"I'm so glad Mama agreed to keep Adrienne and Tammy so we can have our mountain camping trip."

"I think they will enjoy staying home and playing with Cheryl more."

We left after Warren got home from work as usual. Adrienne and Tammy slept most of the night after they got over some of their excitement. We located a small park with picnic tables sometime around 7:00 a.m. "This looks great" I said as we all piled out.

"Let the kids play while you cook the bacon and eggs, and I'll stretch out and snooze for a bit," Warren said as he got the stove going.

Everything seemed to be going smooth until the wind came up. I had bacon in the skillet and was trying to get paper plates on the table. All of a sudden everything started blowing all over. "Warren, Warren, wake up and help me!" I screamed. My plates and pans were blowing all around, and the fire had gone out under the bacon. We finally collected all our belongings, loaded everything back in the trailer, and decided to stop at a restaurant to eat breakfast. The girls liked that idea better anyway.

About mid-morning, we were someplace in southern Illinois, when we heard a terrible noise in the back. "What's that?" I yelled. Warren didn't have to answer because when we looked through the rearview mirror, we saw our trailer about fifty feet behind us.

"Oh no!" Warren screamed. "We've lost our trailer."

We were on a two-lane road so we were able to turn around, go back and pull the trailer to the side of the road. Something in the hitch had broken and would have to be welded back together. "The only thing we can do is for you and the girls to stay with the trailer and I'll go back into the last town we went through and get it welded," he commented. I didn't like the idea but I didn't have a better one.

"I'll bet it's twenty-five or thirty miles back into town," I sobbed.

"It's all we can do," he said as he got into the car. I knew it would probably take him an hour just for the drive, and I had no idea how long it would take to get the part repaired.

"Let me get some of their toys," I said before he drove away. The kids were only five and three so I knew I was in for a fun time.

We played guessing games and all the other games I could think of. I also read their books at least three times. Several times I got very scared when cars looked like they were going to stop. Some did ask if they could help. A couple of cars with only guys really had me terrified. They would almost stop, whistle and make flirty remarks. This was another time I know, without a shadow of a doubt, that God protected us.

"I see Daddy!" Tammy yelled to the top of her lungs.

"It could be," I agreed. We all agreed he had been gone long enough. We were tired and getting very sunburned.

"It is Daddy!" Adrienne screamed as he drove over to the side near our trailer.

"Do you know we have been here for over three hours?" I asked. "The girls are hungry, I'm tired, and we're all sunburned," I cried.

"I got back as fast as I could," he snapped as he started

hooking the trailer up.

We were on our way in a short while. I was very glad to be out of the sun, and the girls were especially happy to get snacks to tide them over until we could find a place to stop for lunch. Mama was getting quite worried by the time we drove into their driveway around 11:00 p.m. We had been on the road for about twenty-three hours. Normally we drove it in seventeen or eighteen. After explaining our ordeal and unpacking enough of our belongings for the night, we hit the bed, all of us bone-tired.

I awoke once again to that wonderful smell of country ham frying. I jumped out of bed and headed to the kitchen for a cup of coffee. Mama was busy putting a huge pan of biscuits in the oven. "I thought you would sleep a little later," she said.

"The smell got to me," I said, grabbing a piece of ham.

"When are you going to the mountains?" she asked.

"I think we decided to leave on Thursday and come back on Sunday."

"Are Pat and Dan still going?" I asked.

"Dan has talked of nothing else for the past week and Pat says she's looking forward to it too. I tried to talk Sam into going, but he just doesn't seem interested," she added.

"I guess when you get almost sixteen, you've got better things to do."

"If Joan didn't have to work, she would love to go, too, but she doesn't have enough vacation."

In a few minutes the commotion began. Everyone was up and gathered around the big kitchen table for one of Mama's big country breakfasts. It seemed really odd without Morris being there. I asked Mama where they were living. "They have an apartment in Scotts Hill for the time being."

Pat and Joan had just gotten up and seated themselves at the table. Joan commented that Morris would probably start building a house in a few months. Louise and Frank had already built one across the road and Morris was building his fairly close to theirs.

Pat would be a senior in high school in the fall, and Joan was now working at the shirt factory in Parsons. Dan and Cheryl were the only ones that had not changed very much. Dan was eleven and Cheryl was now six years old. Pat also had a summer job but was able to get off a few days for our vacation.

Neither of us had ever been to the Smoky Mountains and were very excited about going. We left bright and early on Thursday for our four-day outing. I had cautioned the girls several times to be good and mind their grandmother. The one I was most concerned about was Tammy, She seemed to have more energy than she could contain. Mama assured me she could handle her. "I've managed eight over the years and I should be able to make it four days with your little three-year-old."

"You make her mind even if you have to spank her."

"I will, even if it is just to get the bluff on her," she concluded.

I was a little concerned about something else happening to our trailer but Warren assured me it would be fine now.

Our first obstacle came when we got to the campgrounds, and all the camping sites in the Smokeys were filled up. They said we could have a space the following night, but Thursday night was completely booked. "There's a campground across the mountains in Cherokee, North Carolina," the ranger told us.

"I guess we have no choice but to go," Warren answered.

We had been driving for eight hours already and were all worn to a frazzle. We planned on cooking instead of eating out all the time, but I knew it would be quite late by the time we set up camp and cooked supper.

"Are you hungry?" I asked Dan. He admitted he really was. "Why don't we have a snack before we drive across the mountain?" We dug out some food and ate our snack at a beautiful spot beside a brook deep in the mountains.

We drove for about two more hours before we got to the campgrounds in North Carolina. They had an opening and we were very glad to settle in for the night. It was a beautiful spot, right beside a bubbling brook, with mountains in the background.

I fixed our supper while Warren, Dan and Pat set the tent up for the night. "It's ready!" I yelled just as they put the last stakes down. Everything tasted wonderful. We were all so tired we snuggled in our sleeping bags and were sound asleep by 10:30 p.m.

We had been asleep about two hours when someone let

out a loud scream, followed by a round of profanity. "What in the world is that"? Warren said as he shot out of his sleeping bag.

We all jumped up to see what the commotion was all about. By this time, several other people were standing outside their tents and camp trailers. Whoever it was continued screaming and cursing as he strolled up and down the park. "We should get the manager," one of the men announced. A couple more agreed and they walked over to the office to report what was going on.

The manager drove around later explaining to everyone that this was an Indian from a nearby reservation. He said they frequently got too much to drink and ended up disturbing the peace in his campground. He told us everything was under control, and the culprit had been taken into custody by the police.

It took us a while to get back to sleep, but we were so tired, nothing could have kept us awake.

"What time are we going back over the mountain"? I asked Warren while Pat and I were fixing breakfast. "Let's do some sightseeing here before we leave. There seems to be some unique shops back in town."

We finished everything early and started our sightseeing adventure. Many of the shops had Indian chiefs dressed in native attire, standing beside the doors taking pictures with the customers.

"Let's take your picture," Warren said to Dan. He finally agreed and Warren took his picture standing beside this tall Cherokee Indian chief This picture became a treasure for Dan for many years.

When we got back to the Smoky Mountain National Park Campground, they had an opening and we set up camp for our second night. We did a lot of walking, sightseeing and taking pictures. We were always on the lookout for bears along the roadway.

Late in the afternoon, we were on our way back to camp when Pat yelled at Warren. "Look, look! There's a couple of cubs right beside the road." We stopped, Warren grabbed his camera and took off to get their picture. He ventured out several hundred yards from the car, when all of a sudden, the cubs climbed a small tree. We all heard a noise in the distance when a huge grizzly bear came into view. We all started screaming to Warren to the top our lungs. "Run, Warren, run!"

I had the door open when he got to the car a few seconds later. He started the car as quickly as possible. When we looked out the rear-view mirror, the bear was standing beside the road looking toward the car. We learned a valuable lesson that day: don't take pictures of bear cubs because their mother is usually very close. The park ranger did a talk, before we checked in, about keeping food away from our tent. He said the bears would rip your tent open to get the food.

Our second and third nights were uneventful. We never dreamed the weather would be so cold in July. We slept in our clothes and snuggled in sleeping bags but were still quite cold. The ranger told us the next day the temperature had gotten down to the low forties during the night. "Look, Warren," Dan said, the last morning, "there are tracks around our campfire."

"I guess bears were out looking for food during the night," Warren agreed.

"I'm sure glad they stayed away from our tent," Pat added.

We left early Sunday morning for our trip back to Mt. Carmel. I had missed my girls, but we all agreed it was a great fun time. "Maybe, we can do it again sometime," Dan said just before we got back to Mama's. We all agreed.

Mama was glad to see us. I'm sure she was worn-out from having three little girls, fighting and squabbling for four days. "How were the girls?" I asked.

"They got along good," she said with a smile.

"Come on; tell us what happened," Warren added. She made us promise we would not spank again before she would tell us what happened.

Tammy was quite a strong-willed little girl and didn't understand in the beginning that Grandma would spank if she did not mind. "She started jumping off the high end of the porch. I told her she would get hurt but she just kept on. After about four times, I told her I was going to spank her if she didn't stop. This did no good and I had to give her a little spanking, but after that she has minded every word I've told her." They were glad to see us but, of course, not ready to go home.

We left on Saturday to go back to Minneapolis. This time I was not quite so sad, because I knew we were planning on coming back for Christmas. I settled back into a routine of sewing and being a normal homemaker for the next few months. It was the first time things almost seemed normal: we had finished our house, the girls were growing like weeds, and I had time for myself. I loved to sew; I made all my clothes and most of the girls. I always sewed in the afternoon and after I got Adrienne and Tammy to bed at night.

Ruth and Little Debbie

My routine changed in the early fall when Warren's aunt and uncle that lived next door sold their house to a couple with two kids. Ruth, the new neighbor, was very nice and she and I got to be friends right away. She had a daughter, Debbie, who was about a year younger than Tammy. We started having coffee together almost every afternoon after Warren left for work. She worked nights at Munsingwear, the same place Warren's dad had worked before he died. The girls seemed to play together quite well, or at least we thought so.

One day we heard a scream. We ran to the room where they were playing to find little Debbie holding her arm. "What's wrong, honey?" we both asked. She wouldn't answer, but when we looked, we saw a huge bite mark.

"Did you do that?" I immediately asked Tammy. She started to cry but wouldn't deny it.

"She wouldn't give me the doll, and I had it first," she sobbed.

I took them home and gave Tammy a good spanking and I tried to explain to her that you should not bite to get your own way. This began a long period of dealing with a real biting problem.

Little Debbie did not complain very much to her mother so we had no idea how bad the problem had gotten until one day, Ruth pulled her arms up and showed me all the bite marks that had accumulated over the past few weeks. "I guess we'll just have to keep them separated," she concluded. I agreed with her and there were no hard feelings between us; we just knew there was a problem. I knew I was the one that had to deal with her. For some reason, she was not biting Kim as much, maybe because Kim was older and wouldn't stand for it.

However, one day she did bite Kim very badly on the leg. I spanked her and did what my mother had told me to do: I bit her on the arm. I did it just enough to hurt, but not enough to make a mark. "Do you see how it feels to other people when you bite?" I asked. It worked and the biting stopped and Ruth and I started having coffee together again.

One afternoon Warren had just left for work when someone knocked at the door. "I'll get it!" Kim yelled. "Mommie, Mommie, someone wants you."

Kevin, Ruth's teenage son, was at the door. "Can you come over?" he asked. "My mom is very sick."

I grabbed the girls and went with him immediately. "Stay outside and play," I told them when we got there. I could hear Ruth moaning and groaning as I approached the bedroom. I followed a trail of blood from the hallway to the bedroom. "Oh, Ruth, what's wrong?" I asked. "I think I'm having a miscarriage. I was going to tell you in a few weeks. I found out I was pregnant about a week ago. I was between three and four months."

"You've lost a lot of blood," I said as I started picking up towels that were soaked in blood. "I need to call Johnny and get you to a hospital," I added. She gave me the number where Johnny worked. After I reached him, I tried to keep her calm and keep the kids out.

He was home in a very short while, and we called the doctor who agreed to meet her at the hospital. I took the kids to my house until Johnny came home later that night. "They are keeping her overnight," he said. "They said she had lost so much blood, they would probably have to give her a couple of units."

"I'm just glad she's going to be all right, "I added.

Our friendship lasted another couple of years, until they moved to a new neighborhood. We visited a few times but finally just drifted apart.

Christmas Train Ride and a Surprise

I always dreaded the winters in Minnesota. We were planning on taking the girls to Tennessee for Christmas, but I kept dreading the drive. I knew the snow could be a real problem that time of year. I checked the prices on a train trip for a family of four. It was quite reasonable. In fact, it would be very little more than it would cost us to drive. My only problem now would be to convince Warren that we should take the train instead of driving.

One morning in late October, I approached him on the subject. "Honey, guess what? I called the train station and we can go on the train to Tennessee and have a good time in the process." I presented my case as best I could but didn't convince him right away.

"Let me think about it."

"We'll need to get tickets as soon as possible, since it's over the Christmas holidays," I added.

The next morning he agreed, and we drove down and got our tickets. I was very excited for the next two months. I just knew this would be our best vacation ever.

"Let's think about getting a movie camera," Warren announced about a week or so before our trip.

"Do you think we can afford it"? I asked.

Bruce and Jan had gotten one a few months before and I knew Warren had the bug to get one. I doubted if we should get it now since we were going on this trip and, besides, there had been rumors of a lay off at Northern Ordinance, where Warren worked. "Sears has a really great deal, a complete package, the camera, screen, and projector for a little over $200. We can always use our Sears credit card and pay it off by payments or when we get our tax refund in the spring."

I gave in and we bought a movie camera, complete with screen and projector. He especially wanted to take it with us on our Christmas vacation to Tennessee the next week.

Bruce drove us to the Milwaukee train station on Thursday before Christmas, which was the following Monday. We were scheduled to be in Jackson Tennessee, on Friday morning. Frank and Louise would pick us up. It was really a good trip down and the girls enjoyed it tremendously. I carried food for several lunches but we ate in the diner car a couple of times. It was so much easier having Warren with me than it was on the other trip by myself. There was beautiful scenery from the dome car and we were even able to sleep some during the night.

The girls were the first to spot Louise, Frank and Cheryl waiting for us at the station. They let out a cry of joy; they were so glad to see them and to be able to get off the train. "Did you have a good trip?" Louise asked.

"It really was," we all agreed.

The ride to Mt. Carmel went by quickly because everyone had so much to share and it was hard to get a word in.

Mama and Daddy were so excited to have us home for Christmas. This was the first time we had been home for Christmas since Kim was about a year old. Warren was taking pictures almost from the time we walked in the door. "Do you have to use that big light?" Pat asked. "It just about blinds us."

"If we want good pictures, we have to have plenty of light," he added. He took pictures for the next couple of days of everything and everybody.

On Christmas Eve morning, he really had a reason to take pictures. We looked out the window and it was snowing heavily. It was so beautiful but we all agreed it would probably stop soon. We were wrong and at noon it was still snowing. "Look at Louise coming up the hill!" Cheryl shouted. "She's having trouble walking in the snow because it's getting so deep." Warren grabbed the movie camera and started taking her picture.

By later that night, we had a foot of snow. In Minnesota a foot of snow is nothing, but in Tennessee that's a different story. It snowed continually throughout the night, and on Christmas morning we had about twelve inches of snow. "I can't believe this," Daddy said as he reloaded our wood heater. "This is our first snow at Christmas in many years."

"I just hope we can get to Jackson tomorrow," I added.

"Frank can put snow chains on if he has to," Louise contributed.

"Let's just enjoy this beautiful Christmas day," Warren said as he got out his movie camera.

By this time the girls had heard the commotion and were up looking to see what Santa had brought. We looked around and Cheryl was crying to the top of her lungs. "What on earth is wrong?" Mama asked.

"My doll is not like Adrienne's!" she sobbed.

"It's a beautiful doll," we all told her.

"It's not like Adrienne's," she kept crying.

"You told Santa you wanted this doll," Louise added.

"That was before I knew what kind Adrienne was getting," she wept.

"We'll swap yours next week for one like Adrienne's," Mama consoled her.

Everything finally calmed down after all the gifts had been opened. I was disappointed as always by Warren's gift. It seemed he always bought me sexy nightgowns and underwear and not the everyday kind I could wear. This year, in particular, I was embarrassed when I opened my present in front of everybody.

"Is everybody ready for breakfast?" Mama asked. We all scurried to the kitchen for a wonderful Christmas breakfast of country ham, eggs, fried potatoes, pans of homemade biscuits and, of course, warm chocolate syrup.

The kids played in the snow and had a wonderful time the rest of the day. I packed up late in the afternoon, hoping the roads would be all right for us to get to Jackson the next morning.

I was not the least bit worried about our train. I thought if we could get to Jackson, the rest of the trip would be fine. How wrong I was. Frank put his snow chains on the car the night before. We also allowed plenty of time for the two-hour drive. We drove up at the train station about forty-five minutes before our train was due. I knew something was wrong when I saw how many people were in the waiting room. "The trains from New Orleans are delayed because of snow," the agent told us.

"How long?" Warren asked.

"The last we heard it was about two hours," he replied.

We told Frank and Louise that they might as well leave but they said they would stay with us since they had nothing better to do. We were scheduled to leave Jackson about 11:00 a.m. and at 3:00 p.m. our train was nowhere in sight.

"You should go on and not have to drive in this kind of conditions after dark," we told Frank.

"We'll miss our connections in Chicago, for sure," I said to Warren.

"We'll just have to wait for the next one," he agreed. Frank and Louise did decide to leave so they could be home before dark.

"Tammy's cough seems to be getting worse," I said to Warren.

"Give her some more cough syrup," he suggested.

"She's just about out, but I'll give her what's left."

We finally left Jackson around 4:00 p.m. and arrived in Chicago about 10:00 p.m. Our scheduled train had left at 8:00 p.m. and another one had just left before we arrived at 10:00 p.m. and the next scheduled one was to leave at 6:00 a.m.

"Do you realize we will have to spend the night in this train station?" I asked Warren.

"I guess we have no other choice do we?"

I took our coats and tried to make a comfortable place for the girls to lie down. The biggest problem was Tammy's cough and she just couldn't seem to stop coughing. The people that were stranded with us were so very nice, especially one lady. "Could I give your daughter something for that cough? I have honey and lemon and it will usually help."

"Anything would be appreciated, since I've given her all her prescription cough syrup," I responded.

The honey and lemon seemed to help, and they both got to sleep before midnight and slept for several hours. Warren slept some, but I tried very hard to stay awake. I read everything I could get my hands on. Several people gave me their magazines after they finished with them.

About 5:00 a.m. we checked to see if the train was on schedule and Warren came back and announced we could board in about thirty minutes. "We'll just wait and have breakfast on the train," I told the girls. Warren decided he had to have coffee instead of waiting until we got on the train. "Get the girls a little something,"

I yelled to him as he left for the coffee shop. We loaded our snacks in our bags and took off to finally board our train. I was never so glad to be on our last leg of our trip. "This was supposed to be a fun, no pressure trip," Warren said as we prepared to depart for Minneapolis.

"It was an experience," I responded.

We called Bruce about 11:00 a.m. to come and pick us up. We had been en route from Mt. Carmel for twenty-eight hours. We arrived at our blue house on Medicine Lake tired, but very glad to be home safe and sound.

The next morning at breakfast Warren announced, "I guess it's about time I tell you some news I heard at the plant just before Christmas vacation."

I looked up and asked, "What news?"

"There's going to be a lay off announced today."

My heart froze before I asked the next question. "Do you think you'll be laid off?"

"The rumor is it will go back as far as those with ten years of service."

It really began to sink in. "I can't believe you didn't tell me this before we went to Tennessee!" I screamed. "You also bought that movie camera knowing you would probably be laid off." I was almost hysterical. "How are we supposed to make it until you find another job, with the little bit of money we have left?"

"I only wanted you to have a good Christmas," he said sadly. "I knew how much you wanted this trip, and I didn't want to spoil it for you and the girls."

The rumor was right, and Warren found out that night he would be without a job in two weeks. We tried to tighten up our belts, rearrange our bills and prepare for it. "You will find a job in a very short while and, besides, maybe you can find a day job," I kept telling him. "Adrienne will start to kindergarten in the fall, and I can have Gloria watch Tammy so I can go back to work if I need to."

His last day at Northern Ordinance came with no job in sight. The next two weeks were about the worst in our lives. I had never seen Warren so depressed. He literally walked the floors, that is, when he wasn't putting in applications or calling all the plants in the phone book. He had been out of work a little over two weeks when someone called and asked for Warren.

"Who was that?" I asked after he got off the phone.

"The personnel office at Central Machine Works wants me to come in for a second interview.

"It would be a day job, wouldn't it?" I asked joyfully.

"I expect so, since they don't have a night crew," he answered.

He did get the job and started work the following week. He had worked nights for seven years, and now he had a normal job working during the day. I was totally overjoyed to have him home nights.

We went camping almost every weekend with couples from the fire department. The kids really enjoyed it and the adults could play cards after we got the kids to bed at night. It was about all of our social life except our Dinner Club once a month.

Adrienne's First Day of School

"I can't believe Adrienne will be starting to school next week," I said to Warren the last weekend of August 1963.

"She's older than some kids since her birthday is in December," he assured me.

"I know she's ready but it still makes me sad."

Adrienne's first day of school was a sad day in my life. It was really hard to let go and know how fast she was growing up. She had a wardrobe of cute dresses I had made for her, but the one she wore for the first day was especially pretty. It was embroidered with different stitches all around the full skirt. I cried for hours but finally decided life goes on.

Opal Phillips Johnson

Accident-Prone

It seemed especially quiet around the house with just Tammy and me at home. Tammy was between three and four years old when her accident-prone period began. Her uncle Bruce used to say if she lived to be twelve, she might make it.

One of her worse accidents happened one Saturday morning when she and Adrienne were playing behind the house with David and Dawn. We tried to keep them away from the area behind a barbed wire fence that was just at the back of our house, but they often ventured back there. "Mommie, Mommie!" Adrienne screamed as she ran in the back door. "Tammy's bleeding really bad." Warren and I both ran out as fast as we could and sure enough, she was in the area behind the fence.

"Oh, Warren, it's really bad," I yelled when I saw all the blood. The calf of her leg was cut about four inches.

"It's really deep," Warren concluded.

By then Bruce had gotten there. "Let's get her in the squad car," he said as he gathered her up in his arms. "Run and get some towels and we'll tie a tourniquet to help stop the bleeding." We were back in the car in a few seconds with the sirens screaming as we headed for the emergency room.

Tammy was fairly calm by the time we got to the hospital. It was a different story when the doctor came in and started the stitching process. He had to stitch it inside and out. All total there were about twenty-five stitches. He said she was a lucky little girl that no tendons were cut and also that we were able to stop the bleeding and get her medical attention as fast as we did.

This was the first of many incidents in Tammy's accident-prone childhood. I guess her guardian angel kept her alive for her special purpose in life. Many of her accidents were a result of her being impulsive and not thinking.

One weekend morning she woke us up standing beside our bed.

"I can't get it out," she said crying.

"What can't you get out?" I asked.

"The little wheel in my nose," she answered.

When I looked, I could see she did have some object in her nostril. "Let's try the tweezers," I said trying not to get too mad at her.

"Why did you put a little wheel up your nose?" Warren asked.

She just kept saying, "I don't know."

The little car was from Cracker Jack they had gotten the day before. The tweezers didn't work and, instead, it seemed to go in further. "I guess we'll have to take her in," I concluded. I called her doctor and the nurse said he wouldn't be in until noon. He told us to come on in and he would work us in. It only took him a few minutes to unlodge it and take it out. He gave Tammy a good talking to about keeping things out of her nose.

Most of her accidents seemed to happen on weekends. Probably the most frightening was her incident with the lawn mower. Warren announced right after breakfast on Saturday morning that he wanted to get the yard mowed before we all went to Brookdale shopping. The girls were playing outside as usual. Warren had no idea Tammy was walking ten feet behind him in the path he had just cut. I heard the mower stop and looked out the window to see Warren bending over Tammy. "What's wrong," I yelled out the window.

"Tammy has something in her eye," he called back.

I ran out as quickly as possible. "Let's get her inside so we can look closer," I said.

We took her inside to the couch and continued to try to see if she had something in her eye. "I think she might have been hit in the eye by a tiny rock," Warren concluded.

"We'd better take her in and let the doctor look at it," I reasoned.

Warren agreed and we left for Wayzata. They had a clinic that was open not only on Saturday but Sundays also. Several of the doctors were Seventh Day Adventist so they did not go to church on Sunday. It was close to noon on Saturday by the time we got there. The doctor said he had to take X-rays to be sure her eye was not seriously damaged and if there was any foreign object still lodged there. He gave us some eyedrops, bandaged it up and told us he would call us the next morning about the X-rays, since the technician was not in on Saturday. Tammy was irritable but made it fine with her eye patch on for the rest of the day.

The next morning the nurse called from the clinic. "Mrs. Johnson, could you bring Tammy in for more X-rays?" she asked.

"Why, is there a problem?", I wanted to know.

"Something showed up behind her eye," she said.

"We'll be right in," I said as I hung the phone up. "Warren!" I screamed, "come here." I told him what she said, still almost hysterical.

"It's probably nothing," Warren kept saying. "Let's wait until we know for sure before we get too concerned."

We spent most of the morning in the clinic, but when we finally left, we had very good news. They did a completely new set of X-rays, and finally concluded the others had a spot on the film. Nothing at all showed up on the new set. She had to wear the patch for several days, but within a week her eye was back to normal.

The next major incident occurred with Bruce's police dog, Duke. He usually kept him chained up in the back yard except when he was working with him. One day Jan and I were in the kitchen having coffee when we heard a bloodcurdling cry. Tammy was standing beside Duke with her mouth bleeding. She had a bite on her nose and lower lip, and I knew if he had bitten her hard, he would have taken part of her face off.

We grabbed her up and took her in for stitches again. "Her scars will fade quickly, since she's so young," the doctor assured us.

Tammy told us later she was trying to take Duke's food bowl away. Needless to say, she was kept completely away from Duke from that day forward.

There were numerous other incidents with Tammy, including the time she poured Clorox from a bottle into her eye. She was looking to see if there was any left in the bottle. Quick thinking probably saved her eye, the doctor told me later. I grabbed her up and ran cold water directly into her eye before I called the doctor. She also got stitches in the top of her head when she pulled a barbecue motor from the top of the refrigerator hitting her on the head. This was another time Bruce took us in the squad car.

My Place In Time

Adrienne was home from kindergarten because of snow, so I knew I could not drive on the roads. I called Bruce and he came and took us in for X-rays and stitches.

Adrienne's accidents were minor compared to Tammy's. She only had two that I can remember. The first one, she was less than two years old when she drank Old English furniture polish. She loved soda pop and this particular brand looked like cherry pop. I was cleaning and left the bottle on the kitchen table, and when I walked into the kitchen, she had the bottle turned up and was drinking. I screamed and grabbed it from her. I tried immediately to get her to vomit and then called the pediatrician. Warren was still working nights so he was home when it happened. The doctor told us to bring her in because we would probably have to pump her stomach. I was about six months pregnant with Tammy at the time. This was one of the worst things I had ever experienced. They had to run a tube down her throat and pump the contents from her stomach.

About half way through, I started feeling dizzy. "Warren I have to leave," I said as the nurse caught me. She put cold towels on my head and made me lie flat for a little while. Warren stayed with Kim and a few minutes later they brought her out.

"We got only about a teaspoon, the doctor told us. You must have gotten most of it when you made her vomit."

The other incident I remember with Adrienne occurred right after they got their new swing set. Tammy came running in one afternoon. "Mommie, Mommie" she screamed, "Adrienne fell off the swing." I ran out as fast as I could.

"My leg hurts,, she kept saying.

"Let's see if you can stand on it," I said to her.

"No, I can't," she cried.

I picked her up and carried her inside. By this time Warren had gotten out of the shower. "Look at Kim's leg and see if you think it is broken," I said. He looked and said he did not think it was, but she still would not even try to walk. "I guess we'd better take her in and have it X-rayed." The emergency room doctors said her leg was fine, probably just bruised a bit. Kim was still not convinced. She did not walk for about two more days and then decided it was fine.

Opal Phillips Johnson

Adrienne's Birthday Party

Kim loved kindergarten and strived for perfection in everything she did. If she got anything other than an "A," she cried her heart out. "Your birthday is in a couple of weeks," I said to her one morning before school. "What do you want to do this year?" I asked.

"Could I have a party"? she asked.

"Sure," I answered, thinking it would be the usual few kids and her cousins.

"Could I invite my whole class?" she asked.

"I'll have to think about that."

Warren and I talked it over and decided probably only about half of the class would come; that would be maybe 15 or 20, including David and Dawn. Janette agreed to help with the games and serving.

The next day we wrote out invitations for twenty-eight kids and the party was to be the following Saturday at 10:00 a.m. I ordered a big birthday cake and we had plenty of favors and all the games planned. "I don't think I've ever seen anyone so excited," I said to Jan Saturday morning as we set everything up. "She was awake at the crack of dawn. I just hope at least a few show up, or she'll be really disappointed.

They started arriving about 9:45 a.m. and by 10:00 a.m. all twenty-eight kids had arrived. Including David and Dawn - we had thirty kids in our living room. We would try to get them organized to play games or to sit while we gave out cards for the games, but it was utter chaos. Finally, Jan blew a whistle and yelled to the top of her lungs, "If you don't calm down and be quiet, we will not serve the cake and ice cream!" This helped a little and at least we were able to play "Pin the Tail on the Donkey" in shifts.

After that, we did a couple more simple games, opened her presents, and then came the really fun time. It was time for refreshments. We seated them in circles on the floor and managed to serve everyone. The parents started arriving to pick them up about noon. This was the longest two hours I believe I've ever spent. Jan helped clean up so about 3:00 p.m. we both were totally wiped out. I made the kids rest for a while so we could go to Ma and Dad's for an adult and family party that evening.

Christmas 1963

Christmas of 1963 was much different from the previous year. It was still a very special time of year because the girls were at such a wonderful age to buy gifts for. This year they both wanted Chatty Cathy, which was a doll that was very popular. She talked when you pulled a string on the back of her neck. We found one right away but spent several more weeks looking for the other one. "I guess we should store these in the attic," I said to Warren, the day we brought them home. We stored them in the attic, never dreaming there would be a problem on Christmas morning. We kept the batteries downstairs, but somehow the moisture did something to one of the dolls.

"I think they are up already," I said to Warren about six o'clock on Christmas morning.

"They can't be up this early; they were up until twelve last night."

"That doesn't matter when you're their age and excited about Santa Claus," I answered.

Warren grabbed his movie camera and I proceeded to put the coffee on. The girls were already looking under the tree. Tammy always looked through her stocking first because she loved candy and already had her mouth full when I came into the living room.

"Oh, Mommie, he brought our Chatty Cathy!" Adrienne screamed. She pulled her string and it proceeded to speak, but when Tammy pulled hers nothing happened.

"Mine doesn't work," she cried.

"It was working last night," Warren said, as he took the batteries out to see if there was a problem there. He checked it with new batteries, but to no avail; it simply would not work. "Honey, we'll take it back and get a new one that will work," he told her.

We found another doll and exchanged Tammy's the following day. They both loved those dolls and played with them for many years.

Church

"Honey, we simply must find a church," I said to Warren, one morning as I filled out another form from Adrienne's school. "They asked again on this form about our religion or church affiliation."

"Put down Congregational," Warren answered."

"I'm not a member of the Congregational church."

"I am still a member and, besides, both the girls were christened there."

"I know, but I still think we should find a church and join together and then take them to church and Sunday school."

"We'll visit some out this direction," he concluded.

In the following months we visited several churches, mostly Methodist, since we were married in a Methodist church. Besides, it was similar to the Congregational church, where Warren was a member.

I had always said I would never join a church just to be a church member. I wanted it to make a difference in my life. When I was growing up, I attended a Methodist church part of the time, but at other times I went to a Pentecostal church. It usually depended on who my friends were at the moment. Both churches were in walking distance of our home. Mama and Daddy didn't go to church when we were growing up, although both of them became Christians before their deaths. Mama became a Christian when I was in my early teens, but Daddy did not accept the Lord until he was about seventy-five years old, only a year before he died.

So here I was, twenty-eight years old looking for a church to join, so the girls would have a place to go to church and Sunday school. I know now it's a valid reason, but not the main reason to join a church.

We visited a Methodist church on Parkers Lake, only a few miles from our home. After a few visits the girls seemed to really enjoy everything so we started discussing joining.

The next Sunday we found out their new sanctuary was almost finished, and they would be moving to it in the next few weeks so we decided to postpone talking to the minister.

Meanwhile, I discussed what we were planning to do with Jan. "I've been thinking about the same thing," she admitted. "We'll visit for a couple of weeks and I'll see if Bruce will consider joining too," she added.

A few weeks later we made appointments to talk to the pastor. He came to our house the following Tuesday and made an appointment with Jan and Bruce later in the week. I had coffee and refreshments ready when he arrived around seven. He was a very nice man, very friendly and easy-going. We discussed the fire department, the neighborhoods, schools and several other topics before we got around to the real reason for the visit.

"Opal, I see you have never joined a church before," he commented. "Warren can transfer his membership from the Congregational Church, but you'll have to join on profession of faith." I remember thinking I guess I know what that means. Many years later, I look back and realize I knew nothing about faith in Jesus.

The following Sunday we stood up as families and joined the church. I repeated all the words, but my heart was no different than before. We started attending fairly regularly. Warren and Adrienne started singing in choirs. They had a children's choir and a great adult choir. I mentioned before how Warren loved to sing so this was right up his alley. I started working with the small children and Vacation Bible School.

We were now very much church members. The sad thing being, we were no different than we were before we joined. Many times we would stop and visit our friends, Carol and Butch, on our way home on Sundays but we never discussed our faith. They attended a Lutheran church fairly close to the church we went to. For the next several years, we were typical Church members, but how I praise God. He did not give up on us.

Opal Phillips Johnson

Joan and Tommy

"Guess who's getting married in May?" I asked Warren one Saturday morning in late April.

"I have no idea," he answered.

"Mama says in her letter, Joan and Tommy Wyatt are getting married May 9th."

"I really wish I could go, but I guess that would be an impossibility at this time."

"If you hadn't started working, it might have been arranged," he concluded.

I had started working afternoons at Gold Bond Stamp Company several weeks before. A friend of mine was keeping Tammy, and since Warren was on days, it worked out great. I had tried working nights, going to work around five in the afternoon and working until eleven, but I never seemed to see Warren so that only lasted a few months. They were so desperate for key punchers, I could almost pick my own hours. Now I had almost perfect hours, I started at noon and worked until five.

"I really wish I could go to the wedding," I said to Warren, for the tenth time.

"I wish you could too, but it looks impossible. I doubt very much if we could afford it, at this time."

I cried off and on for several days but finally came to the conclusion, I just couldn't go. I wrote Mama and told her I just couldn't come, but to please get me lots of pictures.

The pictures she sent were beautiful. Joan was a lovely bride and Tommy was quite handsome. I got even sadder when I looked at the pictures. I loved my family very much, and it hurt to not be a part of something so very important. I was now looking forward to July and our vacation so I could hear all the details.

My job was going quite well at Gold Bond. I had a great boss who allowed me to take off any time I needed, when the girls were ill or had something at school. The extra money really helped out. I had to pay the sitter for Tammy, but I still did quite well and I had time at home to take care of the house and be there for supper.

My Place In Time

I guess it was the perfect job, at least the perfect hours if you had to work. I met several nice girls and got to be good friends with a couple I worked with. One lived in my neighborhood so she and I visited back and forth. I went to a copper party she had and then, of course, I had one. This started my copper collection that I still have today. Helen was a great cook and was always bringing me recipes.

Stuck in the Mud

One day we were getting ready to leave work when she caught up with me as I walked down the steps. "Wait up, Opal!" she yelled. "Why don't you and Tammy come over to my house for an early lunch tomorrow?"

"That sounds great; I guess we could go to work from there."

"I have a wonderful new casserole recipe," she added.

Tammy was excited about playing with Helen's daughter. It was late May and a very rainy season in Minneapolis. "I really wish the rain would stop," I said to Tammy as we loaded in the car.

"Me, too," she answered. "I'd like to play outside."

We went on to Helen's, had a wonderful lunch and left about 11:30 a.m. so I would have time to drop Tammy off and be at work by noon.

It was still raining slightly when we got in the car. Helen lived on a gravel road on a very hilly street. I backed the car off into a very muddy section and the wheels started spinning. I knew immediately I was in trouble. The more I fooled with it, the worse it got. I told Tammy to stay in the car while I went back in to make a phone call. "I guess I'll call Bruce," I told Helen. "I know he's home. He's only working part-time since his accident."

When I got him on the phone a few minutes later, he said he could come and get me out, but it would be a few minutes. "Why?" I wanted to know. "She only lives a couple of miles from us."

"I know," he answered, "but I don't have a car home; I'll have to ride my bike." He insisted that he didn't really mind coming even though it was still drizzling rain.

"I'd better call work, and Gloria, Tammy's sitter," I said to Helen before I went back to the car to wait for Bruce.

He got there in about fifteen minutes, riding his bike in the rain. We worked another fifteen minutes getting the car unstuck. I was about an hour late getting to work, but I learned a lesson about family and how wonderful it is to have people you can depend on.

This was just one of many times I had called on Bruce in the past for help, and he was there many more times before we moved away in 1968.

July 1964

We went to Tennessee as usual the first two weeks in July. It was now 1964, and our family had undergone some drastic changes. We had been in Minneapolis since 1956, almost eight years. Sometimes it seemed much longer. Morris and Janice had been married for two years and had a beautiful daughter, named Pamela Jean, who was born February 9th. She was such a beautiful child. The girls and Cheryl were really taken with her. They loved to swing her and push her in her stroller. Joan and Tommy seemed very happy in their new marriage. They bought a house, fully furnished, down by White's Creek only a few miles from Mama's. I really envied them all being so close. Morris and Janice had built a house below the road from Mama and Daddy's. Louise and Frank also had a house next door to Morris and Janice's. I really missed being a part of it all even though everything was great when I did get to come home. Warren knew how much I wanted to move back to Tennessee and always said we would eventually get back.

One of my most unusual friends also worked at Gold Bond. She was a tall, thin girl with long, dark hair. Her name was Royce. She started work after I did and at first seemed very reserved. She worked very close to me, and we started having our breaks together. After I got to know her a little, she started opening up.

My Place In Time

She told me she and her husband were race car drivers. They lived out about thirty miles on a farm. They owned two horses, besides their race cars.

"Guess what I got invited to"? I asked Warren one night. Before he had a chance to answer, I blurted out, "Royce, my new friend, is having a Tupperware party, and she wants me to come. Maybe Jan will go with me," I continued.

The Tupperware party was the following week and Jan did agree to go. Even though we had good directions, we got slightly lost. We stopped and called and managed to get there shortly after it started. It was a fun time. The next day at work, Royce surprised me by asking, "Why don't you and your husband bring the kids out to ride horses on Sunday?"

"That sounds great," I told her. "I'll talk to him tonight and get back to you tomorrow." We did decide to go. On Sunday after church we rushed home, changed clothes, and started for our outing in the country. Both girls were ecstatic because they had never been around horses at all and were very excited. "Shall we stop for a hamburger?" I asked. Of course, they were ready for that.

We got there around 3:00 in the afternoon. Adrienne and Tammy both had a great time. Adrienne was a bit leery of the horses at first, but warmed up later. They both had rides and enjoyed it tremendously. Royce fixed a picnic before we left. We all agreed it was a great time. They talked about what great race cars they had and Tammy, of course, said she would like to drive one.

The rest of the summer went by very quickly. We went camping almost every weekend with couples from the fire department. The kids loved it because there was always a lot of swimming and playing with other kids. Meanwhile, the grown-ups spent a lot of time playing cards. We developed lasting friendships during this time.

I met Warren at the door one day in early September. "Honey, guess what? I just had a phone call, and Mama and several others are coming for a visit in October."

"That's great; who all is coming?" "She said probably Joan, Tommy, Louise, Frank, Mama and Cheryl. She also said Joan is pregnant. She's only a few months along so the doctor said it would be fine for her to travel. She also said Pat might be able to work it out so she can come. She's in her second year at Lambuth College now."

"That's really great news," Warren concluded.

The second week in October, the crew arrived. This time it was quite a bit different. The house was finished, and we had so much more room than we did the previous time they visited. What a great time we had. All except Joan. She had morning sickness really bad but didn't complain too much. Tommy kept us laughing half of the time. We shopped, cooked big meals, went out to eat, and just had a great time.

"Pat's birthday is next week," Louise commented.

"Then let's get a cake and have an early birthday party," I suggested.

We all sang "Happy Birthday" and celebrated Pat's twentieth birthday. Cheryl, Adrienne, and Tammy had a ball. They slept in sleeping bags in the living room, playing until they were totally exhausted. It was all over too quickly and they had to leave. It was so wonderful for me to have them visit, and see our house, and see the life I was living in Minnesota.

Warren and I seriously discussed moving back to Tennessee the week after they left. "Maybe we can leave the kids with your mom in July next year and look for a job in Memphis or Nashville for one of the weeks we are there,"

"Oh, honey, that would be wonderful," I agreed.

Christmas 1964

Christmas 1964 was routine. We did have a great time with our friends on the fire department. I was now Chairman of our Women's Auxiliary. This year in particular, we had decided to make an afghan and auction it off at our Christmas party. We usually had at least one fund raiser each year. About six of the ladies were able to knit, so we found a pattern with squares and decided we could all work on squares and then put them together.

"Carol, is this ever going to work?" I asked one day when I stopped at her house for coffee.

"I'm afraid some squares will be bigger than others," she agreed.

"Maybe Grace can put it all together so it will look like it's supposed to."

It took us a couple of months but by the time the Christmas party was held, it was a work of art to behold. It was absolutely beautiful.

"Wouldn't it be better to sell raffle tickets than to just auction it off?" Grace asked at our last committee meeting. We all agreed and set out on a campaign to sell five hundred raffle tickets at one dollar each.

"Would you believe we have sold over five hundred tickets?" I asked Warren on our way to the party and he agreed it was a great idea. We had coverage from the local papers and they took pictures of Carol, Grace and me with our beautiful afghan and ran it in the paper a couple of times. This turned out to be our greatest fund-raising success. We used the money the following year to buy things for our kitchen at our local volunteer fire department.

Early 1965

We had a tremendous amount of snow the early part of 1965. It seemed to never stop and the weather was extremely cold. A few months before, I had switched my hours at Gold Bond and was now working from 5:00 in the afternoon until 9:00 or sometimes 10:00 in the evening.

Tammy did not like staying at Gloria's, and I needed to be home when Kim got home in the afternoon since Bruce and Jan moved. They sold their house and moved into an apartment for a while before deciding to buy a mobile home. It was quite an adjustment getting used to not having them next door.

One cold Saturday morning, we had slept late, as usual. Warren brought me coffee back to bed and laid down to talk. "The kids have probably been up for hours," I said.

"Isn't it wonderful they can get up and watch T. V. and let us sleep?" he added.

I agreed it was sure a better age than when they were younger. "By the way, have we given up completely the idea of trying one more time to have a boy?"

"Do you realize Tammy starts kindergarten in the fall?" I asked.

"I know, so it's now or never."

"I'll be thirty years old in June" I commented. "I'm perfectly content with two girls," I said as I got out of bed and headed to the kitchen to make breakfast.

I knew this was not the end of this subject. We had discussed it on occasion for the past three or four years. I did conclude by telling him that I would think seriously about it for the next month or so.

Jan and Bruce had been spending more time at the lake, since he had recuperated so nicely. I guess the results of too much time on their hands would be a new bundle of joy. She was pregnant with their third child, due later in 1965. This fact alone seemed to spur Warren on with the idea of our having another baby. I had such a hard time delivering Tammy that even thinking about going through it again made me cringe. I was going to a specialist for a cyst on my ovary so I wasn't even sure I should get pregnant. "I'll talk to Dr. Hamel when I go in next week," I told Warren the following day.

The following week I sat in Dr. Hamel's office wondering how I would approach the subject of whether or not I should have another baby. After my examination he came in to discuss his findings. "Everything looks almost normal, and I think the procedures have been successful."

I just blurted it out, "Dr. Hamel, what would be your opinion of my getting pregnant again?"

"The cyst would probably not be a problem, but I would have a little concern about the R. H. factor. Since your husband is 0 positive blood type and this is your third child, there could be complications. However, we could monitor the blood regularly and be ready to do a transfer, if necessary."

"My husband really wants to try for a son, so I told him I

would discuss it with you."

"We would do everything in our power to ensure a successful pregnancy. This would mean monitoring your blood quite frequently, probably on a monthly basis." I thanked him and told him we would discuss what he had to say.

I told Warren what the doctor had said as soon as he got home that afternoon. "He also told me there is a good possibility I might not even be able to get pregnant since I have a cyst and a very tipped uterus."

"Do you want to try?" Warren asked.

"I know I trust this doctor much more than I did Dr. Nash, the other one I had with Kim and Tammy. I believe he would keep the pain to a minimum and also the risk. Let's go for it," I said before I went to bed. "You know we will probably end up with three girls," I added.

Warren was very positive, "It will be a boy." he concluded.

It only took between two and three months after I went off the pill before we had results. I woke up one morning with the same awful feeling of morning sickness that I had with the girls. "I sure hope this doesn't last the whole time," I said to Warren as I grabbed crackers and went back to bed.

We had agreed I would quit work as soon as I became pregnant. I was excited about that, since everything had gotten very stressful at work. I really hated to leave my friends but was delighted that I would be home with Warren in the evenings.

We got a call from Mama on April 6th, 1965. "Guess what?" she asked. Before I could answer she continued, "Joan had her baby this morning."

"She did?" I yelled. "Is it a girl or boy?"

"It's a boy and they named him Steven Edward and will probably call him Steve."

"That's great and I'm sure she's glad it's over. I can't wait to see him."

"It won't be that long until July," she continued.

I didn't tell her I thought I was pregnant because I hadn't been to the doctor yet and figured I needed to be sure before I told anyone.

The morning sickness continued for the next couple of

months. It was even worse than with the girls. Dr. Hamel confirmed that I was indeed two months pregnant. He calculated it would arrive around the third week of January. "I'm so glad I'm not working," I said to Warren one morning as I tried to finish his breakfast. He thought he had to have bacon and eggs every morning of his life before he left for work. I would get about half through and get sick and vomit every single morning. He finally agreed he would fix his own or eat cereal with the girls until I got to feeling better.

Adrienne had gotten to be such a big girl; she was finishing up first grade. She was such a perfectionist, always had to make A's. Tammy would be starting kindergarten in the fall. I was looking forward to two or three months at home by myself, before I started the process all over again.

July 1965

We had a great time on vacation in July. We had two little ones besides the three girls. Pam was a little over a year old and Steve was almost three months. He was such a cute baby but very, very active. He was a lot like Tammy had been, colicky and very fussy. We had a lot of picnics and spent a lot of time swimming at the river. My morning sickness was better, but I still did not feel very good. I felt sad about giving up my dream of moving back to Tennessee, at least temporarily. I knew with the new baby coming, everything would have to be put on hold. I also knew I wanted to move while our family was still young before they got too attached to life in Minnesota.

"Warren, do you know they really are going to put a house right in back of ours?" I asked one morning shortly after we got back from Tennessee.

"Do you know for sure?" he asked.

"I had talked to Deanna Faber and she said they are planning on starting in a couple of weeks. Jack, her husband, is the son of Mr. Faber, who owns a farm and all the land near Medicine Lake. He's giving them two acres to build their house. I have no idea, why they have to put it so close to ours. Although she does seem very nice," I continued. "They have three children, and she is expecting another. They have two girls, about Adrienne and Tammy's age, and a son that is four. I've heard that Mike, their son, is a rounder."

By September, the Faber's house was finished. There were some problems, but the good outweighed the bad. The main problem was Mike. He was always fighting and throwing rocks at the other kids. On the positive side, Deanna and I got to be very good friends. She and Jack were very good neighbors and would go that extra mile to help you out.

Fall of 1965

Tammy started school right after Labor Day in 1965 and she was so excited. She always wanted to do everything Kim did, so it was difficult for her to be home when Kim got to go to school. "You will never believe what I have to tell you," I said to Warren as we sat down to supper, a few weeks after school had started.

"Just tell me."

"They called from Tammy's school today, and they want to have her tested."

"What kind of testing?" he asked.

"Basically, I.Q. skills, to see if she is gifted."

"Go for it," he concluded.

They called us in for an appointment the following month to talk to us about the results. Her I.Q. was very high and, in fact, she tested in the top ten of the whole Wayzata School District They suggested she stay where she was but to make sure she was evaluated regularly.

All my family were really excited about another baby. They were worried things would not go as well as with our other two. Mama especially seemed very concerned, especially about the blood problem. I tried to assure her Dr. Hamel seemed to think he had it all under control. Jan's sister-in-law had the same problem when her son was born. They changed his blood completely, and

I knew he was doing fine. I tried not to be overly concerned, but I knew I felt really bad. I had very little appetite and kept losing weight. It was very hard to tell I was pregnant because I weighed less than I did when I got pregnant.

My biggest problem turned out to be a very delicate one. I could not sit without a pillow and was told by the doctor to stay off my feet as much as possible. I was able to do this for a short period of time, but things changed drastically when Adrienne and Tammy came down with the red measles at the same time.

"The doctor says they have to have complete bed rest in as dark a room as possible for the next couple of weeks," I announced to Warren, the day I got back from their doctor visit.

"I thought Tammy had a measles shot when she was two."

"She did, but he said somehow she had contracted it, but she would probably have a milder case than Kim."

He was right; Kim was much sicker than Tammy. It was impossible to keep Tammy quiet, since she didn't feel too bad. I had a very hard time during these two weeks. I had no choice but to take care of the girls, but my condition got much worse. Warren did his best to help on weekends so I could stay off my feet.

However, when I went for my appointment in early November, Dr. Hamel immediately announced he was going to put me in the hospital for a few days. "You need rest desperately, and I want to have a surgeon examine you and see if he can possibly do a procedure that will give you relief and let you carry this baby for the next two months."

"Ma said she would come out and help with the girls while you're in the hospital," Warren said, trying to assure me. "How can they do surgery and put you to sleep when you are almost seven months pregnant? he wanted to know.

"He said it would be a local, so it would not affect the baby,"

The nurse that put me in my room and got me situated asked, "What are you in for?"

"They will probably do a minor surgery so I can get through the rest of this pregnancy," I answered.

"I had no idea you were even pregnant," she replied.

I just looked like I had a little tummy but most of the baby seemed to be toward my back and was giving me terrible lower pressure. After two days of bed rest the surgeon decided they would do surgery the following day. "It will be very painful," he told me as he explained what they planned to do. "There is no way we can give you any medication orally, but we will use a local anesthesia. This will deaden the area to any pain during the procedure. However, the shots will be quite painful. I really wish we could do more than that."

He was completely on target; I had never felt such intense pain in my entire life. Tears rolled down my cheeks, and I clinched my hands together until they were bleeding. The attending nurse was so kind and compassionate; she was almost crying too.

Later, in my room the surgeon came in to talk to Warren and me. "This is one of the worst cases I've worked with," he said. "You will need extensive surgery sometime after the baby comes. I know how hard it is to stay off your feet with two small children, but this procedure will be in vain unless you do. The first few weeks after delivery will probably be very hard," he continued. "The pressure from labor and childbirth can be very difficult and must be dealt with carefully."

"Dr. Hamel has agreed to be with me during the last part of labor, and do all the examining himself," I answered. "He says, he will not allow me to suffer too much," I concluded.

Mama called regularly to check on me, especially right after the surgery. One day out of the blue, she announced, "Louise and I are thinking about coming up when the baby is born. We would take the train up and maybe stay a week and help out with the kids and new baby."

I started to cry. "I can't believe you would make such a trip in the middle of a Minnesota winter to do this," I sobbed.

"Maybe we won't get lost, if Warren will pick us up at the train station," she concluded.

Christmas 1965

Christmas of 1965 was very difficult. Christmas shopping had to be done, presents mailed to Tennessee and the task of taking care of two very active little girls. There was also the constant fighting with the new neighbors. Tammy and Mike, their son, seemed to clash. Mike was forever throwing rocks and causing other problems. Deanna and I had gotten to be very good friends, so we tried very hard not to let the kids' fighting spoil our friendship.

She and Jack were wonderful neighbors. They had volunteered to clean up storm damage from our yard the prior summer when we went on vacation. We had the car packed and were leaving early the next morning when we had a tremendous storm. There were tree limbs all over the yard, even a few lying on the house. Jack insisted we leave as planned and he would do everything necessary until we returned. That's the kind of neighbors they were, always there in time of need.

"Warren, do you think I should try to go to our Christmas Party for the fire department?" I asked in early December. "It's only a week away and the doctor still insists I stay off my feet as much as possible."

"Maybe if you rested most of the day, then we could go for a little while," he reasoned.

I knew how much he wanted to go so I agreed that sounded like a good idea. I had managed to get most of my shopping done by early December. I did quite a bit of catalog shopping that year.

We did go to our Christmas party even though I knew I would probably need to leave early. This was our social event of the year. A few years before, we started having the event at a local night club where we could have a dance. We had a wonderful dinner and a great band for dancing. I knew I would not be dancing very much although I still loved to dance.

I managed to make a beautiful party dress for the occasion. Straight shifts were very much in style, so I had selected a straight, loose-fitting dress that was very flattering. "You hardly look pregnant," Warren said before we left.

"I sure feel it," I answered.

I was also very flattered later in the evening, when our fire chief asked me if I wanted to dance. I told him I had better sit the rest of the evening out, or I might end up in the hospital. He asked me why and said he had forgotten I was pregnant and that I did not look it. I was very thin, having lost weight during the whole pregnancy. At this point, I think I weighed about one hundred and thirty pounds.

The girls were excited over the Christmas holidays. They got a new puppy that Tammy named Chico. He wasn't housebroken so we had a new series of problems. "What is your Grandma Phillips going to think about us having a puppy in the house?" I asked Tammy one day as she cleaned up after him.

"She'll think he's great," Tammy answered. My mother had never allowed us to have a dog in the house.

She and Louise were still planning on coming after the baby came. I knew I would stay in the hospital for five days. Warren planned on calling them when I went to the hospital so they could leave and be there before I came home.

Trying to stay off my feet during Christmas was an impossibility. Adrienne and Tammy seemed to have a great time, especially with their new puppy. We spent less time than usual at Ma's due to my condition.

"Carol called and wondered if we could go out to eat with them and Don and Gladie on New Year's Eve," I announced to Warren after he got home from work the day after Christmas. "She says they have to make reservations, so they need to know by tomorrow."

"Let's go," he answered. "We can cancel if you don't feel like going."

We went out to eat on New Year's Eve, even though I felt weird. "I still have three weeks to go," I said to Carol at the restaurant. "I feel like I will probably go early," I continued. I ate very little and we left right after midnight to go home.

Eric

Warren got up with the girls on New Year's Day and let me sleep in. I stayed in bed most of the day, and I was having contractions off and on but decided it was just false labor. "Honey, when are you coming to bed?" I asked Warren about eleven o'clock.

"I'll be in soon, just as soon as this football game is over," he called back.

About fifteen minutes later, I got up to go to the bathroom and suddenly I knew something was terribly wrong. I started screaming for him to bring me towels. I didn't realize for a few minutes that my water had broken. "I'll call the doctor and see if we should come on in to the hospital," Warren said as he handed me more towels.

"Call Jan and see if we can drop the kids at their place," I added.

A few minutes later we were on our way to St. Mary's Hospital in downtown Minneapolis. "Are the roads slippery?" I asked Warren.

"They aren't bad and the traffic is light this time of night," he answered.

It was after 1:00 a.m. on the second of January when we got to the hospital. "I guess I'm in for a long wait," I said to the nurse as she got me settled in my room. "I'm having mild contractions, but they aren't regular."

"I've talked to Dr. Hamel and he says he will be at the hospital shortly. He wants us to make you as comfortable as possible until he gets here."

Dr. Hamel arrived around seven in the morning. The contractions were regular and beginning to get very painful. He examined me and decided it would be quite a few more hours. He gave me a shot of Valium to try and help me relax. The next few hours are best forgotten. I was in very intense pain, but I was also very thankful to have Dr. Hamel as my doctor. He would not let the nurses examine me. He did it all himself and stayed close by in case I needed him. At 11:45 a.m. he examined me and said I would probably be a couple of more hours before I was fully dilated. He told Warren to go to lunch and that he had plenty of time.

Fifteen minutes later, I screamed for the nurse. "I feel like I have to push," I told her as she came in the room.

"You're not ready," she yelled back.

"I will not hold back." I told her. I did that with my second daughter and I almost died, so this time when I feel like pushing, I intend on pushing.

"I'll get the doctor," she said as she walked out.

Dr. Hamel came in, looked at me and said, "Let's get her in delivery."

When we got to delivery, the baby's head had crowned and a few minutes later, he laid my son on my arm. "It's a beautiful seven pound boy," he said smiling. "Everything looks great with the blood and I think he's going to be just fine."

As he wheeled me out of the delivery room, Warren came running in, and they let him see Eric before they took him in to clean him up.

"I'm glad we decided on a name," I said to Warren later when he came into my room.

"Eric Warren Johnson fits him perfectly," he agreed. "I called your mother and she said they would leave by day after tomorrow and be here before you go home. I've got to call some guys from the fire department."

He spent the next hour calling almost everyone he knew and he always began by saying, "Guess what? I had a boy."

I finally laughed and said, "Just who had a boy? Maybe you should say we had a boy, since I had a little to do with it."

The next four days were heaven. Peace, quiet and someone waiting on my every need. My appetite was back and I was beginning to get back to myself. I was very, very sore and had to sit on a rubber tire, but I knew I was on my way back. When they brought my little boy in, I knew it had all been worth it.

"Opal, where on earth is Warren?" Louise almost screamed into the phone.

"Where are you?" I asked. "Warren called a few minutes ago and said you weren't at the Milwaukee train station and said he had been waiting for over an hour."

"I think we're at a different station," she concluded.

"As soon as he calls again, I'll tell him where you are, so just stay put and he'll be there soon."

"I hope so," Louise added, "I wouldn't want to be out in this temperature. Someone just said it's about twenty below zero."

I laid in my hospital bed for the next hour, worrying and fretting because it was taking so long for them to get there. Around

9:00 p.m. the door opened and there they were. I was never so glad to see anyone. They were tired but excited about seeing the baby and, of course, getting to see Adrienne and Tammy.

A little later, I went with them to the nursery to see Eric before they left to go to our house for the night. "I can't wait to get him home, so we can hold him," Mama said, on our way back to the room.

"I've been here four days and Dr. Hamel says I can go home now that I have some help for a few days. Warren, be sure you get here sometime before eleven tomorrow," I added.

By 10:00 a.m. the following morning, I was dressed and waiting for Warren. He was there shortly afterward. He had taken care of all the paperwork before he came up to my room. "I'll get your son and you can be on your way," the nurse announced.

"I have never been more excited about anything in my life," I said to Warren. "I never realized how much I missed my girls, until I started thinking about going home. I'm also very glad to be taking home a wonderful healthy baby boy, aren't you?" I asked.

"I sure am, and now our family is complete," he added.

"It had better be," I remarked, "because if we have another one, you will probably have to have it, because this is definitely my last one."

The next few days were great, having Mama and Louise with us. They not only helped with Eric; they had a great time with Adrienne and Tammy. They were on Christmas holiday for the first few days they were with us. Mama gave Eric his first bath and, of course, we took lots of pictures.

I still worried about the weather. It was a typical Minnesota January. The first night I was home the temperature got down to thirty degrees below zero. I had trouble sleeping at night, always worrying that our furnace might go off. "You worry too much," Warren kept telling me. "You know we have a brand new furnace and the house is nice and warm, so why worry?"

"How can you stand this puppy?" Mama asked for the tenth time. "You know how I hate dogs in the house," she added.

"It's my puppy and its name is Chico," Tammy yelled.

"You had better start training him, or he'll ruin your mom's carpet."

"He doesn't like to go outside," Adrienne chimed in. "It's so cold outside so we're trying to make him go on newspapers."

"He sure misses the papers a lot," Mama laughed.

Mama and Louise stayed a week, but it went by so quickly. I was so thankful they were able to come, but I was really sad they had to leave.

The girls went back to school the day they were leaving. They said their goodbyes early and left for the bus, teary-eyed and sad. "At least, Eric will be here when we get home," Adrienne said, as she walked out the door. I cried for a long time after Warren took them to the train station.

It seemed really strange to be with my baby all by myself. I remember sitting there, just looking at him for a very long time, I thought to myself, I'm going to spoil you if I want to. I have loads of time, so I'll play with you and rock you to sleep and do all the things I never had time to do with the girls.

Eric was a good baby and he had occasional colic, but the doctor was able to give him medication that helped. He cried very seldom and dearly loved attention. I kept my vow to spend time with him. I would play with him sometimes for hours in the afternoons. Warren was now working days, and the girls were in school, so I had my days to devote just to him.

Deanna, my neighbor, had a little girl, Lynne, almost the same age as Eric. We would get together several mornings a week and have coffee. As they grew, Eric and Lynne learned to play together quite nicely. I sewed very little and had very few other projects so the first year or so of Eric's life I devoted almost entirely to him. He was a very well adjusted and contented baby. Jeanette also had a son, Dean, a year older than Eric. However, we didn't get to see them as often since they moved. We did get together some on weekends and holidays. I did miss Jan, but by this time Deanna and I were very good friends.

I was so glad to have Warren home at nights. I was able to ignore how unhappy he was where he worked. He worked for Central Machine Works in northeast Minneapolis. His only enjoyment seemed to be his hours spent on the Plymouth Volunteer fire department. He had taken on more and more responsibility and seemed to be gone almost every night of the week. He worked with Civil Defense, taught Red Cross classes and was at two or three meetings a week for the fire department.

I was very active in the Women's Auxiliary for the department. In fact, I served three years as its chairman. We did fund raisers, planned teas with other clubs, and had quite a few social events.

1966

By the end of 1966, Warren and I very seldom saw each other. Carol and I went for coffee one night after a meeting with our auxiliary. "Is Butch gone as much as Warren?" I asked.

"Probably more," she answered. "It's getting to be a major problem with several of the other wives." I remember thinking that night, this *is not what I want for the rest of my life.* We were still attending Parkers Lake Methodist Church. Warren and Adrienne were singing with the choirs. I worked with the nursery and the kindergarten Sunday School. I remember thinking, I wish we could just quit; it only adds more pressure and takes a lot of our time. But somehow I felt it was something we should do, even though the sermons were boring and I was always glad to get home.

My Place In Time

Mama called the last of May to tell us Morris and Janice had their baby. They had a baby boy, named Tony Glynn Phillips. "We'll now have three baby boys in the family," I said to Warren that night after he got home.

"They should have a lot of fun playing together" he agreed.

July 1966

It was a great reunion in July when we got to Tennessee. Steve was the oldest baby; he was a little over a year old, then Eric was close to six months, and Tony was only a couple of months old. Adrienne, Cheryl and Tammy thought they were hot stuff, running around trying to take care of the three babies. It was all great fun; we had picnics, swimming parties at the river, and several get-togethers at various houses. Pat was engaged to Carver Wentworth, and they planned on being married the next year. Before we left to go home she said, "I want you as one of my bridesmaids."

"I sure hope I can work it out to come to Pat and Carver's wedding," I said to Warren on our way home.

"Maybe it'll work out," he agreed.

"Are we ever going to move back to Tennessee?" I asked Warren. "I used to think we would, but now, I'm not so sure."

To my surprise he said, "I'm ready. We'll need to do some planning but I'm certainly ready to quit the job I'm doing now."

Early 1967

It was early 1967, and things seemed to be worse instead of better with Warren at work. There seemed to be so much pressure and I had never seen him in this state. He seemed agitated, cross with the kids, and gone with the fire department as much as possible.

One spring morning in early April, I approached him again

about moving back to Tennessee. "We could store our furniture in one side of Pappy's house until we find a house and you get a job," I said almost casually.

"Where would we live with three kids, until all this happens?"

"Mama says we could stay there; it would be no problem."

"Let's think about it for a while," he concluded.

A month or so later, Warren approached me on the subject. "If you still want to try this, let's see if we can save some money, say maybe a thousand dollars, within the next year."

We could then put the house up for sale and see what happens. I was elated! I knew I could save the money if I put my mind to it. We now had a plan and somehow I just knew it would work out.

Later in the spring, Mama called to say Pat and Carver had set their wedding day. "It will be on December 17th," she added.

"Why are they getting married so close to Christmas?" I wanted to know.

"She wants to have a Christmas wedding with everything red and green," she replied. "She also wants you to be in the wedding, if at all possible." We talked about it a while longer and I found out she was having seven attendants and a very large wedding. "She plans on everyone making their bridesmaid dresses, so I guess you could do yours when you get here," she concluded.

I told Warren all about the plans when he got home from work. "There's no way I could take off work at that time of year." He also said that his vacation was in July and even if he could take the time off, it would be without pay.

"I guess I could take the kids and go by myself," I threw out.

I was surprised when he added, "You could check it out."

Summer 1967

We took our vacation as usual in July and all the talk was about Pat's wedding, and the fact we were considering moving back to Tennessee in the near future. We had a great time as usual with lots of picnics and social events. Leaving was not as bad as usual. I had great hopes, not only of coming back in December, but maybe of moving permanently within a year or so.

Warren and I discussed possibilities about my going to Tennessee in December almost continually for the next couple of months. One of the major problems, of course, was money. I had managed to save some toward our venture, but I also knew if I used any of our savings, it would be difficult to have the thousand dollars by spring of 1968. "We're going to start working nine hours a day, beginning next week," Warren announced one Saturday morning.

"That's great, maybe we can use part of it on my trip to Tennessee. I guess I'll probably try to go on the train again" I concluded.

"That would be a hard trip with three kids," he added. I agreed but also knew I probably couldn't afford to fly.

Christmas 1967 and Pat and Carver

In mid-September, I started checking prices, not only on the trains but also the airlines. To my great surprise, I found a special on Delta that was very close to the train prices. It was a family rate, where two of the kids could fly free. Warren agreed that it was the best way to go. We checked with Pat about getting someone to pick us up in Memphis and it was settled. We were flying to Tennessee for Pat's wedding. I had never flown in a jet before and, of course, the kids hadn't flown at all. Needless to say, we were all very excited for the next few months.

I dreaded leaving Warren for two weeks but we had agreed

I would come home before Christmas. I was going over a week before the wedding and would stay a few days afterwards. This would work out so I could be back with Warren for Christmas. "This means I'll have to do all my Christmas shopping quite early," I commented to Warren.

"You'll manage," he laughed.

He was right. I did manage to have all the kids presents bought and wrapped, all my shopping done for the family in Tennessee and even some baking done by the time December ninth rolled around.

Kim had just celebrated her tenth birthday on December fifth. I knew she would be a big help with Eric on the plane. Eric was not quite two years old so I dreaded trying to keep him still on the flight. Warren took us to the airport an hour or so early. "I've never seen the kids so excited."

"Look who's coming," I said to Warren, as Carol and her daughter, came toward us.

"I brought you some treats for the plane," she announced.

"They look wonderful and I know the kids will love them," I commented as I took a box of homemade cookies from her. She stayed with Warren until we boarded the plane.

The stewardess was wonderful with Eric and the girls. They treated them really special, giving them treats and pilots' wings. They had a great time but were ready to get on to Grandma's house by the time we landed in Memphis.

Carver met us at the airport, collected our bags and had us on our way in a very short while, "This sure beats traveling on the train," I commented.

"Pat had a meeting tonight; otherwise, she would have come," Carver commented.

Everyone was tired and keyed up by the time we drove into the driveway at Mt. Caramel, some three hours later. Of course, Mama and everyone were very glad we were able to come. Pat was especially happy I would get to be in the wedding. "Maybe you'll be able to make Cheryl, Kim and Tammy matching dresses so they can serve at the reception," Pat announced after we settled down.

"I should have time, if we can find the material pretty soon,"

I answered. Pat was making her dress with help from Mrs. Poppa John, a lady who had moved from Memphis some time before. Our dresses were green velvet with red muffs.

We spent the next few days running from cloth shoppe to showers and working every spare minute sewing dresses. I made Cheryl, Kim and Tammy red lace dresses. They looked really, really cute.

Before we knew it, it was December 17th and wedding time. It was a beautiful wedding, and I was so thankful it had all worked out for me to be a part of it. I missed Warren so very much but I also knew he was glad for me to be able to come. I tried to take movies with the movie camera, but the ones I trusted with the movie camera knew nothing about it so they didn't turn out very well.

We opened our Christmas presents the night before we flew home. The kids were totally wiped out and still had Christmas to look forward to in Minnesota. The flight home was not quite as exciting as coming down but, all in all, it was an adventure I knew they would never forget.

Warren was very glad to see us. "I can't believe you bought so many presents," I said to him when we started opening our gifts."

"I had loads of time on my hands," he said, as he handed us each a package.

"Look, Mommie," Tammy yelled, "red pajamas."

"I have some, too," Adrienne cut in.

Eric and I opened ours and we had matching ones. Warren went in the bedroom and came back carrying his pair. "Let's all put them on and I'll take a picture," he continued. It was a wonderful Christmas.

Spring 1968

"If we plan on putting the house up for sale, we had better get busy with our saving plan," I said to Warren in the early spring. We had managed to save about half of our goal. I went into real action after that and by late April, we were almost there.

"We'd better wait until the house sells first," Warren added.

"It'll sell," I said under my breath. I skimped and saved and managed to put some in our savings every week when Warren got his check.

I'll never forget the afternoon I presented our passbook savings account to Warren. "Look, honey, it says one thousand dollars. Can you believe it?" I was almost in tears.

"I guess this means we'll put the house up for sale," he added.

The next week we called a real estate agent to come and evaluate our house. Jan and Bruce used the same agent a year or so before when they sold their house, so we felt comfortable using him. We had a few repairs to make in order for the house to qualify for an F.H.A. loan.

By May 1st our house was listed and an ad ran in the Sunday paper. We got a contract that very first Sunday. "I hope this works out," I commented to Warren. "I'm really tired of trying to keep the house in perfect order."

The next week they backed out of the contract. I was devastated but felt confident the house would sell. The agent regrouped, ran another ad and assured us it would sell quickly. He was right; we had another contract within two weeks. "This is only a contract," he reminded us. "It could take some time before their loan goes through." He was right again. It was mid-July before we knew for sure we would be closing in about a week.

"We have so much to do and such a short time to get it done," I commented to Warren. "It'll all work out," he kept telling me.

I knew he was right, but somehow, I was nervous, on edge and having terrible migraines. "I'm going to the doctor tomorrow," I said to Warren the minute he walked in the door the next day. "I simply cannot take these headaches anymore," I added. "The stress is almost too much."

I did go to Dr. Hamel the following day. He agreed I needed help. I'm not sure he had the answer with his tranquilizers and pain pills, but I also knew I had to try something.

Somehow I did survive the next month. We had a huge rummage sale, selling most of the girls' furniture and many other things we felt were not essential to take down. However, I could not believe we had so much to pack and store.

Louise, Frank and Tommy drove up a couple of days before we moved to help us with driving the truck and numerous other details. "Is this the biggest U-Haul truck they rent?" I asked Warren as he got out of the cab.

"It's the very biggest," he answered.

"Let's hope it'll all go in," Louise added. The living room was stuffed full of packed boxes.

"Let's go get something to eat," Warren commented. "We'll come back and get everything packed in the truck, before we go to bed." The kids were so excited; I knew they would sleep very little anyway.

The Move to Tennessee

After a restless night, we were up early, finishing loading the truck. We had it so full, after putting the girls' bikes on end; if the doors were opened suddenly, everything would have tumbled out. We all stood laughing after we closed the doors for the final time. We had three men and three vehicles to drive. They decided to take turns driving the U-Haul. I knew we were going through Chicago, and that part I really dreaded.

The trip itself is like a blur. I remember waking up with a headache. "I guess I'll load up on tranquilizers and pain pills," I said to Warren, after we finished giving the house a final cleaning. The new owners were moving in the following day. We had a new station wagon, which was nice for the kids. They could play games, etc. I knew this was a big step, but I also knew I had no regrets, as we drove the truck out of the driveway. It would be so wonderful to be close to my family again. I decided I would not dwell on the fact we had three kids, no job and no home. I knew we would not go hungry as long as my family was there.

The trip went quite well under the circumstances. We drove straight through from Minnesota to Tennessee in about nineteen hours. The kids did great, sleeping most of the night in the back of our station wagon. I remember going through Chicago, making a couple of wrong turns, but basically everything went smooth. At least that's the way I remember it.

We drove into Mama's driveway, totally wiped out, but very

thankful we had a safe trip. "We have until tomorrow to get the truck to Jackson," Warren commented as he flopped on the couch.

"We can unload it later this afternoon," I answered.

"Pappy has the other side of his house completely cleaned out," Mama said.

"I hope there's room for everything," Adrienne chimed in.

"I'm sure there will be," I added.

We rested, ate lunch and visited for a couple of hours before everyone was ready to unload our U-Haul truck. We managed to get everything stored and had the truck ready to return the next morning.

"What an adventure," I said as we got ready for bed.

"All we need is a job and a house," Warren concluded.

The next six weeks were stressful, to say the least. Warren and I had our own room; the girls and Cheryl slept on a hide-a-bed in the living room. We chipped in with groceries and I helped with cooking and other chores. I look back now and wonder how Mama could have survived. She never complained or made us feel we were in the way but actually seemed glad to have us.

We had looked at a nice house in the neighborhood when we were visiting before. It was only about a mile from Mama's and would be a very good buy. Grady Crawley and his family lived there but were building a house in Decaturville. Grady was a judge for Decatur County, therefore, when he told Warren he could find him a job in Decatur County, we felt confident about it. "I love the house," I said to Warren for the fourth time. It has such potential."

"It's certainly big enough", he answered. It was almost twice the size of our house in Minnesota. It was a three-bedroom brick with beautiful hardwood floors. There was also a three acre lot.

We had been in Tennessee for several weeks when Grady and Mary Ann told us they were moving and if we were interested in the house, we could go ahead and move in and they would wait until our G.I. loan went through for the rest of their money. Warren had interviewed for several jobs, but most did not pay near what we needed. Grady kept assuring him he had several leads and he was certain something would pan out.

"Are you sure this is wise?" I asked. "We're buying a house without a job."

"I'll get a job, even if I have to drive back and forth to Jackson," Warren answered.

We discussed it back and forth for the next few days, before deciding it would be great to live in the country even if Warren did have to drive sixty miles to work. We still had hopes he would find a job in Parsons.

We signed a contract with Grady and Mary Ann and also filled out the necessary paperwork for a G. I. loan. We paid them most of our money we had left from the sale of our other house and took possession of our beautiful new home. I knew we had loads of painting and repair work to be done before we could move in, but Warren was more interested in finding a job than helping me get the house ready.

Warren's New Job

"The girls are in school, so I'll go with you to Jackson tomorrow," I said to Warren on Sunday night in early September 1968.

"I guess it's time to give up on Decatur County," he concluded. "I'll apply at several plants in Jackson."

"They have to be paying more than they do around here," I added.

The weather was very nice, so I was quite comfortable sitting in the car reading, while Warren went to several plants and filled out applications. He came back from the first few, quite discouraged. "They are just not hiring at the present, but they'll keep me in mind if something opens up," he told me as we started to McDonald's for lunch.

"You still have one more prospect this afternoon," I said trying to cheer him up.

"Someone did say they might be hiring at Rockwell," he added.

We finished lunch and headed for Rockwell. "This should be a great spot to park," Warren commented as he parked the car under a shade tree. I read for what seemed like hours, before

My Place In Time

I saw him approaching the station wagon. He seemed to be smiling, so I knew he must have good news. "It looks pretty good. It seems they have an opening for machine repairman in the maintenance department. They want me to get a local reference and since we don't know anyone in Jackson, he's sending me to someone the Personnel Manager knows at one of the local banks. He'll talk to me for a few minutes and then give a reference to the company. They will also accept my other two references from Decatur County."

We took the references back to Rockwell, and within an hour Warren came out and announced he had a job.

"When do you start? How much does it pay?" I was more excited than he was and I had a million questions.

"We'll talk about it on the way home," he said as he got in the car.

The pay was much more than he could make in Decatur County but not as much as he was making in Minnesota. He would be starting the following Monday.

Settling In

We finished up all the painting and moved our furniture the weekend before he started to work. I was very excited about our new house and all the room we had, but I also knew right away we had some real adjustments to make. We would only have one vehicle for the time being, since it would be costing so much in gas for Warren to drive over sixty miles one way to work. I knew not having my own car would be a problem but decided I could live with it, since Joan and Louise both had cars and lived fairly close. I felt I could also do some running around after Warren got home from work.

A couple of months went by before I began to realize this was going to be a real problem. First, Warren was very late getting home at nights, since they were working lots of overtime. Mama was not feeling well, so Joan spent most of her time with her. She picked Eric and me up several mornings a week so we could go to Mama's, have lunch, then watch the stories together, while Steve and Eric played. The only problem was, I did not have time to do the things I wanted to do and was used to doing before we moved here. I loved to sew and made most of my clothes plus all of Adrienne's and Tammy's. Now it seemed, every time I started sewing, I either needed thread or machine needles, or something I could only get in town, which happened to be thirteen miles away. Louise did have a car, and she did invite me to go with her on occasion, but she was always in a very big hurry. I did go a few times after Warren got home, but it was usually so late; the stores would be closed or I was too tired after supper to get out.

"I'm beginning to feel trapped," I said to Warren on more than one occasion. Our loan had gone through and we officially owned our house, so I knew it would be no small matter to move. Houses in the country did not sell easily. I had taken up doing most of the yard work, because Warren just did not have time to get it done. He worked almost every Saturday until noon. When he did get home, he was worn out.

Christmas 1968

Our first Christmas in Tennessee was wonderful. It was so nice to spend Christmas with my family and not have to worry about the long drive back to Minnesota. The kids seemed happy and well-adjusted. I was probably the only one that felt a little apprehensive. I hoped things would be better in 1969. I was to find out that 1969 would be one of the most difficult years of my life. It was also the beginning of my spiritual journey that would change my life.

I struggled with money issues, not having a car, and worried continually about Warren driving sixty-four miles each way to work. In the past six months, he'd already had one major accident.

One morning early, about eight miles from our house, a horse was in the road as he turned a curve. He killed the horse and did major damage to the station wagon. I was very thankful he wasn't hurt and that we had insurance to fix our car. However, it added to my worry and anxiety. (Bills and car expenses were tremendous.)

My Family in the 1970's
Standing: Sam, Morris, Pat, Cheryl, Joan, Dan;
Sitting: Opal, Mama, Daddy, Louise

Mrs. Poppa John and Bible Study

One Friday afternoon, as I waited for Warren to get home from work, there was a knock at our front door. *Who could this be*? I asked myself as I started for the door. Mrs. Poppa John, the Sunday school teacher at the Mt. Carmel Methodist Church, stood there. "Opal," she began, "we're starting a Bible study on Wednesday nights at church, and I wanted to invite you to come. I can pick you up," she continued.

"I'd have to leave the girls and I'm never sure what time Warren will get home," I protested.

"I'm sure they'd be all right for an hour or so, and the church is so close, and Sharon would be home, in case they needed her."

"Let me talk to Warren and I'll get back to you on Sunday."

On Sunday I told Mrs. Poppa John I would begin the Bible Study the following Wednesday. On Monday afternoon, she was back at my house; this time she presented me with a new Scoffield Bible. "I want everyone to have the same version of the Bible," she said as she handed it to me. I thanked her and told her, I was looking forward to coming. I was certainly not looking forward to going to a Bible study, but I felt I should at least give it a try.

There were eight or ten people there for the first night of the study. "We'll be studying Romans," she announced. I knew almost immediately there was something different about this study. I concluded, it was the teacher. I had never met anyone like her. She talked as if she knew the Lord personally. She seemed to care about each one of us and said she would be praying for us the next week.

That night I as I thought about the study and Mrs. Poppa John, I knew there was something there I wanted to know more about. I decided I needed to read my new Bible. *If she could spend her money and buy me a Bible, the least I could do was read it,* I concluded. So I started reading the New Testament. It was hard to put it down. Then I started in the Old Testament. I kept thinking how horrible these people were. The problem was I never saw myself in any of it, only other people. "Now at least I can discuss the Bible, intelligently," I said to Warren one night.

For the next few months, I studied my Bible at home and attended Bible study on Wednesday. I thoroughly enjoyed it and decided Mrs. Poppa John had something in her life that I really wanted. I somehow missed out on learning how one can live the Christian life, or even what makes you a Christian. I decided I wanted to be a Christian and set about in my own strength to be one. This was a frustrating and trying time because I learned later we cannot be a Christian in our own strength, but it must be done by the power of the Holy Spirit of God. It's Christ in you. I praise God that if we're open, he doesn't leave us in that predicament.

More Accidents

In early spring, the telephone rang about an hour after Warren had left for work. The girls were getting ready for school, so Adrienne grabbed the phone. "Mom, it's Dad," she yelled.

I answered the phone with a lump in my throat, knowing something was wrong. "I'm at the hospital," he began. "They think I have a mild concussion, nothing more. I'm in Lexington and I had a pretty bad accident; the station wagon is in a ditch, or rather a small creek, a few miles from Lexington. If you can call Frank or Morris and get one of them to bring you up here, I think they will release me from the hospital."

"Stay put, we'll be there as soon as I can get everything worked out."

Frank and I were in Lexington in about thirty minutes. The nurses at the hospital told us to watch him fairly close for the next twenty-four hours. Warren felt well enough to call a wrecker and make arrangements for the station wagon to be hauled in.

When we stood on the bridge, looking down at the wagon, upside down in a small creek, I began to cry. "Warren, the Lord is telling us something," I remarked. "I think He's saying stop the commute, stay in Jackson. It hasn't been but a month or so since Tommy Rushing went to sleep and wrecked his car and miraculously neither of you were hurt. I guess I can't blame him for giving up his job." I continued, "I just think something must change."

Moving to Jackson (Almost)

Warren agreed to rent a motel by the week and stay in Jackson from Monday until Friday. He did this until early June. One day he came home all excited. "Guess what?" he asked.

"I have no idea."

"I found a house trailer I can rent for what it's costing me for motels and you and the kids can stay."

"That should work great," I added.

"We can come back to the house on weekends until it sells."

"This is not a bad place," I remarked as we placed our clothes and personal items around the two-bedroom trailer. We bought a rollaway bed for Eric to sleep in the living room. The worst part of the whole situation was the fact it was in a trailer park, and everything and everybody was so close. You could hear the guy next door playing his drums. There was a lot of kids fighting and adults having marital problems. "It's much better than you staying away from us for four nights at a time," I told Warren after our first night there.

"Maybe our house will sell soon" he commented.

The following weekend we got a contract on our house. We didn't know how long it would be before we could close. My cousin was killed in a truck accident some time before, and his widow was waiting for her insurance check and planned to pay cash for our house. *Eventually things will work out,* I kept telling myself as it got harder and harder to pay all the bills. "Honey, I don't know how long we can keep paying two utility, bills, two telephone bills plus two house payments," I said to Warren for the

tenth time since we'd been in Jackson.

"Maybe she'll get her money soon," he answered.

August rolled around and the girls had to be enrolled in school. We continued to go to our house in Mt. Carmel on weekends, hoping this would all end soon. Adrienne and Tammy went to different schools so transportation became quite a problem, since we still only had one car. Sometimes Tammy would ride to school with a girl that lived down the street, and sometimes Adrienne would ride the bus with a friend she now knew.

"Warren, I'm truly at my wit's end," I cried one Sunday night as I thought about the following morning. Many days I would get up, load the kids in the car, take Warren to work, then drop the girls at school. Later in the day, I would pick them up and Warren later at work. "Do you really think we should let Christine and her family move into our house until we have our money in hand?" I asked Warren.

"We could rent a house, and our bills would be less," he answered.

"Do you think we can find a house to rent on a monthly basis?" I asked.

He said he thought we could, and we actually did find one where the guy was in service and his father wanted to rent it on a monthly basis until his son got out of service in a few months.

Our neighbor from Mt. Carmel moved our furniture the following weekend. "I'm a nervous wreck," I kept telling Warren as I watched my lamp shades blowing in the wind on Monroe's flatbed truck. We got everything there safely, and what a joy it was to be in a house again.

I was still driving all over Madison County but, all in all, it seemed much better. We celebrated Thanksgiving in our rented house in 1970, hoping we would close on our house very soon, since we had found a house we wanted to buy a few weeks before. As I walked in the door on Saturday after Thanksgiving, Warren said, "Annette called and wants to see the house we're buying if we have time this afternoon."

"Do you still have a key?" I asked.

"I do," Warren answered. "Reggie said I could just keep it for a few weeks. Maybe we can close on it by the first of the year," he continued.

Our Home on McCool

We showed David and Annette Mount, our good friends from the trailer park, the house we planned on buying if things went according to plan. They loved it as much as we did. This house was like a dream after all we'd been through. The main feature was location. It was convenient to everything. The schools were two or three miles away, and, most important, the mall was about three miles from this house. The house was spacious, not as large as the one in Decaturville, but it appeared larger because of the high ceilings.

"Isn't this the most exciting day?" I asked Warren.

He agreed, "It's like a dream come true."

Christine had gotten her insurance check the week before and we had closed on the house in Mt. Carmel and made a large down payment on this one all by the middle of January.

We settled in quickly, the girls were now able to ride the bus, which made things a whole lot easier. We joined Northside Methodist Church as a family the following month after we moved in. It was close and we liked the pastor. I was still trying very hard to be a Christian, wanting to let my light shine the way it did in Mrs. Poppa John.

I'm Saved!

Warren and the girls joined the choir, and Adrienne and Tammy became active in M.Y.F. I also became involved with Methodist Women. Although I was busy and my life had finally taken a turn for the better, I still felt there was something missing.

One Wednesday night I had a headache and decided to stay home from Wednesday Bible study. "Warren, you and the girls go ahead to choir practice," I said. "I think I'll stay here and watch Billy Graham on television."

They left and I settled down on the couch in front of the television set. The sermon started out much the same as usual, but somewhere along the way I became engrossed in what he was saying. It's like he was speaking especially to me. He was talking about the cross. He said, "If you were the only one on this earth, Jesus would have died just for you. He loved you that much." He also added, "The ground is level at the foot of the cross, everyone is equal, we're all sinners, in need of a Savior. He accepts us just as we are and places his Holy Spirit in us to live the Christian life for us." He said, "We can never live the Christian life in our own strength."

It all made sense for the first time in my life. I had to surrender my life to Him and He would live his life through me. I fell on my knees before the television set and asked God to forgive my sins and for Jesus to come into my heart and fill me with his Spirit. "Jesus, I will go any place you want me to go and do anything you want me to do," I said, with tears streaming down my face. This was my new beginning.

New Beginning

I had a peace in my heart like I had never known before. I began to see my desires changing. I now enjoyed things I had never been interested in before. I now found that going to church took on new meaning. "Warren, you truly do not know the real me anymore," I said early one Saturday. I was trying to explain something I had learned at a Bible study the week before.

"I'm just not interested," he commented as he walked out of the room.

I met so many wonderful Christian friends who were like-minded. I met one lady in particular at church. On a Sunday a few months after I'd committed my life to the Lord, a lady came over to me on my way to the car, "Opal, you are someone I think would be interested in a Bible Study I used to go to."

"I probably would," I answered.

"I'm not able to go any more since I started back to work, but I would love to take you over to meet Becky. I think if you met her then you would feel comfortable enough to go by yourself."

"That would be great," I answered.

The following week, Marguerite called and set a time for us to go meet Becky, the lady who hosted the Bible Study in her home. We went the following Wednesday. She was probably the most gracious, kind, and gentle person I had ever met. I could hardly wait until the following week to attend the Bible Study in her home.

Up until this time, I had completed a correspondence course from Billy Graham, many studies from DeHann, on Day of Discovery, and a weekly study our pastor had been doing, but nothing prepared me for this type group. This whole group of believers were excited about the Lord, much like Mrs. Poppa John from Decaturville. We studied the book of John. It was so great to meet new Christian friends and get grounded in God's word at the same time.

"Could you pray for my husband, Warren?" I asked after I had been attending for several months.

Suzanne stayed over and talked to me after the study. "Do you think he's saved?" she asked.

"He's been baptized and is a member of a church, but he doesn't seem to have a relationship with the Lord."

"Then that's how we'll pray," she concluded.

Christian Friends

This was the beginning of two years of many Christians agreeing in prayer for Warren to have a close relationship with the Lord. I met many friends at this Bible Study that would stay close friends for the next thirty years and up until present time. In fact, I met a friend, Bennie Farmer, at this Bible Study in 1971. She and I have stayed close and still meet on a regular basis for prayer. I thank God for her daily. God blessed me with many other great friends through this Bible Study and through the Christian

My Place In Time

Women's Club, that was started about this time. So many have been such blessings in my life. One in particular, Hanan Hamada, a woman from Lebanon. She had only been in this country a short while. God put us together, along with another dear, departed friend, Lucy Naylor. The three of us spent many years praying together for each other and our families. This was a very special time. The Lord works in mysterious ways His miracles to perform.

Through many frustrating times at work, God began to deal with Warren until one night he fell on his knees before the Lord and asked Him to take over his life. Slowly we began to communicate on a more spiritual level. " Warren," I asked one night, "would you be interested in going to a Bible Study at Hanan's apartment? Her husband Lewis is going to be teaching Revelation."

"I don't see why not," he answered.

We started to attend this Bible Study together and suddenly God began to open doors. "I've been asked to teach the adult Sunday school class," Warren announced the following week.

"I've also been asked to teach the fifth and sixth grade class," I responded.

This was the beginning of God showing us his truths in the word for ourselves. It was a wonderful exciting time.

There was a teenager in this study by the name of Mike Moore. I was very impressed with Mike. He was a junior in high school but had the maturity of one much older. He had a real devotion to the Lord and seemed to stand up for his biblical principles everywhere.

Reggie Smith was another participant in our study. He owned Town and Country Realtors. We had met him briefly when we bought our house. "Warren and Opal," Reggie announced one night at Bible study, "I wonder if you two might be interested in going on a Lay Witness Mission to Munford, Tennessee, next weekend?" We asked some questions and told him we'd pray about it and get back to him.

"Would you like to go?" Warren asked on the way home.

"It sounds great," I answered. "Hanan and Lucy both have been going on these weekends for several months."

Lay Witness Missions

We went on our first Lay Witness Mission the following weekend. It was scary but very exciting. You never knew when you would be called on to give your testimony. We also led small groups and had lunches on Saturday, where we were called on to share. Probably the greatest blessing was staying in homes with the church members. They were complete strangers but in a very short while we felt as if we had known them forever.

This was the beginning of a twenty year ministry. We went once or twice a year. Many times we went as a family, but other times, the kids stayed home with friends. I was also very involved with the Christian Women's Club. I served on the board for many years with two years as chairman. In 1976 I was asked to give my testimony at a club luncheon. For the next ten years or more, God gave me the opportunity to share what He was doing in my life at many clubs throughout the country.

Our Children

The years have flown by so quickly. We saw our children become adults we could be proud of. Our greatest joy in each of them was their decision to accept Christ as their personal Savior. We've been double blessed to see our children's children and our four great-grandchildren.

Adrienne, our oldest daughter, married John Childs in 1978 and had four children. David, their oldest, Matthew, who is now with the Lord, Adrienne "Kim," their only daughter, and lastly their youngest son, Andrew.

Tammy married Eddie Hill in 1980 and became the parents of Candice Marie and Amy Elizabeth.

Eric married Lisa Tabor in June of 1986 and they had two children, Lindsey Katherine and Blake Warren.

The next generation grew up and two of my grandchildren

were married. Candice Hill married Chris Eley and had two children, Anna Marie and Brian Jacob "Jake."

Amy Hill married Max Edmiston and they have two daughters, Adeline Grace and Britton Faith born May 25th 2011.

If grands are wonderful, which they are, then greats are super great!

They say that time changes everything and we have had some changes in our family as well. Adrienne is now married to Jimmy Otto. Tammy is married to John Hurst and has added three more additions to the family – Heather Wright, Maria Blair Moore and Brian Hurst. In 2004 Eric married Emily Clarke and has added two more grandsons, Adam Clarke and Andrew Clarke.

50th Anniversary

Warren and I celebrated our Golden Wedding Anniversary in June of 2005. It was a perfect day. The kids treated us to a day we will always remember. Family and old friends came from near and far. Carol, one of my bridesmaids from fifty years ago, came from Arizona. The night before our anniversary we rented a limousine and went to Nashville to all the places we had been when we were dating. What great fun!

My Family

I must mention some other members of our family at least up to 1971. In 1969 Frank and Louise adopted two boys, Glenn and Randy. Melinda was born to Joan and Tommy in 1970; Sam married Deborah Haggard on March 5th, 1971. They had two daughters, Samantha, 1975 and Mary Beth, 1978 . Cheryl would later marry Doug Harvey in 1983 and become the mother of Jonathan in 1986 and Laura in 1989. Life would then go on to the next generation.

My family decreased over the years by five. My dad, then Mama, next Dan, Louise and then Pat. Frank, Louise's husband, also passed away. I'm very thankful to have been a part of such a wonderful family. Those remaining still get together periodically and have such good times and so many memories.

True Joy!

I truly believe if we delight ourselves in the Lord, he will give us the desires of our hearts. He has allowed Warren and I to travel and see much of his beautiful creation, including a trip to Europe in 1990. We have traveled to eleven countries and 42 of the United States, including Hawaii and Alaska. Warren retired from Rockwell/Porter Cable in 1997, and we've had had thirteen years of togetherness. After a few adjustments, we've learned to truly enjoy each day together. He's my soul mate and best friend. He knows what I'm thinking even before I say it. <u>We have a family handpicked by God. I know He has a great plan and purpose for each of their lives. I truly believe God revealed to me how to end</u>

My Place In Time

my book. He said the rest is their stories.

I love and cherish each one and believe this life is just a vapor; it appears for a little while and then vanishes away. our real life begins!

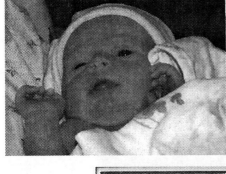

The newest Great-Granddaughter
Britton Faith Edmiston

Eric's Family
Top: Adam Clark, Blake Johnson & Andrew Clark
Lindsey Johnson
Bottom: Eric and Emily Johnson

Adrienne's Family - Updated
Andrew, Kim & David Childs, Adrienne & Jimmy Otto

Tammy's Family Maria Blair Moore, Tammy & John Hurst, Heather Wright

My Place In Time

**Tammy's Daughters:
Candice Eley & Amy
Edmiston
Bottom:
Great-Grand Kids:
Addie Edmiston, Jake
Eley, Anna Marie Eley**

*25th Anniversary
Eric, Adrienne, Opal, Warren, Tammy*

2004 - Opal & Warren 49 Years Together

My Place In Time

Warren, his sister Marlene and brother Bruce 2005

**Siblings and Spouses as of 2011:
Morris & Janice, Debbie & Sam, Opal & Warren, Cheryl & Doug,
seated: Joan & Tommy**

ABOUT THE AUTHOR

    Opal Johnson is a dedicated Christian lady, whose faith is first and foremost in her life. Next, she's a devoted wife to Warren, and a mother of three children, grandmother to eleven, and "Great-Ma" to four.

    She's retired from many endeavors in her life. She taught Bible studies, Sunday school, and has given her testimony on Lay Witness Missions, Christian Women's Clubs, and many other occasions.

    Before moving back from Minnesota, she was a key punch operator off and on for many years.

    She went back to school in her forties, took several psychology classes. She then decided to do volunteer work instead.

    Her last endeavor was a decorating and floral design business, which lasted around ten years. In 1997, Warren retired and they moved to the country. A wonderful place on a lake, that God provided for them. Opal also retired from her business but has been busy with all the opportunities the Lord puts before her. They've also been blessed to travel and see so much of God's beautiful creation. This was also a passion of theirs. They truly believed if they delighted themselves in the Lord, He would give them the desires of their hearts.

Main Street Publishing, Inc.
206 E. Main Street, Suite 207
P O Box 696
Jackson, TN 38301

Toll Free #: 866-457-7379
or
Local #: 731-427-7379

Visit us on the web:
www.mainstreetpublishing.com
www.mspbooks.com

E-Mail: editor@mainstreetpublishing.com